CW00797652

MADE IN AMERICA! 🇺🇸

PONTIAC
FIREBIRD
THE AUTO-BIOGRAPHY

For post publication news, updates
and amendments relating to this
book please visit
www.velocebooks.com/books/V5003

www.velocebooks.com

First published in 2003. Second edition printed February 2007. This third edition published November 2016 by Veloce Publishing Limited, Veloce House, Parkway Farm Business Park, Middle Farm Way, Poundbury, Dorchester DT1 3AR, England. Fax 01305 268864 /
e-mail info@veloce.co.uk / web www.veloce.co.uk or www.velocebooks.com. ISBN: 978-1-78711-003-8; UPC 636847010034.
© Marc Cranswick and Veloce Publishing. All rights reserved. With the exception of quoting brief passages for the purpose of review, no part of this publication may be recorded, reproduced or transmitted by any means, including photocopying, without the written
permission of Veloce Publishing Ltd. Throughout this book logos, model names and designations, etc, have been used for the purposes of identification, illustration and decoration. Such names are the property of the trademark holder as this is not an official publication.
Readers with ideas for automotive books, or books on other transport or related hobby subjects, are invited to write to the editorial director of Veloce Publishing at the above address. British Library Cataloguing in Publication Data – A catalogue record for this book is
available from the British Library. Typesetting, design and page make-up all by Veloce Publishing Ltd on Apple Mac. Printed in India by Replika Press.

MADE IN AMERICA! 🇺🇸

PONTIAC
FIREBIRD
THE AUTO-BIOGRAPHY

NEW 3RD EDITION

VELOCE

MARC CRANSWICK

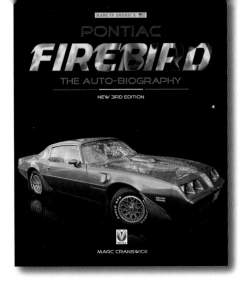

MADE IN AMERICA

PONTIAC
FIREBIRD
THE AUTO-BIOGRAPHY
NEW 3RD EDITION

MARC CRANSWICK

Contents

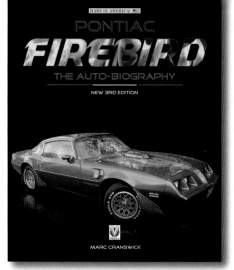

– Dedicated to Matt Moore –

Introduction

Over a 40 year period the Pontiac Firebird has earned a unique place among speedy domestic cars. What started out as another contender in the 'me too' Mustang pony car race ended up becoming so much more. Only Pontiac could have come up with a coupe like the Firebird, and it was the Firebird that kept the performance fires burning once the mighty GTO was gone.

The Firebird has garnered a reputation for being larger than life, and many have come to regard it as a large car, but that was not always the case. Pontiac's Firebird was originally a small car, classified as a sport compact in the days when the terms personal car and specialty car were used. However, after the first major gas crunch, viewpoints altered. One thing that didn't change was Pontiac's commitment to keeping its Bird flying high.

Rather than trade on past glories, or play games with nameplates, the Firebird stayed true to form and never gave up. Perhaps it's that persistence that has made many regard the Firebird as a model in a certain mold. The truth is that, over its life, the Firebird has altered significantly, reflecting general changes and trends in the auto world at large. The Firebird's tale reflects the development of the mainstream domestic car in the modern era.

V8, turbo V8, turbo V6, HO V6, overhead cam I6 and even a Super Duty four banger: if there's a performance avenue to be explored then the Firebird has been there, and Pontiac never quite gave up on the hope of using a transaxle! So it isn't just a story about V8s, or even Pontiac, for that matter; icons always seem to have a wide influence. Popular with car fans and in the sales charts, the Firebird has had a high profile both in television and at the movies. The Pontiac Firebird has also received its fair share of attention from hot-rod shops, tuners and car customizers.

As for racing, well, the Firebird was there, too. Then again, Pontiac has always stamped its authority on the street. As per Pontiac tradition, the Firebird delivered what folks expected in the real world. Even during the lean years the Firebird kept the 400-cube, 4-speed dream alive when others had moved on to paint and tape specials. Fast cars didn't die out in 1973, they just started wearing the 'Screamin' Chicken' on their hoods!

As a collector car the Firebird has all the right credentials. A strong fan base, wide variety of power team and trim options, various low volume and commemorative models, and a healthy helping of nostalgia thrown in for good measure. A number of Firebird models are already valuable classics, but certain younger versions can be counted on to be some of the fastest appreciating collector cars of today and tomorrow.

*The band Chicanery
with 1968 Firebird 400
Convertible.*

From the go-faster 1960s to the gas mileage and pollution controlled 1970s, the performance renaissance of the 1980s, to the indifference of the 1990s, the legend just gets bigger: the Firebird was always there and this is its story.

Marc Cranswick

1

Enter the Pony Car – Pontiac's new Firebird

Room for another player in the specialty car arena?

The Firebird story has two beginnings. The first centers on performance and the second relates to a certain style of automobile. Look to the enterprising exploits of Mr John Z DeLorean, Pete Estes and Jim Wangers over at Pontiac Motor Division (PMD). These brave souls were able to break the anti-performance GM family rule, and maneuver the 389 V8 from the full-sized Pontiac line into the intermediate Tempest to create the immortal GTO. Suddenly, going fast never looked so good; the 1964 Pontiac GTO was a runaway success, sparking hoards of imitators. It also warmed the hearts of senior management by boosting regular Tempest sales by 76.4 per cent.

Far from being frowned upon, performance was now something to be embraced. Pontiac was pleased to see rivals create their own hot intermediates because imitation is the sincerest form of flattery.

The second beginning to our story was the moment when Lee Iacocca peered over Don Frey's shoulder at Ford and suggested that a rear seat should be added to the sketch of that week's automotive dream on wheels. Add a

*The Pontiac Tempest GTO borrowed a Ferrari nameplate and awakened Detroit's interest in performance. This 1965 example has Hurst rims and Reef turquoise paint.
(Courtesy Bob & Edie Mohalley)*

8

Three 2-barrel Rochester carbs, a Poncho 389ci V8 and one brave pilot allowed the Goat to feverishly fly down the quarter-mile. (Courtesy Bob & Edie Mohalley)

The first generation Firebird made a 1967½ model year debut and notched up 82,560 sales. Pontiac's street performance image was consolidated by the new Firebird. (Courtesy San Diego POCI)

Pontiac got the right to use the 'Firebird' name through the GM gas turbine-powered show cars of the 1950s. The Firebird III pictured was shown at GM's 1959 Motorama show. (Courtesy Fred Teufert)

rear seat; it didn't matter if it could hold only little Fido or your favorite hat, it had to have that rear seat! One piece of inspired marketing led to another, and before one knew it, North America had fallen in love with the new 1964½ Mustang. Compare the little pony's first year production total of 121,538 to the 53,277 Thunderbirds sold during the T bird's first three years, and the value of a rear seat becomes obvious.

With performance and sport compacts in the air, it wasn't long before the two were blended to create hot pony cars. The term 'pony car' was coined by contemporary *Car Life* editor Dennis Shattuck. A sporty coupe, reasonably small in size that could be custom ordered by the individual purchaser, it was a sure-fire hit, and GM, plus everyone else in car land, wanted to get in on the act. The Chevy Corvair and Pontiac Tempest had introduced interesting technical concepts, like rear air-cooled flat sixes, transaxles and bent driveshafts. However, why risk controversy when a simpler and more lucrative path lay elsewhere? GM bosses could see that a Corvair with the Monza or turbo sport packs was no commercial match

for Mustang. Plans were afoot for a real rival, the GM F body.

Two heads are better than one
Responsibility for the F body was first the sole preserve of the Chevrolet division. What started as the proposed Panther ultimately became the 1967 Chevrolet Camaro. However, in view of the market size the Mustang had revealed, GM reasoned that two heads would be better than one. The Mustang was complemented by the upscale Mercury Cougar, and GM decided that its Camaro could also use a partner in crime. Pontiac seemed the likely GM family member to be called on for reinforcements. The Great Ones had been flying high since the GTO arrived, and had achieved an enviable performance image. It made good sense that Pontiac should supply GM's second pony car for the sport compact sales race.

Landing the job of creating GM's second F body was a mixed blessing for Pontiac. The new sport compact would bolster PMD's already solid image and take its style of performance into a new and growing market segment. It was inescapable that

Pontiac's new F body would not only complement the Camaro, but also its big brother, the Tempest/

The 1967½ Firebird was available in hardtop or convertible forms, with optional power top. The big inch Poncho 400 allowed the Firebird to stand out from the pony crowd. (Courtesy Brett Liukkonen)

GTO line. Unfortunately, the new F body also spelt the end of John Z DeLorean's hoped-for 2-seater sportscar. The XP-833 prototypes were probably considered too close to the Corvette by management heads, so it was buried. While the chance to be part of GM's pony car adventure would have brought some cheer to Pontiac, it was hardly full compensation for the loss of what might have been a unique, specialized sportscar.

Pontiac's new four place pony express made a February 23 1967 entry as the new Firebird. However, this wasn't the first name suggested for the latest youth market coupe. Banshee was a much mooted earlier choice, but a little study showed that this might not be such a good idea. The name had Celtic origins, where it meant fairy. In addition, Banshee was also connected to funeral wakes. All that glitters is not gold and, what was initially thought to be a very macho nameplate, was given the heave-ho and in stepped the Firebird tag.

Firebirds I-IV were GM gas turbine-powered experimental vehicles. These show cars were attractions at GM's 1950s Motorama shows. It was through such GM experimental cars that Pontiac acquired the right to use the Firebird name. Around 82,500 Pontiac Firebirds rolled off the production line during what remained of the 1967 model year. In 1968 that figure escalated to 107,112: a record that would stand until the 1976 model year.

This volume should come as no surprise because the late '60s saw the commercial zenith of the specialty car in general, and the sport compact in particular. Indeed, after a rocket-like start in 1964, sport compacts accounted for 13 per cent of new passenger car sales during the 1967 model year. Substantial variation in makes, models and specification occurred to meet the upsurge in interest. Manufacturers were eager to fill price gaps that may have existed.

By 1970 the specialty car field spanned anything and everything from a plain sub $3000 Mustang I6 to a loaded $9000 plus Continental Mk III V8. Somewhere in all the rush the Pontiac Firebird made a start. Buyers knew a promising newcomer when they saw one, and that explained the Bird's solid market entry. In keeping with the custom order nature of the specialty car segment, Firebird offered a host of engine and trim options. Initially, the new model was touted by PMD as The Magnificent Five, alluding to the similarly named cinema motion picture, and the fact that five initial engine options were on offer. Not content to just fit in with the status quo, Firebird had some tricks that made the opposition sit up and take notice.

The availability of a large 400-cube motor in a car of this size, plus the refinement of a 3-speed automatic where previously it had been usual to offer 2-speed boxes, must have spurred Ford and even Chevrolet to review their product lines. Pontiac's powerplants went a long way towards entrenching the newcomer in the hearts and minds of sports fans everywhere. It might have been feared that the new Bird would come off second best, seen as no more than the Camaro's twin brother picking up missed sales. The heart of a car is its engine, and Pontiac's overhead cam I6 and 400 V8 could be counted on to set apart the Firebird from its GM cousin, and the madding crowd as a whole. Buyers soon discovered that unique power teams and the special touches bestowed upon the Firebird by PMD, gave the car a spirit of its own. After all, the Firebird came courtesy of the same folks that had put the GO in GTO! They knew what they were doing.

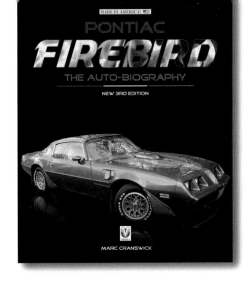

2

Engineering & design
– what made the new Firebird fly

GM didn't have much time to get the F body ready for production. To reduce the time lag before a Mustang competitor could be launched, engineers turned to computer aided design (CAD) to fast track the new pony car's development. Computer-based modelling helped to test out a bunch of ideas quickly and inexpensively, a method that became common in the years ahead. While the GM F body has always been a very conventional car, the partial unibody was something of an engineering highlight.

Here was a successful, volume produced car that partly used unit body construction and a separate chassis, hoping to combine the unibody's rigidity with full frame shock absorption. The new car had a separate subframe composed of two parallel rails and three cross members that were secured at four locations. The rest of the structure was pure unibody. Wes McCallum and company made the front subframe concept a reality. Large rubber washers acted as mounting point dampers between the frame and body structure.

Beyond the partial unibody it was sport compact business as usual. The front independent suspension consisted of unequal length A-arms, plus coil springs and tube shocks. At the rear lay a conventional live axle with single leaf springs. If you're thinking that single leaf springs might not provide the last word in ride comfort and rear-wheel control, then you'd be right. Unfortunately, the design computer suggested single leaf springs as the optimal solution and the engineers followed this electronic decision. Pontiac could see that single leaf springs would be as useful as pogo sticks in taming wheel hop on a Firebird 400, so they selectively employed special trailing arms, depending on the particular Firebird at hand.

Rather than have the trailing arms pivot at the axle housing and underbody, Pontiac used an adjacent bracket rigidly attached to the axle housing. The trailing arms only came into play when the rear axle rotated, and, when combined with special geometry, rubber bushings, sandwiches at pivots and contacting surfaces, the axle helpers partially addressed the axle hop expected from single leafs and big engine torque. The Firebird received axle aid on a needs basis. 326 autos, Sprint 6 autos and ordinary OHC I6 motivated models with optional 3.23 to 4.33 gear ratios all got one right side trailing arm. All Firebird 400s, stick shift 326s and Sprint 6s received double the help with two trailing arms. Convertibles were also singled out for special consideration. Open top Firebirds used four weighty sealed containers at the corners to combat scuttle shake, that annoying body flexing associated with fresh air motoring.

The GM F body successfully utilized partial unibody construction. It combined unibody rigidity with 'body on a frame' shock absorption. (Courtesy Eran Redick)

Looks are everything

Styling – an element that plays a big role in the fashion conscious world of the pony car – was a worrying thing for Pontiac and the Firebird. The problem for Pontiac was: how to give the car an identity, especially when development time ran to just six months and the Firebird had to largely share the Camaro's sheet metal?

In the end Firebird managed to find a different style, and, when combined with Pontiac's motor line-up, the finished car had managed to distance itself from Chevy's Camaro. Accentuating the long hood/short tail pony car look, the Firebird received a combined bumper/grille beak-like extender that added four inches in length when compared to Camaro. There was also the 'ironing board' hood, hash marks on the rear fenders and GTO influenced double slit taillights.

It was enough to stop people shouting 'Camaro clone,' despite Pontiac being on a budget. The Firebird was one short order special that looked like it just might make it big. Credit PMD for rescuing what might have been a forgettable concept and giving it wings. The Bird's instant appearance was symbolized by the new B F Goodrich space saver spare. Add some freon gas from the can provided and, before your very eyes, that licorice-like band of rubber clinging to the steel rim popped into an instant temporary tire! An instant tire and an instant sport compact; both took the public by surprise.

Playing it fast but safe

A truncated development period didn't mean that PMD skimped on primary and secondary safety. Firebirds came with collapsible steering columns, dual circuit

Computer modeling suggested the use of single leaf rear springs. Pontiac combated wheel hop on more powerful Firebirds with selective use of trailing arms. (Courtesy Eran Redick)

brakes, flexible door handles and four-way hazard warning lights. Front/rear lap belts and front shoulder belts were available. Firestone Wide-Ovals were the standard Firebird tire, and were generous for the size and weight of car. The wide section nature of the tire gave good roadholding,

and the aesthetic benefit of filling out the wheelarches. While regular OHC I6-powered and 326-engined Firebirds were delivered with 9.5in drum brakes all round, the Firebird 400 and Sprint 6 editions were marketed with single piston caliper Delco-Moraine front disks. This option was essential if repeated

hard braking was to be followed by straight, fade-free stops.

The swerving under-braking that overheated 4-wheel drums caused was something that called for a cool head, and not a small amount of guts. Pontiac's Delco-Moraine option mirrored the Kelsey-Hayes setup that was

Only 1967½ Firebirds had vent wings, and only 400-powered models wore the Pontiac shield logo on the combined bumper/grille beak. (Courtesy Eddie Pettit)

The 230-cube Pontiac I6 was the first overhead camshaft inline six with a cambelt produced at Detroit level production volumes. Plans were afoot to make a version with an aluminum head and place it in the proposed XP-833-derived Pontiac sportscar. (Courtesy Select Motor Company)

available on Ford's Mustang. It didn't take long for the majority of buyers to prefer the benefits of front disks over the then common, all-drum systems. Apart from fade-free stops, power front disks gave the ergonomic benefit of a lower brake pedal. On the minus side disks didn't have the natural assistance experienced on all-drum setups. This implied that the sport compact was the largest and heaviest car one could order non-power assisted front disks on. In contrast, non-power assisted all-drum setups were feasible on even family-sized cars. As with other cars, the power assisted brakes on the Firebird had too much assistance. Panic stops were hard to modulate without brake lock-up.

A most unusual engine in the motor city – Pontiac's OHC I6

Worthy of special mention is the use of Pontiac's overhead cam (OHC) I6 in the Firebird line. This was the first overhead cam inline six to be made at Detroit production volume levels, and came as an option on the 1966 model year Pontiac Tempest. This single overhead cam engine

used the Chevy 230-cube inline 6 as a starting point and featured a replaceable fiberglass-reinforced Gilmer belt. One would have to travel to West Germany and visit Hans Glas GmbH to encounter a similar contemporary design. Glas was a pioneering company which demonstrated the advantages in cost and refinement that a cambelt could bring compared to a conventional chain drive.

Pontiac gave its new engine a respectable air of durability by making provision for the Gilmer belt's protection and adjustment. The belt was housed within a diecast aluminum cover with sheet metal backing. A tensioning sprocket, near the crank sprocket, had attached to it an integrated accessory package. Oil pump, filter, fuel pump and distributor were all carried by an aluminum housing and driven by the sprocket. The whole package was attached to the engine block with six cap screws and could be removed as a single convenient unit for routine maintenance.

More innovative thinking lay with the OHC I6's valve gear.

When launched the Poncho OHC I6 became the first overhead cam motor in the world with automatic valve lash adjustment. Rather than use a pivot shaft Pontiac placed a partially spherical pivot between the cam lobe and valve stem, allowing the pivot to move freely and keep close contact with the cam lobe surface in the interests of minimizing wear. A search for greater performance caused Pontiac to depart from the modified 'bathtub' combustion chamber present on the Chevy I6. The combustion chambers assumed more of a wedge shape, and the incline of the valve stem plane was increased to 15 degrees. Larger valves were present on the OHC I6, compared to the Chevy 230-cube OHV I6, and combustion chambers were machined rather than left as-cast.

Both Pontiac and Chevy inline sixes shared seven main bearings and a nodular cast iron crankshaft. However, Pontiac extended the cylinder block past the crankshaft centerline by 2.38in. Although the new OHC I6 had both a cast iron block and cylinder head,

Somehow the Firebird V8s, like this 1967½ Firebird 400 hardtop, always seemed a more natural form for the Firebird to take than the I6 models. (Courtesy Hugo)

230 I6 and 326 V8 kept the Allstate insurance man at bay, as Firebird made a flying 1967 start! (Courtesy Rick)

aluminum was in evidence. The cam carrier, accessory pack and cambelt cover all used the lightweight metal, and it was on the cards for PMD to make the cylinder head out of aluminum, as well. It was in connection with the XP-833 sportscar project that Pontiac engineers installed the Poncho OHC I6 into a Jaguar XKE!

The Corvette's future and GM management ended John Z DeLorean's dream of the XP-833 funster, but the one-off, Pontiac-powered Jaguar gave an indication of where PMD wanted to take the pushrod free motor. Unfortunately, the OHC I6 never did get to play in that rarefied group,

destined, as it was, to finish its days in more down-to-earth machinery. The reality was that the OHC I6 had more technology on offer than the average buyer in the Firebird and Tempest market wanted. A bold design, but technical overkill for mainstream Detroit and the audience it actually found.

Another 1966 model year newcomer that made a bigger splash was the four barrel Quadrajet, brought to market courtesy of GM's Rochester Products Division. GM laid down the law that, from here on in, any sporty cars coming from its subsidiaries would be limited to four carburetor throats. Forget the war cry of the Goat, as it cleared its

triple two barrel carb 389 V8 throat on yet another sprint towards the horizon. Such extravagance was deemed evil, and triple deuces were consigned to history for good.

On the plus side, power levels didn't exactly plummet, and the new Q-jet was an easier creature to keep an eye on. Rochester's new pet had small primaries and big secondaries. The promise was of good general economy with the motor chugging along, and an instant shot of adrenaline when the pedal was floored and those secondaries kicked in. Rochester delivered on the promise and the Q-jet was part of GM's corporate furniture for many years to come.

Visit Veloce on the web – www.velocebooks.com
Special offers • Details of all current books • Gift vouchers • New books

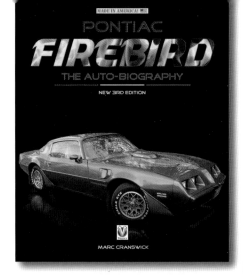

3

The magnificent five ride – the Firebird model range

Pontiac began the 1967½ proceedings with what it claimed were the magnificent five – or was that five and a half? Make that a qualified half because Firebird 400s with the optional L67 Ram Air package were rare birds, indeed. The zenith of pick-and-mix car ordering was open to one and all. Endless power team and color/trim possibilities stretched as far as the eye could see. Make no mistake: PMD had a more than passable option list, but somehow the Firebird packages seemed more like stand-alone models than other cars in the Motor City. A Firebird Sprint 6 was a certain kind of car, and so, too, was the Firebird 400. Perhaps PMD knew something about the rationalized model lines of the distant future?

The range kicked off with the innocuous 165bhp OHC I6 base Firebird that wouldn't offend anyone. Next up in ponies was the Firebird Sprint 6, a sporty incarnation of the six-cylinder Firebird that used the OHC I6 in 215bhp high output form. The 2bbl Firebird 326 came in as the first of the V8 models with a fair 250 horses. Warmer still was the 4bbl version of the 326, boasting 285bhp. The 326 HO was

Four weighty containers located at the convertible's four corners helped keep scuttle shake at bay.
(Courtesy Brett Liukkonen)

16

Pontiac pinned sales hopes on Firebird 326s, like the car featured. It was something the kids could afford without incurring the full wrath of insurance companies. (Courtesy Eran Redick)

the Firebird PMD pinned its youth market hopes on; quick enough to hook the junior racing crowd, but not so powerful that the insurance companies would join the party and scare all the guests away.

Climbing to higher altitude one encountered the Firebirds that dreams were made of: 400in in such an itzy bitzy little car! PMD put the cat among the automotive pigeons by releasing the 325bhp Firebird 400. Well, if Pontiac could borrow the 400 engine from the full-size Catalina, then Chevrolet could state before GM management that it was only reasonable for the Camaro's option sheet to have a box next to the

The Firebird 400 didn't need to rely on European associated names or terms to convey its effectiveness. Floor the gas pedal, open up the 4bbl 400, and the world was your oyster. (Courtesy Frank Thomas)

numbers 396. There was no danger of the Firebird entering Camaro copy territory. In spite of shared A bodies, the public never mistook the Pontiac GTO for the Chevy Chevelle SS 396. It could see that the Firebird was no Camaro hiding behind Pontiac's shield.

Continuing with the notion of stand-alone versions, let's look at a couple of Firebirds that were making the headlines back in those early days: the Firebird Sprint 6 and the Firebird 400 V8.

Pontiac's track stars – the Sprint 6 & Firebird 400

Look upon the Firebird Sprint 6 as a high-spirited ground coverer

Singer Nancy Sinatra owned a new special order 1968 Pink Mist-colored Firebird 400 ragtop. (Courtesy Elizabeth)

falling within Pontiac's 'European' phase of the mid '60s to early '70s. Much has been written about how the Great Ones took European terms and imported them to Michigan soil. There was a Ferrari called the GTO, Grand Prix were races conducted mainly in Continental Europe, and Le Mans was a big adventure where combatants with insomnia piloted sportscars for 24 hours. However, with a little bit of imagination, and even more cheekiness, these great names might also serve as Poncho nameplates on models that many know and love. Why stop at the name? Why not adopt an entire

concept? Give it a home and make it one of the PMD family. In the Pontiac Firebird Sprint 6 PMD was hoping buyers would find the great European road machine.

High revving high jinks, floor shifts, resilient suspension and, at the top of the list, balance. Such were the qualities attributed to European sporty machines; could PMD hatch a Firebird that put speedy ground coverage ahead of ¼ mile strip work?

Pontiac's recipe started with a special version of its overhead cam six. Compression on the 230-cube motor was raised to 10.5 to one, making premium grade 99 octane

juice the rule. A bigger cam put even more daylight between the Sprint 6 and regular single barrel inline six edition. Valve timing alterations were responsible for boosting the Sprint 6 engine's output from the 207 horses found in a 1966 Tempest to the 215bhp of 1967. One benefit of the OHC layout was the opportunity to go for a peppier top end without killing low speed torque. Due to higher valve acceleration rates, OHC can achieve this high/low end compromise without the extreme valve timing overlap associated with OHV motors.

The Sprint 6 engine featured one Rochester 4-barrel sitting on

a special intake manifold with internal dividers that directed concentrated airflow to each of the six cylinders. A freer flowing dual exhaust manifold completed the list of changes made to the base OHC I6. In light of its sporting pretentions, the Firebird Sprint 6 came with both single leaf taming trailing arms, and firmer than stock suspension. The $9.32 #621 'Ride and Handling Package' standard on Firebird 326 HOs and 400s was optional. A rakish mid-body height $14.22 #491 Rally stripe decal, in the style of the one available on the Tempest Sprint, was also on offer.

1967's all-new Rally IIs, together with a floor shifted Muncie 4-speed box, were frequently seen on Sprint 6 cars. In fact, the four on the floor Muncie box had special ratios of 3:11, 2:20, 1:47 and a direct top fourth gear. All to eke out a tractable power delivery from the highly strung Sprint 6 engine. At first glance the Firebird Sprint 6 specification suggested European-style performance on a low budget. Firm, wallow-free suspension, four forward speeds, a high output overhead cam inline 6 that did its best work at higher engine revolutions, and a raspy exhaust note. The trouble was, spec sheets can lie ...

The Firebird Sprint 6 was in no way a bad car. Indeed, it was laudable that PMD should create something that put aside all-out firepower in the interest

At first the Firebird Sprint 6 had '3.8 litre' insignia, but 1968 saw the arrival of the 250-cube OHC I6 and a badge change to '4.1-litre.' The larger motor had Pontiac crank and rods.
(Courtesy Select Motor Company)

of finding balanced performance. Could this recipe really be served to a wider audience than those visiting Triumph and MG dealers? Unfortunately, the Sprint 6 concept was at odds with the underlying car. One can't help but think that the Firebird and Tempest would have been happier devices when fitted with a sensible Poncho V8 motor and a nice automatic transmission. As things stood, the unperturbed high speed grand tourer wasn't there. The '6.5 litre' and '3.8 litre overhead cam' badges adorning the sides and hoods of the 1964 GTO and 1967½ Firebird Sprint 6 respectively shouted European-style, but the driving reality said something else.

The Firebird Sprint 6 handled well on smooth surfaces, but the Motor City's traditional suspension

lacked enough compliance when the going got rough. In this respect the optional Koni shock absorbers and BFG radials only made matters worse. The pleasant Muncie 4-speed was partly downgraded by an indifferent GM shift linkage. The Sprint 6 lived up to its name in acceleration, but that linkage implied the occasional missed shift. The 230-cube overhead cam 6 possessed reasonable torque and made good power when revved, but it really would have been more at home in that lightweight sportscar John Z DeLorean wanted. However, in an era when anything not connected with the ¼ mile was thrown aside, the Sprint 6 was a bold effort to be different. Unfortunately, this was one Firebird that was a decade before its time.

The first generation Firebird was very much a car of its era. Escalating horsepower, bold styling; these were the hallmarks of the late '60s pony car scene. PMD had a capable exponent in the Firebird 400. The Sprint 6 was a nice little diversion, but the 400-powered cars represented what the sport compact performance scene was all about. The Firebird 400s were the highest flyers in the original Firebird flock. The inline 6-powered cars took care of low cost ownership and cut-rate European performance dreams. The 326-powered V8s catered for most mainstream performance demands, but the 400 motivated Firebirds were the image makers.

This Australian right-hand drive 1968 Firebird 400 hardtop automatic has the rare D port Ram Air I engine. The Ram Air option wasn't readily available until the March 1968 introduction of Ram Air II. (Courtesy Larry McGrath & Chicanery www.youtube.com/watch?v=7A2UVh52uI8)

For those who wanted – and could actually afford – it all, life started with 400in. Once again, think of the Firebird 400 as more than just an engine option; there was more to it than that.

Firebird 400s had twin scooped hoods, four tail pipes and PMD's

Homer Simpson bought a red '68 Firebird convertible from the Springfield police impound lot auction, the car belonged to career criminal Snake! (Courtesy Jim Thomson)

The hood-mounted tachometer, initial mini rear traction bars and 4-barrel Q-jet marked the Firebird 400 as a creature of Woodward Avenue. A bird of prey ready to strike at some impromptu street race. (Courtesy Jim Thomson)

handling pack thrown in for good measure. In 1964 the GTO acquired PMD's full-size car V8, and now the compact Firebird was getting a 400-cube motor. Were everyday cars really going to reach the moon before astronaut Neil Armstrong? Well, they just might have if it wasn't for a few corporate edicts that GM management laid down.

We already know about the ban on anything wilder than four carb throats, so GM's power-to-weight house rule should come as no surprise. If you consider the original Pontiac GTO as a lapse in concentration; GM was still anti-racing. It was decreed from on high that no family member, except the Vette, was to pack more than one gross horsepower for every 10lb of bodyweight. A 3000lb vehicle could have no more than 300 ponies.

While the contemporary GTO had 335bhp and a Ram Air assisted 360 horses, the equivalent 400 motors offered for the Firebird 400 were both rated at a mere 325bhp. GM's power-to-weight rule had resulted in the comic situation of buyers paying more for an optional engine that created the same horsepower at 5200rpm rather than 4800rpm! GM liked to keep up appearances. There's no doubt that PMD underquoted the power level of what has come to be known as the Ram Air I 400 motor. If a plain Firebird 400 hardtop coupe weighed in at 3250lb, then GM family law stated that it shouldn't look like it had more than 325bhp. Great, I

hear you say, does this mean the lighter Firebird could be purchased with GTO go? In theory, yes, but in practice, no.

There was a performance pecking order to be honored at PMD, and this implied that the finest 400s Pontiac could muster were bestowed upon the GTO. Both the Goat and the Firebird 400 shared the same block, premium gas hungry 10.75:1 compression ratio, 2.11in intake and 1.77in exhaust valves, plus identical cylinder head porting. Even the cam profiles chosen came from the same quartet of options. However, there was just no way that PMD would let a showroom Firebird 400 complete the 1320ft sprint first. Choose a certain cam, add a metal tab to prevent the throttle linkage from opening up the Q-jet's secondaries all the way, and that little Firebird was always going to be in the GTO's rearview mirror.

To add insult to injury, major motoring journals often tested the lead sled Firebird 400 convertible rather than the relatively lithe

hardtop. Those four heavy sealed containers may well have limited convertible scuttle shake, but they also reduced the Firebird's terminal speeds on the ¼ mile flight path. The rarity of Ram Air assistance in that very first truncated model year also widened the perceived performance gulf between a well tuned GTO and the new Firebird 400. *Hot Rod* magazine's prototype 1967½ Firebird 400 ragtop with 3-speed hydramatic came in at a positively corpulent 3855lb. It's little surprise that the mini beast registered 15.4 seconds in the ¼ with a trap speed of just 92mph. As if to emphasize that the search for performance always rests on the margins, *Car Life* secured a 1967½ Firebird 400 hardtop with four on the floor that was happy to fly down the ¼ mile strip in 14.7 seconds at 98mph.

Impressive figures for an out of the box pony with a hydraulic lifter V8, but it was never going to catch the Goat ... in stock trim. Then again, no self-respecting racer left his car in stock trim,

This loaded 1968 Firebird 400 convertible has the rare distinction of being a genuine factory 400 ragtop that came with air conditioning. (Courtesy Shane Pierce)

Pontiac styling cues, unique powerplants, and the flow-on effect of the GTO's image, distanced the Firebird from its F body sibling, the Chevrolet Camaro. (Courtesy Larry McGrath & Chicanery www.youtube.com/watch?v=7A2UVh52uI8)

unless he wanted to hitch a ride home after losing his pink slip. This was the late '60s, the heyday of Woodward Avenue, and helpful Royal Oaks dealer, Royal Pontiac, who just loved to put a tiger in your tank. The solid lifter fraternity may have frowned upon your mode of transport, but with 400in in the lightweight Firebird, the sky was the limit. Metal tabs could be removed, Royal Pontiac was ready to mill the heads and sandwich some super slim gaskets between cylinder head and block. Add a spot of judicious ignition timing tuning and you were all set to secure ownership of a rival's pink slip during the dead of night.

If the Firebird Sprint 6 was a nice change of pace, then the 400 was the Firebird's destiny. If you liked participating in Pure Stock, fitting glass paks, playing with alternate gear sets and generally raising a little hell, the Firebird was for you. Royal Pontiac's Bobcat versions summed up the mood of the time. A tuned engine with sky high compression, half white painted roof and thoughtfully positioned Royal Bobcat insignia left no doubt in the minds of onlookers. Here were

rough and ready street brawlers designed to prowl quiet night-time roads looking for fresh prey.

Somehow it didn't seem to matter that your Royal Bobcat Firebird 400 possessed drum brakes all round, there was no replacement for displacement and brakes just slow you down! For ¼ mile devotees front disk brakes just heaped on unwanted unsprung weight and incurred greater wind resistance. Those optional 11.1in front disks might have been all that was separating you from your pink slip in a close fought contest of speed.

The first generation Firebird's hood-mounted tach, Rally II rims, big inch V8 and floor shift went together as well as lox and cream cheese. However, the need for speed carried its own price. There's no doubt that the early Firebird was a handling car capable of scooting around corners with the best in town, if the road was smooth. Add a few bumps in the fairway and holding a particular cornering line was hardwork. Pony cars were sporty cars and were not expected to ride as well as family transport. The trouble was that the first generation

F bodies were stiffly sprung, and harsh riding even by sport compact standards. PMD valiantly tried to tame those single leaf rear springs, but they just lacked enough compliance. As things stood the additional trailing arms fitted to sporty Firebirds stopped a bad situation from getting worse.

Please don't hold onto the dream that Firebird's four seats could actually accommodate four adults in comfort. As with most sporty coupes before and since, rear seat space was tight and should only have been used in emergencies. The driving position also wasn't above criticism. Pony cars usually have the habit of placing the steering wheel too close to the driver's chest and the pedals far away. The hood-mounted tach tended to fog up in damp weather.

Improved through-flow ventilation allowed 1968 Firebirds to do without vent wings. (Courtesy Jim Thomson)

1967½ Firebirds were built at Lordstown, and, by 1968, the Van Nuys factory also. By 1969 Firebird assembly was carried out at the Lordstown, Van Nuys and Ohio Norwood factories. (Courtesy Chris Hall)

While the Firebird wasn't perfect, it did stamp its authority in acceleration and sure-footed smooth road-handling, plus the availability of hardware that was initially uncommon in sport compacts, like a full-size car motor and 3-speed automatic. It was a sporty, affordable, cleanly styled, small personal car that could be optioned up with comfort and performance features found on larger model lines.

The manner in which your particular Firebird made its way down the road depended upon the way it was specified. It was possible to round off the rough edges by specifying such things as power brakes and the 3-speed hydramatic box. The only downside with greater choice was lower assembly line quality. As the Motor City's output expanded through the 1960s, vehicle build quality suffered. The many trim, convenience features, and the power team combinations, only made vehicle build quality harder to control as production volume grew. The cost limits imposed by big car makers on component suppliers also can't be ignored.

Revisions to the Firebirds
The most significant change to the Firebird for the 1968 model year was a redesign of the single leaf live axle rear suspension. Out went the teeth rattler and in came softer multi leaf springs and staggered shocks. The right side shock absorber was positioned ahead of the live axle and the left shock unit sat behind. Instead of the almost vertically mounted 1967½ shocks, the 1968 versions had more angle to their pose. Kids filled with drag racing dreams must have been sad the day the single leaf trailing arms were banished. Those trailing arms with adjustable positive stops may have resembled mini traction bars, and fueled ¼ mile fantasies, but they hardly kept axle tramp

1968 saw the introduction of side marker lights; the front turn signals were redesigned to accommodate them. A 1968 change that could be felt was adoption of rear multi-leaf springs and staggered shocks. (Courtesy Jim Thomson)

in check or netted the Firebird owner better ride comfort.

The most visually significant change for 1968 was the elimination of noise-provoking vent wings. Dumping that additional opening glass pane cleaned up the Firebird's line, especially in ragtop form. More importantly, it heralded an age when an increasing number of motorists expected full fresh air ventilation supply from dashboard vents. So it was that circular swivel dash vents were placed at the lower edges of the dashboard ends; a great way to keep the interior well ventilated at speed without the wind noise associated with vent wings. No other changes were made to the well-padded safety

dashboard borrowed from the Camaro.

1968 also saw an expansion in Firebird engine sizes. PMD took the 230-cube overhead cam six out to 250ci by lengthening the stroke quarter of an inch. The inline six now had the bore and stroke dimensions of 3.88in by 3.50in with the base six up to 175bhp and the Sprint making 230/235bhp by 1969. These internal changes meant that the Sprint 6 could now display new '4.1 litre overhead cam' hood badging in place of the previous 3.8-litre insignia. The faithful middle order 326 was up-gunned to a full 350in. Standard and HO versions of the Pontiac 350 produced 265 and 320 horsepower

respectively, and featured smoother combustion chambers and larger valves. As ever the Poncho V8 could gain displacement by alterations to the bore and stroke. The V8 block retained its external size, regardless of whether the engine at hand was a 326, 350, 389 or 400. Speaking of 400s, the horsepower rating of the Ram Air edition was up to 335bhp.

Both engine power and displacement were increased, but driveability was down. The 1968 model year brought with it the first national wave of pollution regulations, and motorists noticed that the 1968 model year cars didn't start, idle or run as smoothly as in previous years. Engine behaviour and the emissions hardware

The 1968 Firebird dashboard had larger gauges, more safety padding and 'Astro Ventilation.' (Courtesy Jim Thomson)

necessary to meet the laws varied. Innocuous PCV valves and lean carb settings were precursors to more heavyweight future remedies, although some 1968 models did require smog pumps. As things stood, the 1968 Firebird fell into the category of cars that could be tuned out of their driveability depression. Many owners, unhappy with the way their new cars ran, had service departments alter carb and ignition settings. Although not legally permissible it was often the only way to get a 1968 and later model year cars to function properly.

1969 brought the first major restyle since the Firebird landed as a 1967½ model. This may sound odd but 1969's Bird got

bigger, without actually getting bigger. The Firebird had its exterior sheetmetal reskinned upon the existing dimensions and wheelbase.

1969 brought the first major Firebird restyle since the car was launched: there were elements of the 1969 Grand Prix in the latest Firebird. (Courtesy Hugo)

Since the dawn of the 1960s, the average domestic car had gotten larger; a trend that accompanied the successively larger and more powerful motors introduced as part of the horsepower race. Apart from the need to periodically freshen up styling, car makers in such a competitive marketplace felt compelled to make their new model year versions stand out and have greater presence. Ford's Mustang was puffed out into a physically larger car in spite of retaining existing underpinnings. The 1969 Firebird didn't quite take matters to that level, but it sure did look imposing.

The 1969 Firebird received new front and rear styling. The

1969 Firebirds featured this one-piece Lexan front bumper/grille. Although the latest cars were physically larger, they were still built on the same 108in wheelbase. (Courtesy David McGuire)

rear fender hash marks were jettisoned, and long stampings now rode over the rear arches. The new styling touches matched the look of the successful new budget Eldorado-chasing Pontiac Grand Prix and contemporary GTO. The visual changes gave Firebird a more muscular look and, as ever, there was no mistaking the latest Bird for anything but a Pontiac. The new look polarized popular opinion; some really taking to it and some with reservations. Regardless of practicality, function took a back seat to shape with the latest Firebird.

The new nosecone didn't match the earlier car's decorative stamping when it came to serving double duty as a front bumper and aesthetically appealing front view. 1969 also saw the start of the 'Rally Shifter' option for the 3-speed THM autobox. This gadget permitted the driver to manually shift between second and third gears without overshooting into neutral. Move the shift lever to the right and there lay a second plane with detents that allowed only one ratio change per hand movement. Very much like Hurst's Dual/Gate or 'His & Hers'

aftermarket design, except without the visible second gate.

In 1967 and 1968 the Firebird's fuel filler was located between the rear taillights and behind a little trap door. As part of the 1969 revisions it now resided under the rear bumper, behind the license plate. While creating a cleanly styled tail the new provisions made filling the 18½ gallon tank more difficult.

The interior was fitted with a new style dashboard. Earlier incarnations made do with the Camaro's control center, but the 107,112 1968 model year sales

All 1969 Firebirds, like this Firebird 400 convertible, had a new rear facia with the fuel filler relocated under the rear bumper and behind the license plate. (Courtesy Hugo)

Even models like this 1969 Sprint 6 were available with the versatile GM THM 350 automatic. The public had come to expect the refinement and performance advantages a 3-speed autobox offered. (Courtesy Select Motor Company)

permitted a little more extravagance for 1969, including optional wood trim. Add to this power windows, 8-track cartridge player – and even air conditioning – and luxury could be blended with power, even if it was at the expense of vehicle weight.

The versatile 3-speed Turbo Hydramatic was no longer limited to the Firebird 400 but could be chosen for versions like the Sprint 6, too. Here lay the Firebird's problem. The high level of outright performance offered by some versions, combined with items from the extensive option list, often led to comparisons with vehicles costing a great deal more. This was especially true when the Firebird was tested overseas. As mentioned by Britain's *Motor* magazine in 1971 when evaluating the 1970½ Formula 400, the performance with the luxury available belied the Firebird's price. Even when priced far above domestic levels by overseas distributors, a well specified Firebird could meet exalted coupes head-on in some areas.

Visit Veloce on the web – www.velocebooks.com
Special offers • Details of all current books • Gift vouchers • New books

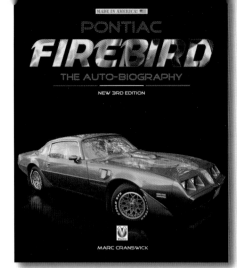

Pontiac's budget Caddy Eldo, the '69 Grand Prix. (Courtesy Andy)

4

Sport, courtesy of the Great Ones

PMD went through a role reversal as the 1960s progressed. Once the purveyor of quiet, conservative sedans, the GTO saw to it that street performance would become PMD's new hallmark. The world was looking at Pontiac through GTO tinted glasses, and things were rosy enough to elevate Pontiac to number three in the sales race. The GTO's market explosion, Grand Prix's winning entry into economy

By the late '60s Pontiac had used its 'Wide-Track' performance image to break out of the Chevy/Olds divide and attain third place in the sales race. (Courtesy David McGuire)

Continued sales success with 107,112 units produced in 1968 meant that revisions for 1969 could include a new dashboard. Up to that point the Firebird had shared its dash with the Camaro. (Courtesy David McGuire)

Eldorado/Continental land, could PMD do no wrong?

For a company, and a corporate parent, that kept its distance from the racetrack, PMD was involved with a number of models and areas close to the enthusiast's heart. Special Firebird versions, engines and some involvement in motorsport, were all in keeping with PMD's established 'Wide-Track' performance theme. Those cunning characters at PMD were attacking from almost every angle: if there was a hot car to sell then Pontiac wanted to sell it. Not content with the Firebird Sprint 6, itself already further than anyone was prepared to go in that segment, Pontiac

played with the PFST or Pontiac Firebird Sprint Turismo. While the engine didn't receive anywhere near the attention lavished on the 303 motor, it could be said that the PFST was close in spirit to a six-cylinder version of the 1969½ Firebird Trans Am 303 that never really was. With insurance rates for V8 motivated performance cars spiraling, Pontiac explored the idea of a white hot performance pony with six cylinders.

Six in a row doesn't go? The PFST & Fitch Birds

Whatever the Firebird Sprint 6 was and did, the PFST went a step further. At a time when the

Detroit had discovered that all things sporty could sell. The Firebird was flying high in an era when one could even get a Hurst shifter on a Buick! (Courtesy Select Motor Company)

Pontiac replaced the Firebird's 326 with a 350 V8 in 1968. By 1969 the 350 V8 was still rated at 265bhp, but the L76 HO version made 325bhp. The car shown is a 1969 Firebird 350 in Sweden. (Courtesy Christer Jonsson)

OHC I6 motor was displacing 230 cubes, Pontiac gave the PFST a 250ci version, a preview of what all Pontiac's inline sixes would be like in the 1968 model year. A new rod and crank assembly achieved the longer stroke, but, of even greater interest, was the carburetion: three DCN downdraft Webers perched on a custom tube and plate intake manifold. Dual branch extractors went into a free flow exhaust system. An exposed large capacity air-box peeked through the hood, and its presence was partially camouflaged by the single blue racing stripe running the length of the car's body. This was all functional, the high performance inline six needed a great deal of air and the air-box had a rear aperture similar to the rearward facing hood scoop on the 1970½ Pontiac Firebird Trans Am. The exposed air-box did need to be that large and aerodynamics dictated that a high pressure concentration of air lay at the base of the windshield. So the extra plumage was all in a good cause.

The PFST had heavier duty springs and adjustable vacuum controlled shocks made possible by a vacuum reservoir and dashboard adjuster. All rubber bushings were replaced by nylon and steel equivalents and were accompanied

by thicker sway bars. A Muncie 4-speed with Hurst linkage and 4.33 to one gears allowed the ¼ mile to be crossed in top gear at the OHC I6's peak power rpm of 5800. An interior roll bar, Hurst rims, Goodyear Speedway tires and rear brake scoops rounded out the PFST picture. ¼ mile times were in the low 15 second bracket and the zero to sixty sprint was a tad under 8 seconds. Handy improvements over the stock car's high 16s and 10.5 second times.

Various barriers prevented the PFST from seeing production. GM's 1966 edict against multiple carbs was at odds with the PFST's triple Webers, and that exhaust system didn't stand a chance of meeting legal drive-by noise standards. Pontiac Engineering did create a 230-cube PFST with a single four barrel, in deference to GM family law. There was also the inescapable fact that short stroke motors have an easier time of things winding out to high rpms. (This last point was of some importance because Pontiac was considering the PFST for future SCCA racing duty.)

A second special entry was John Fitch's Fitch Firebird, a low volume custom Firebird that took over from Fitch's Corvair conversions. By the late '60s the

Corvair's life was drawing to a close and any aftermarket activity concerned with it was fading. John Fitch had connections with notable racing entities such as the Briggs Cunningham, Corvette and Mercedes-Benz racing teams. This former racing ace had his own ideas about what form a specialized street Firebird should take. Fitch expressed his thoughts and intentions to PMD's John Z DeLorean. The upshot was the supply of two Firebirds, a Sprint 6 and Firebird 400. Once again Fitch's plan revolved around the Firebird Sprint 6, but a need to attract media exposure and mainstream performance buyers meant that a Fitch Firebird 400 was also on the drawing board. John Fitch aimed at creating a balanced Firebird, an automobile with sufficient power and improvements in every facet of driving at a reasonable surcharge.

The fundamental difference between the PFST and the Fitch cars was in the approach to suspension modification. The PFST largely selected PMD's heavy duty suspension option, whereas Fitch chose the Firebird's stock suspension and added long, soft jounce bumpers for both front and rear suspension. There was a single inch of free spring movement before the jounce bumpers touched the suspension members. Once engaged the double-doughnut bumpers progressively stiffened up the suspension. The PFST rode

A 1969 Firebird Ram Air III 400 hardtop coupe in Norway. The three 400s for 1969 were the 330bhp W66, 335bhp Ram Air III and 345bhp Ram Air IV. 1969 was the last year of Firebird production at Lordstown. (Courtesy Timo Krop)

stiffly all the time, possessing a level of harshness that even the performance-minded would have found hard to swallow. The Fitch Birds were intended to maintain normal ride comfort on undemanding road surfaces, saving the heavy duty suspension feel for when drivers were really pushing their steed.

The PFST and Fitch Firebird showed two ways to improve the handling of a rear drive live axle pony car. Whereas the PFST strove for flat cornering, the Fitch cars exhibited greater roll. Indeed, the additional roll stiffness brought by the jounce bumpers would increasingly come into play at greater cornering angles. Both were compromise solutions which demonstrated that improved handling on domestic live axle cars was often acquired at the expense of ride comfort. A more sophisticated solution than the Fitch's jounce bumpers would have made the finished car much more expensive.

Fitch also altered the Saginaw power steering's gear valving to limit boosted assistance and increase road feel. The same applied to the power brakes; adjustments were made to the brake booster in the interests of better feel and reduced over-assisted pedal sensitivity.

It was the little changes that made the Fitch Firebirds special.

The Firebird Trans Am made a mid 1969 model year entry. Tick the WS4 option box and your new 1969 Firebird 400 looked like the car T/G Racing wanted to campaign before the SCCA rule book beat it to it. (Courtesy Richard A Clatterbuck)

Rear Koni shocks, Engelbert Radials, a tachometer, Lucas 'flame thrower' headlamps, column stalk-mounted headlamp dip switch – and even a one-touch facility for the windshield wipers. The Lucas lamps and column headlamp dip switch were technically illegal, as were the wire mesh grille headlamp protectors. Added rear buttress fiberglass pillars leant a fastback air to the Fitch Firebirds. When made functional the buttresses had apertures to aid fresh air cabin ventilation and rear brake cooling.

One thousand dollars over the particular stock Firebird chosen for conversion created a Fitch Firebird. Unlike the PFST the Fitch modified cars did actually enter the marketplace. However, the 1969½ Firebird Trans Am overshadowed both the PFST and Fitch cars. In a market segment that didn't exactly reward subtlety, the PFST and Fitch entries paled next to the high output V8-powered opposition. Grand tourers would gain popularity in the mid to late 1970s but, for now, pony car buyers wanted horsepower, and lots of it!

SCCA Trans Am duty
What could offer a better showpiece for glamor and horsepower than the Sports Car Club of America's

Former Shelby team driver Jerry Titus was persuaded by Canadian industrialist Terry Godsall to leave Ford and establish Titus/Godsall (T/G) Racing for the 1969 racing season. (Courtesy www.historictransam.com)

Trans Am race series for production sedans? Watch the imports battle it out in the under 122-cube class, leaving the rest of the festivities to domestic V8-powered machinery wielding motors of less than 305in.

Racetrack prowess spelt showroom success, and this category's stable was just full of hot ponies. The trouble was, one had to pack the right hardware. It was all well and good building production coupes with large block V8 motors, but that wasn't going to help you at the track. Forget about shoe horning a full-size engine into a compact's engine bay, this party was definitely a high output/low displacement affair. If there wasn't a small displacement, high rpm V8 jewel on the manufacturer's parts shelf, it was game over.

Pontiac used a Canadian back door into the Trans Am series. At the time GM supplied Canada with Chevy-based Pontiacs, and this proved a quick way to secure a competitive runner. The Canadian Firebird piloted by Craig Fisher for Terry Godsall during the 1968 Trans Am season was actually a Camaro Z/28 in disguise: under Canadian market sheet metal beat the heart of a Chevy. The Camaro was a successful road racer and, in the Z/28's 302 V8, Chevrolet had a race-ready, sub-305-cube engine. This Canadian trojan horse provided an early Trans Am series foray for Pontiac and greater things were in store for the 1969 racing season.

Toronto heavy equipment industrialist, Terry Godsall, secured the services of Shelby team driver Jerry Titus. Titus left Ford to start T/G (Titus/Godsall) Racing, where he partnered Craig Fisher. The whole enterprise was looking quite promising.

Starting behind the eight ball, the mini Ram Air IV motor that would have to be developed for the 1969 SCCA Trans Am season, would have to overcome the Ram Air's inherent problems. Pontiac's V8s had marginal high speed lubrication, something that wouldn't trouble a domestic production car, but certainly an Achilles heel on the racetrack. Also remember that the Poncho V8 dated back to the mid 1950s. It would take a few late nights to get a race engine that could match firepower with Chevrolet's and Ford's high-output designs.

To tackle these concerns T/G Racing contacted engine guru Al Bartz. Bartz restricted the rocker arm bleed hole at the main bearings to limit the chance of oil collecting in the valve covers. 0.0015in bearing clearances would look after the bottom end of the race motor. The racing Poncho

V8 didn't retain the Ram Air IV's hydraulic tappets, but became a solid lifter powerplant. However, the Ram Air IV's cam profile did make it through the development sieve. Out of eight different cam profiles Bartz chose to retain the stock Ram Air IV's 0.520 lift, 308 degree intake duration/320 degree exhaust. The Ram Air IV cam gave the best torque delivery up to 8000rpm without the dreaded valve float. 12.5 to one TRW forged aluminum pistons with deflectors were part of the build sheet. The piston deflectors filled a combustion chamber that was a smaller version of that possessed by the contemporary Ram Air IV 400.

In the end Ram Air IV junior had dimensions of 4.12inx2.87in, giving an interesting cubic capacity of 303in. Compare these measurements with the regular Ram Air IV 400's 4.12x3.75in. The 303 motor drew upon the Ram Air V's four bolt main bearing caps and cylinder heads. The Ram Air V received cylinder heads that placed the motor's pushrods at the port's center; the racing 303 adopted this design at first. Much like Ford's NASCAR 427, BB Chevys and Mopar

The road-going versions of the Firebird Trans Am 303's 1970 season SCCA Trans Am series rivals.

1970 Ford Mustang Boss 302.
(Courtesy Steven Johnson)

1970 Dodge Challenger T/A 340.
(Courtesy Ann Seip)

1970 Plymouth Cuda AAR 340.
(Courtesy Mark)

1970 Chevrolet Camaro Z/28 350.
(Courtesy Mike & Brenda Le Jeune)

Hemis, tunnel port heads greatly improved breathing, Pontiac was able to almost triple the diameter of the intake port. Intake and exhaust valves were sized at 2.19in and 1.73in respectively. Forged Carillo connecting rods had a wide base to resist bending.

Al Bartz added an open-plenum ram manifold that would connect with dual 600cfm Holley four barrels. The highly-strung 303-cube Poncho V8 was producing over 430 gross flywheel horsepower on the dyno as matters drew to a close, although by now the 303 was using non-tunnel port Ram Air IV heads.

All this good stuff would be bolted to a real 1969 Firebird Trans Am shell, complete with rear spoiler, twin hood scoops and body length blue racing stripes contrasting with a white paint job. Factory spot welding gave way to arc welding for the subframe. Oilless nylon bushings and aluminum spacers replaced stock items, and, for the front suspension, the regular Firebird spindle was junked in favor of a forged steel item with higher placed axle stub. As with the Camaro Z/28, braking was left to 4-wheel Delco-Moraine disk brakes. The planned Pontiac 303 Trans Am racer rode on Koni shock absorbers.

One might have expected the new 303-powered 1969 season Pontiac Trans Am to light up the track, accompanied by the soundtrack of a real Poncho V8. The trouble was it just never happened.

The new 303 wasn't ready in time to meet SCCA rules, so, in a bizarre twist, T/G Racing was forced to campaign with Chevy power yet again. Technically, the 302 motor was a 1968 model year Canadian Firebird option, so the car's styling had to be backdated to match that theoretical option.

In spite of the hurdles put in the way by the powers that be, T/G Racing had a great 1969 racing season, with an overall third place in the Trans Am series; a welcome coincidence of number three on the track for a Pontiac, and number three in the sales race for PMD. The 1970 racing season would be very different. An all-new Firebird and a very different SCCA rulebook necessitated a fresh start for many.

The SCCA finally permitted a sub-305-cube racing motor to be created from any member of an engine family by playing around with bore and stroke dimensions. Chrysler was allowed to destroke its hi po 340 V8 so that the new Mopar E body siblings – the Dodge Challenger and Plymouth Barracuda – could participate. Naturally, this implied that nothing would hold back the baby Ram Air 303 from being slotted into the all-new second generation 'European'-look Firebird body for the 1970 racing season.

When combined with all the free areas permitted by the SCCA's revised rulebook, designing a racer for the new season was like starting from scratch. Unlike in 1969, crankshaft, rocker arms, connecting rods and main bearings could all be non-stock items. Carburetion was now limited to a single four barrel, with carb throats restricted to 1.687in in diameter. Restrictions on roll cage design were lifted, and neither the brakes nor the rear axle had to be sourced from production hardware. Aerodynamic aids were also given a freer design limit.

Jerry Titus had difficulty in 1970 getting Terry Godsall to supply sufficient funding for a competitive Trans Am series entry. This contrasted with sponsorship by *Hot Wheels* of the Mopar cars, and Chrysler tacking on a million US dollar sweetener into the bargain. T/G Racing's racing season was plagued with mechanical gremlins. GM and Pontiac weren't officially into racing so PMD's involvement in the series was limited to engineering assistance from Pontiac's Herb Adams, Tom Nell and Skip McCully. When T/G Racing blamed the engineers for the car's poor showing, it put the kybosh on factory assistance.

The whole sad tale culminated in Jerry Titus' crash at Road Atlanta when he collided into a concrete abutment with locked brakes. Ford took the 1970 Trans Am series with the Boss Mustang, and, after that, the whole series sagged.

As ever, racing requires a great deal of the folding stuff and declining sport compact sales made any manufacturer/privateer

The Poncho 303 V8 finally hit the track with the second generation Firebird body shape in the 1970 SCCA Trans Am series. (Courtesy www.historictransam.com)

involvement harder to justify commercially. There would be no Chevys lining up for the 1971 season, Mopar muscle was absent, and Ford also waved goodbye to one and all at the end of the 1970 Trans Am season. For the remainder of the decade the Trans Am series became dominated by imports such as Jaguars and Porsches.

A notable track spin-off – the Firebird Trans Am

That was the racetrack, but what of the road-going versions? Did Pontiac offer an equivalent to the production Camaro Z/28 and Mustang Boss 302? Yes and no: Firebird Trans Ams were available in 1969 and 1970, but they weren't in the mold of the models offered by Chevrolet and Ford.

Say hello to the 1969½ Firebird Trans Am, best described as a natural extension of the popular Firebird 400. The new Firebird Trans Am combined the visual excitement of the SCCA Trans Am series racer with the practicality of a big inch proven performance power team. Apparently, triple World Driving Champion Jack Brabham was involved with the Firebird Trans Am project, and

there was even talk of naming the new model after him.

Certainly an extrovert by today's 'street sleeper'-loving standards, it had dual body length 4in-wide stripes, a 60in rear wing and two broad hood scoops. Under the fiberglass hood lay either the 335bhp L74 Ram Air III 400 or the new L67 Ram Air IV 400 rated at 345bhp. Those hood scoops admitted cool outside air to give extra pep in the ¼ mile, and elsewhere. A large plenum unit was sealed to the hood by a plastic foam seal and four cap screws, and sat upon the familiar Rochester Q-jet. Gearbox choices

Top speed and acceleration depended upon the rear gears at hand; with the Ram Air III and IV 400s available, the Firebird Trans Am wasn't slow in a straight line. The WS4 pack also included the Y96 heavy duty suspension, so corners weren't cut, either! (Courtesy Richard A Clatterbuck)

Rather than use the small displacement, high horsepower 303, Pontiac gave the road-going 1969½ Firebird Trans Am the tractable Ram Air 400s. This is a 1969½ Firebird Trans Am Ram Air III 400 4-speed. (Courtesy Richard A Clatterbuck)

697 cars were built in the Firebird Trans Am's first model year. Manual or automatic transmission could be combined with the Ram Air III or IV motors. This is one of the 114 manual Ram Air III coupes produced. (Courtesy Richard A Clatterbuck)

The Ram Air designation started off on the '60s Firebirds and carried on to the first year of the second generation cars. After the 1970½ models Ram Air didn't return until the 1996 WS6 Firebirds. (Courtesy Paul Prestidge)

36

ran to a 3-speed manual, close ratio 4-speed with Hurst shift linkage and the versatile 3-speed THM autobox. The even power delivery of the 400 motor meant that, when it came to real world driving, any of the gearboxes would have ensured rapid progress. Rear axle ratios ranged from a sensible 3.55, to a passable 3.90 and ended with the frantic 4.33.

The Firebird Trans Am was a swift performer, generating ¼ mile times in the low 14s and a top speed in excess of 130mph. It was expected to have powerful engines accompanied by multiple gearsets, but what really separated the Trans Am from hot shot rivals was the Pontiac's refinement. It looked like a racer, sounded like a racer, but this was no raw bones ride. Comfort didn't take a back seat and whatever go the Trans Am had on tap was delivered with minimum fuss. The 1969½ Firebird Trans Am Ram Air IV 400 would smoothly surge past its 5200rpm redline on to 6000 engine revolutions plus. It might throw an alternator belt at 6500rpm, but there were no other ill effects.

The Y96 handling pack, with 1in thick front sway bar, resilient bushings and F70-14 bias belted tires on 7in-wide Rally II rims, struck a happy compromise between all-out track star and grand tourer. Pontiac's new for 1969 variable ratio power steering, moving between 16:1 to 12.4:1, ensured accurate and light control of the helm. 697

1969½ Trans Ams were built, and that figure included eight ragtops. Look to the Trans Am decal call-outs on the rear spoiler and front fender to identify this rare car on the outside, not forgetting the Ram Air (IV) hood decals on L67 motivated editions. On the inside scrutinize the leather padded, three-spoke, 14in steering wheel that readily falls to hand. On the bottom spoke was engraved the car's serial number. A tactile piece of auto history, the very first Pontiac Firebird Trans Am.

Now comes the sad tale of the 1969½ Firebird Trans Am that never quite was. Remember the racing 1969 Firebird Trans Am 303 that was going to slay all comers during the SCCA's 1969 Trans Am series? Cost and the SCCA rulebook meant that it didn't get to grace the racetrack in time. What a shame because the Firebird Trans Am 303 was a direct equivalent to the high revving Camaro Z/28 302 and Boss Mustang 302. The road-going Pontiac would have received most of the hardware that made the racer special, like the solid lifter 303 engine and optional 4-wheel disk brakes. Keeping the final price down meant that sand cast pistons and a single 4-barrel Holley would have figured in the production Firebird Trans Am 303.

The Y96 handling pack was available and, when combined with a motor capable of over 7000rpm, was the recipe for a serious open road car. It was a bit slow off the mark with 0 to 60mph and

¼ mile times coming in at just under 9 seconds and the low 16s respectively, but wind that little engine out and nothing could hold back the Firebird Trans Am 303. *Motor Trend* sampled one in October 1969 and reported that top speeds in excess of 140mph were a safe bet.

Unfortunately, history must record that this was one Firebird Trans Am that didn't make it into series production. The SCCA may have felt it was doing Pontiac a favor by allowing the use of the Trans Am tag for Pontiac's new coupe for $5 per car sold. However, it played a major role in depriving sports fans of what would have been a very interesting addition to the late 1960s pony car scene.

Better breathing – the Ram Air family
It's only right that special attention should be devoted to the Poncho Ram Air V8s that were so much a part of the pre-smog era.

The very early Firebird 400s were available with the Ram Air I. We have seen how GM performance policy, and rising insurance rates, made both the base 400 and Ram Air I 400 officially rated at 325 gross horsepower. Both 400s were said to have the same 10.75 to one compression ratio, which was highly unlikely given that the Ram Air edition possessed a bigger cam, greater compression, freer flowing heads and cold air induction. A special air cleaner base plate had an outer foam ring that sealed to the

This 330bhp W66 400 was the hottest motor one could order with a/c in '69 MY; a/c was unavailable on Sprint 6 and Ram Air motors. (Courtesy David McGuire)

As powerful as the Ram Air III and IV engines were, emissions law was becoming stricter all the time. Receiving heated air through special ducts during warm up was just a little glimpse of things yet to come. (Courtesy Richard A Clatterbuck)

This is one of the 46 Ram Air IV/4-speed 1969½ Trans Ams built. The 345bhp Ram Air IV engine was never fitted to the 1969½ Trans Am convertible. The eight Trans Am ragtops were Ram Air III motivated. (Courtesy Eric J Vickers)

metal hood, keeping warm under-hood air out of the air cleaner. Ram Air I was quite rudimentary with the hood scoops open permanently unless the hood scoop inserts were swapped for the factory closed scoops. The same story spilled into the 1968 model year, although at least availability of the Ram Air package improved.

In 1968 the base W66 400 motor was rated at 330bhp, with the Ram Air I edition weighing in at 335bhp. These engines were joined by the 335bhp L74 400 HO. The new 340bhp round exhaust port Ram Air II took over from D port Ram Air I midway through the 1968 model year. From now on Ram Air engines had the refinement of

cable actuated 'flapper doors.' The scoops opened to welcome cool air when necessary, rather than being permanently open or closed. Once again the Ram Air II 400s were claimed to have the same 10.8 to one compression ratio as lesser Poncho 400s, but that wasn't likely. Ram Air III appeared in the 1969 model year, but didn't receive four bolt mains until the following year. Ram Air III was actually 1968's L74 400 HO under a new name.

As a concession to emissions, the 1969 model year even saw Ram Air 400s get special heated air ducts that reduced emissions during warm up. Not even 1969's 345bhp oblong combustion chambered Ram Air IV 400 was spared

this emissions-decreed warm up routine.

The Ram Air IV 400 had an aluminum intake manifold, plus redesigned rocker arms for greater valve travel and improved breathing. It should be remembered that all 400ci Ram Air motors described so far have been hydraulic lifter engines. However, that doesn't include the Ram Air V engine. We have already met the solid lifter 303 that was intended for the SCCA's Trans Am series, but there was also a big brother 366 that ventured forth into NASCAR competition. Indeed, the NASCAR Grand American Firebirds made good use of the 303. Buck Baker and H B Bailey had competitive Firebirds in the

1970 NASCAR Grand American series. Tiny Lund won the 1972 NASCAR Grand American race at Talladega in a Firebird. The 585bhp NASCAR Baby Grand Firebird 366s battled against restricted Ford 427-powered cars in the smaller NASCAR divisions. The 366 V8 never reached the Grand National Circuit level.

Pontiac Special Projects Group did cook up a 1969 Ram Air V 400 that had much in common with the subsequent 1973/74 SD 455 motor. Main bearing web areas were toughened. Strengthening ribs were used down the block's right side, and in the lifter gallery. However, unlike the SD 455, a cross-drilled forged crank was used with the Ram Air V 400, made from SAE 4615 material. Forged steel connecting rods (SAE 4340) with special attention to beam and cap areas were present. The connecting rods had a very wide base and employed an aircraft-style 12-point bolt to pass through the bearing cap and connecting rod. Forged 11 to one

TRW pistons, with forging of the cam-ground slipper design and tin plated exterior and a 3/32 moly coated ring lay at the top.

The Ram Air V 400 used tunnel port heads and a single 800cfm Holley 4-barrel. Plus, as with any out and out race motor, it was a solid lifter engine. Hollow stemmed chrome-plated valves measured 2.19in for the intake and 1.77 for the exhaust side. As per the 303, there was no better cam profile than that belonging to the Ram Air IV design. The pushrods went straight through the center of the intake ports, but, unlike the SD 455's magic steel tube, the Ram Air V 400 used cylinder head deflector foils. The foils directed airflow around the pushrods.

The Ram Air V 400's output might have been as high as 500bhp gross, using 99 octane premium leaded gas. This motor was never an official option on a Pontiac automobile, but around 200 crated motors were sold. The few that didn't wind up under the hoods of GTOs

and other Pontiacs might have been fitted to a few 1969½ Trans Ams, plus 1970½ Firebird Formulas/ Trans Ams. The cover charge for this take-no-prisoners engine was $2000.

The 1966-69 Ram Air V program also included a 428 with dual 4bbls and probably 510bhp, once again using the Ram Air IV cam. It's believed 500 Ram Air V motors were built in total, with 20% being the 428, so keep your peepers peeled for a stray crate motor!

It wasn't long before the US government decreed the phasing out of leaded gasoline. What was a high comp motor to do without leaded high test? Factor in two future gas crunches and it's easy to see how the Ram Air V motor could only be a temporary visitor. Pontiac had to redesign the cylinder heads on the low compression 1971 455 HO engine for the 1972 model year. If this already smog era motor had to receive poorer flowing heads to get by emissions-wise, where would that have left the Ram Air V 400?

Visit Veloce on the web – www.velocebooks.com
Special offers • Details of all current books • Gift vouchers • New books

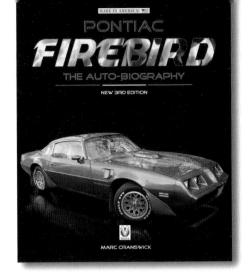

5

The second generation European-look Firebirds – Pontiac's all-new Firebird for the '70s

You have to admire GM's persistence with the F body. On the face of it the first generation cars were a good shot at taking on Mustang, and all the other players in the sport compact league. The trouble was that, by 1968, pony cars didn't look like they had the future marketing once anticipated.

With the pony car scene quietly deflating this didn't seem like an area that a car maker could trust. GM had other ideas; demographic studies showed that all might not be lost. It was apparent that while some models gathered great loyalty, the average sport compact buyer liked to shop around. Pontiac GTO buyers only had eyes for the GTO, but a Barracuda prospect might have considered a Javelin, or a Firebird or ...

Part two of marketing 101 suggested that pony cars were a great way to rope in the young set. Bait them with that sporty little red number and, before they knew it, they would be trading up to larger, more family oriented model lines. Today's Firebird buyer was tomorrow's Bonneville owner, or so the logic went.

While contemporary sport compact sales were running out of steam, GM could see a bright future. The percentage of young car owners would be increasing as the '70s progressed, so it made sense to invest in GM's F body. The upward spiral of Firebird sales after the 1974 model year leant credence to the theory.

Under the microscope – second generation Firebird design detail

Attracting the masses requires good bait; something special. The second generation F body was a well designed, polished and refined example of pony car art. There would be no afterthoughts like Chrysler grafting a fastback onto the Valiant. Pontiac's all-new

Apparent on this 1970½ Formula Ram Air III is the 'European-look' styling introduced by the second generation F body. (Courtesy Bill Marulis)

Firebird didn't rely on imitation stripes. Bold, graceful styling was at the center of the Firebird's game plan. The new GM F body was billed as possessing 'European'-look styling. In the Firebird's case that implied an appearance reminiscent of yesteryear's Maserati or Ferrari.

An unfortunate consequence of the long hood, short deck school of thought was limited trunk

The new Firebird's dashboard continued with the padded safety theme of earlier cars. The restrained style and materials gave a feeling of luxury. (Courtesy Bill Marulis)

Second generation Birds with air conditioning had two extra vents to the right of the heating/ventilation/air conditioning control panel. (Courtesy Michael Russell)

space. Use of the space saver spare increased capacity from 8.8 to 10.3 cubic feet. The restyle for 1977 caused those figures to drop to 6.6 and 7.1ft³ respectively. As bad as that may sound, remember that the contemporary Mako Shark Vette's trunk made the Firebird look positively utilitarian! Whilst on the subject of the body beautiful, it should be noted that there were no factory convertibles with the second generation Firebird. Slowing sales and the specter of government safety rollover tests put the final nail in the ragtop's coffin.

Let's examine the points of design distinction that set the Firebird apart from the sport compact crowd. There was the integrated heating, ventilation and air conditioning system. Demisting, bi-level and other duties could be performed from a simple control panel. There was no need to manually open or close vents to derive appropriate airflow. Firebird had features to ease maintenance. A removable lower dashboard panel on the driver's side gave access to bulbs

and speedo cable, two coin turn fasteners permitted speedy access. Another panel on the passenger side secured by five screws revealed fuses for headlamp, wiper switches, heater controls, air conditioning and cigar lighter. GM once again doubled up with an ignition key that locked both the steering column and transmission.

A buzzer sounded if a door was opened with the key still in the ignition. Plus, the GM Delco radio had its antenna sandwiched between the laminated layers of the front windshield for neatness.

It's the little touches that make living with a car that much more enjoyable once the showroom glow has faded. On the subject of responsible design, the Firebird had a number of good features relating to primary and secondary safety. Front vented disks measuring 10.9in were made standard on all Firebirds. There was the continued use of the pedestrian-friendly Endura nosecone. The padded interior and energy absorbing dash featured well placed controls and round, clear gauges in front of the driver.

A major safety component is a car's chassis. Pontiac took conventional hardware and added refinements to produce a sound ride/handling compromise. The steel unibody continued to use a separate front subframe and front independent upper and lower wishbones with coil springs. The familiar multi leaf sprung live axle was present at the back. However, there was greater rear suspension compliance thanks to GM abandoning the idea that the F body could be an occassional 5-seater. The driveshaft tunnel was raised and now divided the rear seats. The driveshaft was allowed greater freedom of movement and there was an additional 0.75in of upward rear-wheel travel. Combine this with a jounce bumper that progressively snubbed the rear axle on its ascent, and greater refinement was assured.

Greater front and rear-wheel travel permitted softer spring rates. The Firebird turned to multi leaf springs for the 1968 model year and no second generation cars featured single leaf rear springs.

This 1970½ Formula has the Ram Air III/3-speed manual power team, implying functional scoops for the Formula's fiberglass hood. (Courtesy Jack Loria)

The well appointed interior of the 1970½ Formula. Unfortunately, adjustable seat backs didn't arrive until the 1981 Turbo Trans Am Daytona 500 Pace Car. Three-point inertia reel seat belts became available in 1974. (Courtesy Bill Marulis)

In another move towards improved roadability, shock absorber valving was altered to stiffen downward wheel travel in relation to upward movement, as per European practice. Finally, staggered shock absorber placement did its utmost to curb axle tramp. Add together the improvements and you have a sport compact with some ability to deal with imperfect road surfaces.

The use of non-power assisted recirculating ball steering was standard, but, at 5.4 turns lock-to-lock, it was probably best avoided. As for the fast manual steering, that was for the Chevy Camaro Z/28 only by this stage. The steering of choice for the Firebird was the optional variable ratio power-assisted system. It was light in action and retained adequate road feel. The whole steering mechanism on the second generation Firebird was moved forward. Shifting the firewall and passengers 3in rearwards meant greater frontal crush space, and two shock absorber couplings for the collapsible steering column.

Engineers resisted the temptation to over-boost the optional power assisted GM Delco-Moraine front disk, rear drum brakes. The ability to touch the brakes without standing the car on its nose was appreciated.

Motor magazine noticed how the 1970½ Firebird Formula 400 owner's handbook was peppered with cautions and caveats. The safety lobby had put car makers on notice. The new F body encompassed a number of worthwhile features. From the generous tire/rim combinations to the well designed 2-speed windshield parallelogram linkage that swiped right to the screen edge on the driver's side, there was attention to detail. However, there were still some minor annoyances in common with the general auto scene.

Continued use of 2-piece lap and sash seat belts was both a nuisance and a hazard. The inconvenience of having to secure two sets of belts, only to find that, once harnessed, it wasn't possible to reach heating and vent controls, or use items like wipers and headlight

switches without difficulty, was contrary to good sense. If belts are hard to use, or make controls difficult to reach, they tend not to be worn. From the start of 1972 federal law made it mandatory for cars to be equipped with three-point front outboard seat belts and a warning buzzer. It wasn't until the 1974 model year that Firebirds got one-piece, three-point inertia reel front seat belts.

Disappearing windshield wipers looked neat, but the raised hood edge that concealed said wipers could move back and crack the windshield during low speed shunts. This trench at the base of the windshield could also become filled with snow in cold climates, compromising wiper action. Continuing with function following form, Firebird rearward vision was limited until the wraparound rear window was introduced in the 1975 model year.

Most of these design problems were common to sport compacts in particular, and the contemporary car industry in general. Even though sport compacts have never been the

A 1970½ Firebird Trans Am racing replica keeps a Cobra at bay using a Ram Air IV 400 and heavy duty Richmond Super T10 4-speed. (Courtesy George & Sherry Siegel)

last word in practical transportation, the new Firebird refined common problems which made for a nicer car. Even Consumers Union at the height of its puritanical zeal gave a 250ci I6 Firebird first place in a July 1971 group test of domestic and imported sporty cars: "If a specialty car is what you want, you could do a lot worse than a Firebird (or the basically similar Chevrolet Camaro). We found the Firebird far more satisfactory, overall, than the Mustang."

The new four tier model Firebird range

The second generation Firebirds were introduced at the Chicago Auto Show on February 26th, 1970, as 1970½ models. Some assert that the timing of their release was linked to the departure of Bunkie Knudsen to Ford. Then again, a mid-year release helped the Firebird avoid the mob of 'all-new, never seen before' releases that flood the scene at the start of each model year. Not that the new Firebird would exactly become lost in the crowd, you understand. In a market segment where cars live and die by their styling, the Firebird had the look that got noticed.

There was new styling and marketing with the new model range. With the first Firebird, matters became muddled. Newbie showroom prospects outside the loop had a tough time working out what each Bird did. With the second generation models there was a clear hierarchy – a Bird pecking order, if you will.

To kick off proceedings turn to the base Firebird. Think of it as a blank canvas, a starting point from which great automotive dreams could be created. While not exactly spartan by low level sport compact standards, there were still many blanks on the order form devoid of ticks.

After this light starter we could move on to the Firebird Esprit. A natty coupe which automatically came with the otherwise optional Custom Interior Trim. The Firebird

44

The flamboyant Firebird Trans Am continued as the Firebird's top model. This 1970½ Cameo white Trans Am has the standard Ram Air III 400, and optional THM 400 autobox with Rally Shifter. (Courtesy Stephen R Frantz)

Esprit was the luxury variant. A well appointed compact personal car, discreet in behaviour, price and most matters. For those into luxury with spice, Pontiac had the Firebird Formula. The plushness of the Esprit blended with the hardware required for a serious road car.

Those who can recall the banker's hot rod will know the Firebird Formula's measure. Not a stripped out racer, but a comfortable coupe with a premium fuel motor and enough suspension for dignified travel. Exterior signs of the Formula's accomplishments? In

keeping with the model's character these were limited, but note the well padded, leather rimmed, 14in steering wheel known as the 'Formula.' As for the exterior, the eye was drawn to the twin scooped hood, crafted entirely from fiberglass. Auto extroverts would have to look elsewhere.

Common sense told the casual observer that the Firebird Formula would be the pinnacle of the Firebird range. Never jump to conclusions. Waiting in the wings – wearing wings – was a transformed creation that many considered did not belong on the public highway – the Pontiac

Firebird Trans Am. What was this car's mission statement? To deliver the best driving experience by a US designed and built production car. Look beyond just ¼ mile times and skidpad figures, consider everything, then decide. For only then will such a car be truly appreciated. The engineering refinements of the second generation Firebirds were combined with a more focused Trans Am. Think of the 1969½ Trans Am as a great pony car, but know that the new 1970½ Trans Am was an all-purpose, road-going racer.

The 1970½ cars were tuned to run on premium 99 octane gas. The Ram Air III and IV were still rated at 335bhp and 345bhp respectively, but the distinction between manual and auto spec motor cams was gone. Color choices expanded to include Cameo white and Lucerne blue for 1970½ Trans Ams. (Courtesy George & Sherry Siegel)

Early model specifications

Continuing along the lines of the first generation cars the new Firebirds were very much discrete models. The four levels of Firebird could be custom ordered, but within limits that reflected their different natures. After all, the 345bhp premium fuel Ram Air IV 400 was hardly appropriate on a base Firebird.

F body spring rates were computer tailored for given models and the equipment they might possess. Beyond this base level, Pontiac engineers did have some freedom to distance their car from the new Camaro. I6-powered Firebirds used 14x6in rims shod with E78-14 tires. 14x7in rims and F78-14 tires, standard on V8 Firebirds and Firebird Esprit, were optional on the base I6 Firebird. The Firebird Formula came with Firestone E70-15 tires, with the option of F60-15 tires on 15x7in Rally II rims. F60-15 tires and Rally II rims were standard equipment on Trans Ams.

Engine choices also matched the nature of the various Firebirds. Things began simply with the single-barrel 250-cube Chevrolet I6. Pontiac's overhead cam I6 motor was not used on the second generation Firebirds. Pontiac's 2bbl 350ci V8 was optional on the base Firebird. The Firebird Esprit came with the 2-barrel, 350-cube V8 and had the 2-barrel Poncho 400 as an option. The Chevrolet I6 made 155bhp, next up was the 255bhp 2-barrel Pontiac 350 V8 and 265bhp 2-barrel Pontiac 400.

All were docile powerplants that didn't incur too much heat from insurance companies. However, for the Firebird Formula and Trans

The 1970½ Formula's base engine was the 330bhp L78 400; the Ram Air III 400 was optional. In a June 1970 report Car and Driver's 0-60 and ¼ mile times for a 1970½ L78 400-powered Formula automatic with a/c were 6.4 and 14.7 seconds respectively. (Courtesy Jack Nichols)

Formulas received 'Formula 400' badging on the front fenders, and Ram Air equipped cars had 'Ram Air' decals on the functional hood scoops. (Courtesy Jack Nichols)

Am there were more potent V8s. The 330bhp L78 4bbl 400, 335bhp Ram Air III 4bbl 400 and 345bhp Ram Air IV 4bbl 400. The L78 400 was standard on the Formula with Ram Air III optional. The Trans Am came with Ram Air III as standard and Ram Air IV was optional.

Gearbox choices were slightly unusual. The base Firebird could have a 3-speed manual, 2-speed auto or the THM 3-speed auto. Naturally, the 2-speed auto belonged to an earlier era and limited performance and economy in contemporary GM cars. The 1960s Corvette Stingray 327 was a possible exception. Even here, having just two ratios made the engine spin too quickly at cruising speeds, adversely affecting noise levels and economy.

To keep power team combinations rational the 2bbl Poncho 400 was not available with manual transmission. That's ok for a Firebird Esprit, but hot pony cars are usually associated with manual transmission. Curiously, Pontiac continued to offer 3-speed standard transmissions on its hot V8s. It was possible to order a 1970½ Firebird Formula with the 3-speed manual and Ram Air III 400. However, the Trans Am was only available with the GM wide ratio 4-speed Muncie as standard, with the close ratio 4-speed Muncie and THM 400 as options.

Visit Veloce on the web – www.velocebooks.com
Special offers • Details of all current books • Gift vouchers • New books

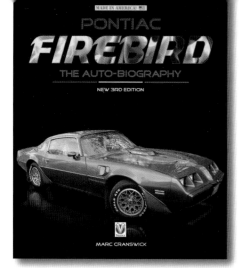

6

The tiger still lives in the tank – Firebird performance in the early 1970s

1970½ Firebird Formula & Trans Am – last of the premium fuel motors

The second generation Pontiac Firebird Trans Am had a strange start. Strange for a car with a sporty nature and coming from a car maker associated with hot street cars, that is.

The Pontiac GTO was considered the hottest car on the street, but zooming forward to 1970 shows that legend and reality can be distant relations. The GTO was hot and it did boost Tempest sales, but it wasn't really campaigned in motorsport. In much the same way, Pontiac's involvement in the SCCA's Trans Am series was limited. The

Racing 1970 Pontiac Firebird Trans Am 303 had minimal impact on the Trans Am series.

However, let's not confuse racetrack dominance with the worth of a car. Modern motor racing involves large cash injections, plus a well run and supported team. Ford bankrolled the Boss Mustang 302 and it certainly helped that car become Trans Am champion in 1970.

The third 1970 season Racing Firebird Trans Am 303, the car concerned with Jerry Titus' death, was crushed after an inconclusive inquiry. Only the trunk lid was saved from the car. The earliest and second 1970 season car were

This genuine 1970½ Firebird Trans Am 303 pictured at Thunderhill Park was the earliest car constructed by T/G Racing for the 1970 SCCA Trans Am racing season. Two additional race cars were built by T/G Racing for the 1970 season. (Courtesy www.historictransam.com)

Today, the earliest 1970 T/G racing car has been restored to its original state, and is owned by Mark and Linda Mountanos. (Courtesy www.historictransam.com)

absorbed into the B F Goodrich 'Tirebird' program for 1971. The earliest car raced at Daytona and the Bryer NH Trans Am during the 1971 season. Car number two notched up a major event win on-street radials in late 1970.

After such trials by BFG the second car was converted to a Camaro by 1971's Sebring race, still wearing BFG livery. This car was subsequently bought by Alfie Reys De Perez and campaigned by the Mo Carter Camaro team over the 1972-75 period. The remaining 1970 racing season Firebird Trans Am 303 was also under Canadian ownership; it was raced by Derrick Johnson at Watkins Glen in 1970. The car's history after that is unknown. The same applies to the 1972 Adams/Minter Firebird Trans Am that Pontiac's Herb Adams created for the 1972 SCCA Trans Am season. This car followed up Adam's successful Tempest/GTO 'Gray Ghost' of 1971, and produced the Firebird's only SCCA Trans Am win during the 1968-72 era.

On the street the GTO still bathed in the warm glow generated by those early triple deuce 389-powered GTOs. The trouble was that past success and marketing will only go so far. By 1969/70 the GTO was quick but there was swifter machinery around, and the kids on the street knew it. There were the Boss 429s and Chrysler were feverishly working on its own 'GO' angle. Pontiac had the hardware and know-how, but speed didn't seem central to business. Management didn't want to go there and, while the new GTO or Trans Am looked very handsome, they were at a disadvantage on Woodward Avenue if left stock standard. Still, with a bit of fine tuning, your new car from the Great Ones could surprise

Above: The first and second race cars built by T/G Racing for 1970, were absorbed into the B F Goodrich 'Tirebird' racing program for the 1971 racing season. This is the second race car T/G Racing built.
(Courtesy David Tom & www.historictransam.com)

many, Transmission Controlled Spark notwithstanding.

This complete indifference to performance seemed to envelop the second generation Trans Am as well. With limited involvement in the Trans Am series, management must have questioned the viability and necessity of a Firebird Trans

After spending a number of racing seasons converted to a Camaro, the second race car T/G racing built was restored to its 1971 BFG 'Tirebird' configuration.
(Courtesy David Tom & www.historictransam.com)

In the SCCA's Trans Am series domestic cars slugged it out in the sub-305ci segment. The public readily identified with the cars in action, and car makers were happy to be involved whilst sporty car sales stayed strong. (Courtesy David Tom & www.historictransam.com)

Am, especially with the presence of the Camaro Z/28 in the GM family. Signs that the Trans Am wasn't long for this world? Well, the Formula got a special twin scooped fiberglass hood and the Firebird's sports steering wheel was called 'Formula.' The Trans Am got a single scoop and steel hood, as if to say the expense of a custom plastic engine lid wasn't justified for one so shortlived.

As before, Ram Air engines implied functional scoops. Rather than inhale horrible warm underhood air, Ram Air III optioned Formulas, and the Trans Am, drew in cool, dense air from outside. On the Trans Am this involved a fiberglass reverse hood scoop fitted with a solenoid actuated door that opened when the gas pedal was floored. At speed there was a high pressure build-up of air at the base of the windscreen that entered the reverse scoop. Rumor has it that the shape of the Formula's scoops actually prevents air from reaching the air cleaner. An air pocket is thought to form at some point along the scoop. However, independent tests have shown that an open scoop on the Trans Am does indeed improve acceleration times.

While the Trans Am wasn't exactly weak, power levels remained

where they were at the end of the first generation car's run. The Ram Air V never became an official option for the new Trans Am. Then again, every Poncho V8 is a high performance motor and not everyone wants to live with a cantankerous, frenetic, solid lifter engine. The 1970½ Trans Am had enough punch, but they could have thrown in a baffled oil pan. The flipside of this story is that, unlike many rivals, the Firebird Trans Am did have a life after the SCCA Trans Am series. It sold in ever greater numbers long after the Trans Am series metamorphosed

into a contest dominated by high class European imports. The Firebird Trans Am's well balanced nature stood it in good stead for life after racing. The public seemed to like it more and more as the 1970s progressed.

Prior to the 1970 model year, two cam profiles were available for Ram Air engines; one for manual transmission cars and a milder one for automatic cars. Due to stricter pollution laws only the 'automatic' cam remained.

More visually apparent was the Trans Am's bodykit set. The

The Firebird Formula combined Trans Am punch with luxury and understatement. Formula collector values are only slightly lower than for the equivalent Trans Ams. In some cases rarity makes the Formula worth more. (Courtesy Will Baker)

body extenders were homologated race items intended to improve the aerodynamics of Firebird Trans Ams campaigned during the SCCA's 1970 Trans Am season. Engineer Paul Lamar's aerodynamic studies brought forth the familiar set of front, rear spoiler and wheelarch extensions. At testing, speeds of 100mph and greater such addendum did reduce front end lift and increase rear downforce. The Formula went without such aero add-ons.

Suspension-wise the Trans Am built upon the sound foundation laid by the Formula. The Formula's 1.13in and 0.63in front and rear sway bars were replaced with larger units measuring 1.25in and 0.88in respectively. Handling on both cars was predictable and neutral. Any signs of understeer could be corrected using 400in V8 torque. Ride comfort was on the firm side; the 60 profile bias belted tires were not the most forgiving of auto footwear. Even so, by street racer standards of the day comfort levels were okay. There were other high-powered cars more adept at loosening a driver's fillings.

In June 1970 *Car and Driver* recorded 14.1 seconds for the ¼ mile and zero to sixty in 5.7 seconds in the 4-speed Ram Air IV Trans Am with 3.73 final drive. Not bad for a car powered by an even-tempered hydraulic V8, capable of coping with a/c and happy to let its driver use second and fourth gears most of the time, and better than the 14.3 and

5.8 second times the same magazine achieved with the 1970 Plymouth Cuda AAR. The famed GTO zest was still there, it just required more fine tuning to find it.

As pollution controls tightened, performance car sales slowed and rivals dropped their heavy hitters. The Firebird Formula and Trans Am looked better with each passing day. The Great Ones refused to let the Firebird backslide into obscurity.

The 455 HO Formula & Trans Am – after the octane has gone

GM and the Californian government influenced the path of pollution control methods towards low compression ratios. As a 1971 GM vehicle the 1971 model year Firebirds had to be capable of running on 91 octane gas. Pontiac's introduction of its 455-cube V8 for the Firebird line partly redressed the decrease in power and efficiency brought about by external forces. For the Firebird Formula there were the optional 300bhp L78 4bbl 400, 325bhp L75 4bbl 455 and 335bhp LS5 4bbl 455 powerplants. The Formula's base engine was now the 250bhp L30 2bbl 350. However , there was only one engine available for the Trans Am, the LS5 455-cube V8.

The LS5 455 V8 had 8.4 to one compression, plus the usual Ram Air intake manifold for 335 gross horsepower. The LS5 had unique cylinder heads resembling Ram Air IV items and a 068 cam. This was 25bhp down on what

In 1971 Pontiac fought emissions regulations and low octane gas with displacement – in other words, the LS5 455 HO-powered Formula and Trans Am. (Courtesy Jim Rotella)

the GTO 455 produced in 1970. The 4-speed Muncie and THM 400 made up possible power teams, but the manual box had a larger 11in clutch compared to the previous 10.4in; after all, low compression or not there was now an extra 55ci in front of the gearbox. Enthusiastic use of the 4-speed on the 1970½ Trans Am could make the clutch slip noticeably, so there was certainly room for improvement in this area.

Even though a LS5-powered Formula or Trans Am could smoke what was left of the competition at the drag strip, noises were already being made that it just wasn't like the old days. A cosmetic highlight that arrived at the same time as the 455 HO option was the Pontiac

The LS5 455 HO powerplant had 8.4 to one compression, and used cylinder heads similar to those found on the earlier Ram Air IV 400. Add in a 068 cam and the 1971 power rating was 305bhp net. Small emissions-related changes meant that fell to 300bhp net for 1972. (Courtesy Jim Rotella)

Honeycomb rim. Basically a steel rim with a painted urethane honeycomb center bonded to said rim, the PO-5 Honeycomb became a favorite in Pontiac circles. 15in Honeycombs were standard on the 1971 455 HO Trans Am, Rally IIs were a no-cost option.

In 1972 the United Auto Workers staged a 174-day strike at the Ohio Norwood plant and only 1286 1972 Trans Ams were constructed. It was possible to order a Formula 455 HO, and the Trans Am continued to be available with just the LS5 motor. Tightening emissions regulations meant some changes to ignition timing, carb settings and minor cylinder head port changes on the exhaust side. Power ratings were now net rather than gross. The 1971 LS5's power rating was 305bhp net; the rating for the 1972 LS5 was 300bhp.

1973 – getting ready for a brave new auto world

1973 witnessed greater alterations to the Firebird line, some by force and some by choice. The 1973 model year was the first time nitrogen oxides (NOx) were considered for engine emissions certification. Two-way catalytic converters could handle hydrocarbons and carbon monoxide, but such devices were powerless over the new kid on the block. GM cars had a reputation for good driveability and 1973 saw a raft of Firebird alterations to maintain this.

A new fresh air duct system allowed more advanced ignition timing without worsening emissions. The choke action on V8 Firebirds was more precise with a richer fuel mix for initial running and shorter choke duration. From 1973 on, all Poncho V8s had Transmission Controlled Spark. A transmission mounted switch meant vacuum advance was dropped to zero in first and second gears. At wide open throttle, performance would be unaffected. This device had been used on GM cars prior to 1973 and had acquired a reputation for harming low end engine response. A package called 'controlled combustion system' consisted of a higher temperature thermostat, pre-heated carb intake air during warm-up and general carb/timing changes. Finally, exhaust gas recirculation (EGR) involved recycling some spent exhaust gases back into the intake side. EGR was the reserve player brought in to fight NOx.

Pollution controls: not an auto glamor zone, but a hardcore reality that was laying low both sporty and non-sporty cars alike.

This automatic, air conditioned 1972 Firebird Trans Am 455 HO was built and shipped the day before the 174 day strike began at the Ohio Norwood plant. Just 1286 1972 Trans Ams were built. (Courtesy Jim Rotella)

1971 Firebirds, like this 1971 L78-powered Formula 400 automatic, possessed non-functional fender louvers behind the wheel wells. (Courtesy Becky Jochman)

As air quality and fossil fuel became increasingly recognized as scarce resources, imported cars were making greater inroads into the performance scene. In the SCCA Trans Am series, IMSA and column inches of car magazines, the imports were appearing. Cars like the Porsche 911, Jaguar XKE V12 and Datsun 240/260 Z were entering national consciousness. The imports played the efficiency card to get out of emissions/economy jail. However, there was a twist in the story. As Detroit turned its back on performance in

search of the ultimate sub-compact and Mercedes grille, Pontiac was prepared to use lateral thinking to come up with a very special Firebird Formula and Trans Am.

The 1973/74 Super Duty 455 package

The large displacement concept still had a home in the 1973 Firebird nest. It all depended on how much adventure you were looking for. The 250bhp L75 455 could be inserted into the engine bay of a new 1973 Firebird Formula or Trans Am. This engine would

still let the owner lay down some nice lines of rubber on asphalt. The L75 455 had enough punch to leave most new cars in the dust, and could be teamed with four on the floor. But, for a few dollars more, there was – the SD 455!

The 455 was something Pontiac created for hauling a full-size Mom and Pop conveyance like the Bonneville: a role where size does indeed matter. All that sheet metal, cargo and passengers asked for torque, and with the long stroke Pontiac 455 one certainly was in torque country. Yup, they upped

54

Continued page 57

1970½ and 1971 Firebirds had a square mesh grille. Whilst the 1971 Formula could be fitted with an L30 350, L78 400, L75 455 or even the mighty LS5 455, only the LS5 was available on the 1971/72 Trans Am. (Courtesy Becky Jochman)

This 1972 Firebird Esprit 350 automatic has the new hexagon mesh grille used on the 1972 cars. The Firebird Esprit, like the Formula, arrived with the second generation Firebirds and was an easy-going luxury coupe. (Courtesy Andrew Benzie)

This 1972 Firebird Esprit shows how the fake fender louvers used on 1971 cars were dropped for 1972. 1972 was the last model year before the first of the federal bumper law make-overs started. (Courtesy Andrew Benzie)

In 1973 Pontiac introduced the Super Duty 455 motor. This action-packed powerplant was available on the Firebird Formula and Trans Am. It created the fastest accelerating Firebirds to that point, and all on 91 octane gas! (Courtesy Larry Navarro)

56

The 1973 SD 455 engine was rated at 310bhp net. It seems that cars submitted to magazines for testing had a Ram Air IV cam. Due to emissions law the 1973/74 cars that customers actually received were in line with the 290bhp spec 1974 SD 455 motor. All customer delivered, SD 455-powered cars had a milder than Ram Air III cam. (Courtesy Larry Navarro)

the bore from the Poncho 400's 4.12in to 4.15in, and gathered the majority of the additional 55 cubes via stroke. The final dimensions for the family 455 were 4.15x4.21in. Now that's awkward because, as everyone knows, sporty motors have a large bore in relation to a short stroke. Long stroke motors tend to lose their place on the hymn sheet when made to sing at high revs.

When GM lifted its ban on 400in+ engines in intermediates, Pontiac was caught off guard. Other members of the GM family had big motors ready for their A body cars, and expediency demanded that Pontiac drop its new 455 into the GTO quickly. The mild

455 complemented the handsome styling of the 1970 GTO, but to make the leap from serving duty to 'Super Duty' required some serious thinking.

Pontiac Special Projects Engineer, Herb Adams, and Project Leaders, Skip McCully and Tom Nell, were associated with the transformation of the 455 into the SD 455, a custom built, largely hand assembled, low volume performance motor that surely had no right to exist in 1973. Although the SD 455 had some engineering touches in common with the SCCA Trans Am 303, NASCAR 366 and Ram Air V engines, here was a road-going

powerplant that could be handled by just about anyone.

A lookalike on the outside for the regular 455, the SD 455 had a special cast block with strengthening ingredients. There were reinforced lifter galleys, extra webbing at stress points, four bolt main bearing caps and forged steel connecting rods that were shot peened and magna fluxed. Cost ruled out a forged steel crank; in its place was a nitrided iron crank that received pressure rolling at journal fillets. An 80psi oil pump and baffled oil pan were included, and there was even provision for dry sump lubrication.

All this intestinal fortitude

In 1973 Brewster green and Buccaneer red joined Cameo white as official Trans Am colors. Unfortunately, Lucerne blue was dropped. 1973 also brought 5mph front and 2½ mph rear impact bumpers. (Courtesy Chris Batson)

was fine, but of equal importance was breathing. With only 91 octane gasoline to work with, any performance extracted from the SD 455 would have to come from intake and exhaust tricks. Pontiac would have to achieve something akin to alchemy because those forged aluminum TRW pistons only gave 8.4 to one compression.

Special heads, like those from the Ram Air IV 400, were combined with a milder than Ram Air III cam, cast iron, dual plane, high rise intake manifold and round exhaust ports. An aluminum intake manifold was ruled out due to poor initial driveability. Valves were swirl

Three GM engineers procured a 1974 Trans Am SD 455 4-speed with 2.56 final drive for Brock Yates' real life 1975 Cannonball Run. The car finished 12th after having problems with its air shocks. (Courtesy Chris Batson)

polished, with the exhaust side larger than stock L75 455 valves by 0.110in.

The real trick came courtesy of a magic tube. To overcome the obstacles of allowing intake passages to make their convoluted way to the combustion chamber, with due allowance for core shift, a steel tube provided a clear shot. The choking effect of using extra cast iron material to seal the intake passage from pushrod holes was done by 'Mr Tube.' So, protective material could be pared down from 0.180in to just 0.030in.

An 800cfm Q-jet was used at a time when a 615cfm unit was fitted to regular Trans Ams. Power was rated at 310bhp net during 1973,

revised down to 290bhp for 1974 due to a smaller cam necessary to meet stricter pollution laws. I did say 'net' and these power claims were conservative because an automatic Trans Am SD 455 with 1973 bumpers running 91 octane gas could slay a 4-speed 1970½ Trans Am Ram Air IV 400 using 99 octane gas.

The SD 455 motivated Formulas and Trans Ams were also faster than a contemporary Vette LS4 4-speed. In May 1973 *Car and Driver* recorded a ¼ mile time of 13.751 at 103.56mph using an automatic, non-a/c 1973 Trans Am SD 455 with a 3.42 gear set. All that was necessary was to walk the car off the line and nail the throttle a little

way in. From that point on it was in the bag. Under full throttle the THM 400 would change up automatically at the yellow line of 5400rpm. (By the way, it was also possible to combine the SD 455 engine with a GM Muncie 4-speed until halfway through the 1974 model year, from which point on the Borg Warner Super T10 4-speed took over.)

Little remained to be done except collect your sub-14 second time slip, and perhaps do a little celebratory dance ... your call as far as what sort of dance. Unfortunately, the release of such latent energy hinges upon one small deviation from stock, a functional hood scoop. Californian drive-by noise standards forced Pontiac to

In May 1973, Car and Driver commented that the automatic 1973 Trans Am SD 455 it had on test displayed the same luxurious interior present in all second generation Firebirds. The magazine also noted that ride comfort was improved if the new optional, steel belted, Firestone GR70-15 radials were chosen. (Courtesy Chris Batson)

build all 252 1973 Trans Am SD 455s and 943 1974 Trans Am SD 455s with non-functional breathing apparatus. Still, the restless could remove the metal plate blocking the Trans Am's hood scoop and improve terminal speed during ¼ mile runs. SD 455 engined 1973 and 1974 Formulas, numbering 43 and 58 respectively, were still available with functional scoops.

Does my car have a functional scoop, is the question you're probably asking right now? 1970½. 1971 and 1972 model year Trans Ams had functional scoops. From 1973 to 1976 the Trans Am's scoop was blocked off by a metal plate and pop rivets. From the start of the 1977 model year until the death of the second generation Trans Am the scoop became a sealed off, hollow fiberglass molding. Between the start and middle of the 1977 model year the Trans Am received a squat hood scoop with pointy center line divider matching the hood crease of the new 1977-shape cars. The Formula had a fiberglass hood and scoops until the end of the 1975 model year. Functional scoops were available until the end of the 1974 model year. The 1976 Formula had a steel hood with reshaped scoops that were broader, and set further back. From 1977 onwards the Formula's scoops became even more discreet.

Returning to the SD 455, this special motor was available on the Firebird and Grand Am model lines only. It was considered for the GTO, but never formally offered on this model. The single Pontiac publicity shot of a 1973 Grand Am SD 455 suggests that this special SD 455-powered car, which Pontiac material described as a LeMans model, existed. One SD 455 engine was inserted into the Pontiac Banshee showcar. SD 455 crate motors were also sent to dealers.

GR 70-15 Firestone radial tires were an option for the 1973 Trans Am, complementing the 60 series bias belted 15 inchers. The GR 70-15 Firestone radials were also seen on the 1973 Chevrolet Monte Carlo S and Corvette. The radials were safer in the wet and gave a nicer ride than the bias belted tires.

Normally, SD 455 Formulas and T/As have the same T/A-style shaker hood. However, at least one factory-delivered SD 455 Formula has come to light with a regular Formula fiberglass hood and dual scoops.

Semi-metallic front brake pads from a police package were also useful to have on a 1973 SD 455-powered Firebird. The stock brakes would fade noticeably during spirited driving; hardly surprising given the power and weight of the car in question.

A mere $521 added to the 1973 Trans Am's base sticker $4186 price secured the SD 455 motor under the hood – fantasy could become reality. However, just as American Motors had canned the 2-seater AMX because it didn't contribute to the bottom line, Pontiac management – in the shape of Martin J. Caserio – wasn't impressed by the SD 455 package. If you think it's strange that a hot 7.5-liter sport compact could be a US market contemporary of the Honda Civic, and continue to be offered as the fuel crisis era

gas lines grew longer and longer, then you'd be right. At least Pontiac added a few visuals to highlight this 4-wheeled rebel.

Up to 1973 the second generation Trans Am could be had in Cameo white with black accented blue stripes, or Lucerne blue with black bordered white stripes. In 1973 Buccaneer red and Brewster green joined Cameo white as Trans Am color options. As if to say horsepower was about to fly away for good, Pontiac's John Schinella came up with the '73 full-sized 'Screamin' Chicken' hood bird decal. This large decal replaced the hood stripe and small, 12in bird decal seen on the nosecone of 1970½, 1971 and 1972 Trans Ams.

This 1973 Trans Am SD 455 enjoys the convenience of automatic transmission, air conditioning and power windows. Manual transmission SD 455-powered Formulas and Trans Ams used the GM Muncie 4-speed in 1973, and the BW Super T10 from the middle of the 1974 model year. (Courtesy Steve Schappaugh)

The SD 455 engine option cost $521. It made this 1973 Brewster green Trans Am faster than it looked, and how often can that be said about a Trans Am? (Courtesy Steve Schappaugh)

A 1973 Formula is shown. However, in McQ, John Wayne's tough guy cop, drove a '73 Brewster green T/A.
(Courtesy Author www.youtube.com/watch?v=DHtTwacRpTI)

And the final change? That came courtesy of the federal government's FSS 215 5mph front and 2½mph rear bumper law. The center of the Firebird's front bumper had 4in of foam backed by rigid steel reinforcements across the top and bottom. The reinforcements were attached to the frame mounting brackets, in turn attached to rubber absorbers placed on the frame's top and base sheet metal. Rear bumpers had smaller changes. With a urethane front the Firebird was better placed than most to meet the new bumper law. The same might be said of other 1970s challenges.

Visit Veloce on the web – www.velocebooks.com
Special offers • Details of all current books • Gift vouchers • New books

7
1974-1981:
the soul survivor

Pontiac Firebird – Detroit's new individual

1973/4 marks part two in the life of the second generation Firebird. Industry heavyweights, once buoyed with happy thoughts of the sport compact/performance scene, and how it would attract buyers and bolster their bottom line, had been having second thoughts for quite some time.

1974 was the last year for Javelin and Mopar marvels the Barracuda and Challenger. The GTO package, heavily utilizing the Ventura as a base, bid the world a deflated farewell. In short, it wasn't the brightest moment in the history

1973 was not the end for the Firebird. The Formula's dual scoops and the Trans Am's shaker lived on into 1974 and beyond, and sales increased! (Courtesy Jeramie Rosencranz)

1974 was the last year for the Pontiac GTO, by which stage it was Pontiac Ventura based. The car that had started the performance fires burning was handing command to the Firebird. (Courtesy Dan Roy)

of the automobile. Even Ford, the company that lit the initial fuse of the marketing mountaineer known as Mustang, was about to throw in the corporate towel. For the next half decade Ford's pony would seek

1974 saw the second generation Firebird's first major restyle. The revisions brought the Firebird into line with the new federal 5mph front and rear impact bumper law. Note the rear bumper pads and the new slatted taillights. (Courtesy Anders Jepp)

It was still possible to get a 2bbl 400 equipped Firebird Esprit during the 1974 model year, but it didn't have quite as much horsepower as the worked unit in this modified car! (Courtesy Anders Jepp)

out a new life as a luxury, mini, personal car bedecked in various finery.

The racer-style adverts of yore promising victory at the next traffic light grand prix and scalpel sharp performance specials were doing little to shake off the dust gathering on full-sized cars at various dealerships. Lee Iacocca was happier pictured with the Monarch and Granada twins, than being associated with Mustang's sequel. Out of all this the F body lived to fight several more days, and not without a modicum of Esprit style!

We should start with the biggest news for the 1974 model year, the first major restyle of the second generation Firebird, a big impetus for which was Federal Safety Standard 208 (FSS 208). It's already been recounted how insurance companies caused the government to initiate the first bumper laws for 1973. In 1974 things went a stage further. The bumper basher test was stepped up to 5mph impacts for the front and rear of most 1974 model year cars. In fact, the revised test brought repeated blows from a narrow,

pendulum-shaped object weighing as much as the average car. The ugly stop-gap methods used by many domestic and imported car manufacturers wishing their products to stay within the letter of the law may have given concern that the Firebird would be scarred for life, but there was no need for sleepless nights ...

The 1974 restyle produced a most agreeable countenance and tail for both the Firebird and Camaro, a look that the public had no qualms with. The Bird had extended about 4in, compared

Unlike many contemporary domestic and imported cars, the 1974 Firebird's 5mph bumpers blended well with the underlying shape. Using a 1973 and 1974 Firebird Esprit for comparison, body length increased by just 3.9in. (Courtesy Anders Jepp)

to the 1973 model year, but the slimmer face and revised tail gave the impression of a lithe, updated creature. Front headlamps continued with circular units within a square frame, complemented by a reduced grille area. The tail featured larger section slatted lamps. After the delicate DeTomaso Mangusta influenced corner units of the 1970½ – 1973 era, the new styling gave the impression that rocket booster flames would issue forth once the gas pedal was stomped!

On a darker note, all 1974 model year cars featured 'interlock,' a mini logic sequence computer that wouldn't permit a 1974 US market car to fire up unless the driver closed the door, buckled up and activated the ignition – in said order. While a good idea in theory, the unforgivably awkward nature of seatbelts in the majority of contemporary cars caused more than a few motorists to despair as the interlock device occasionally succumbed to electronic gremlins. An inability to make profit on safety-related devices motivated car makers to push for interlock's eradication and, by the 1975 model year, the device was no more.

1973-74 Hello Radials!
Firebird was at the cutting edge of domestic radial tire adoption.

American automakers had been slow on the radial, and disk brake, uptake; now the time had come for both features. Radials were seen on 1973 Corvette, in the GR70-15 size. This tire size was optional on 1973 Trans Am – an alternative to the stock bias belted F60-15s. That year, the giant WW7 hoodbird decal also made a debut, as a 55 buck option.

Come 1974 MY, RTS (Radial Tuned Suspension) was standard equipment on both Formula and T/A, but optional on base and Esprit. One received a nifty little plaque, stating same, between the Bird's main dash dials. For years, Detroit had used bias belted rubber, as part of the shock absorption system. With radials transmitting more roadshock to the body, in some operation spheres, Pontiac engineers had to allow more compliance through springs, shocks and bushings.

So it was that the upscale Vette and Firebird rode on radials, whereas '74 Camaro Z/28 raced around on F60-15 kidney punchers! Some missed that locked in, slot racer feel of the bias belted '72 T/A. Others appreciated the ride comfort and wet road adhesion, brought by domestic made (Firestone, B.F. Goodrich et al) 70 profile radials. It blended with Firebird's increasingly refined ambiance. 1975 MY saw RTS

standard on all Birds, starting with FR78-15s, for happy kidneys!

Engine options were much the same as before, but with a few changes. Emissions regulations were getting stricter by the year, at a rate faster than the industry could handle. 1974 was the last year before the Firebird said 'hello' to the catalytic converter. The L78 400 was the standard engine for the 1974 model year Trans Am. The L75 455 and SD 455 were still with us, but the L75 was only available with automatic. Sales of these 455-cube high flyers were not great during the gloom that followed the first gas crunch of 1973/74.

At this point one could be forgiven for thinking that the story was over, that – come 1975 – the shops would be boarded up with a note saying 'gone fishing permanently.' The 1974 model year auto obituaries, and the sight of the 185bhp L78 400 only 1975 Trans Am greeting the motoring press at GM's proving ground, did not bode well. However, in the years that followed the Trans Am did not walk quietly away; technical developments and commercial success sent a clear message that the Trans Am was here to stay. The tough just got going.

The truth is that, by 1974/75, the Poncho 400 was quite a meek device compared to past versions. When *Road Test* magazine encountered a zombie shift L78 Trans Am in March 1975, it recorded a 0 to 60mph time of 11.2 seconds,

This 1974 Trans Am SD 455 automatic is a replica of the 1974 Chicago Car Show Trans Am, that was a precursor to the 1976 Limited Edition black and gold Trans Am which commemorated Pontiac's 50th anniversary. (Courtesy Andrew W Ten Eyck)

Accurate to the last detail. This is the only SD 455-powered replica of the 1974 Chicago Car Show Trans Am Y81/82 precursor in the world. Note that the 'Custom Air Conditioning' fitted to this 1974 Trans Am retailed at $412. (Courtesy Andrew W Ten Eyck)

The 1975 L78 400-powered Trans Am automatic was the first Trans Am to be fitted with a catalytic converter. The space taken up by the catalytic converter meant that only the smaller GM THM 350 automatic could be used. This is a 1976 L78 Trans Am 400 automatic. (Courtesy Ben Deutschman)

Although quick by contemporary standards, the motoring press and public felt that the mid '70s Trans Am 455 HO was misnamed, due to its L75 powerplant. Pontiac dropped the 'HO' by 1976. (Courtesy Rocky Rotella)

For an extra $150 a Trans Am buyer could upgrade to the 1975½ Trans Am 455 HO 4-speed. The L75 455/4-speed power team was just for the Trans Am. This particular car is a 1976 model. (Courtesy Rocky Rotella)

double the time taken for a shiftless 1973 SD 455-powered car. The quarter mile figure was 17.99, or 18 seconds between friends. It should be noted that the car in question was fitted with a 2.56 economy axle. A 3.08 gear set and 4-speed manual box were available, but nothing more radical than that. The 1975 Trans Am's much improved gas mileage, High Energy Ignition (HEI), a lavish option list of power windows, door locks and stereo cartridge deck, were some consolation. The Trans Am was a good place to enjoy concert sound if the purchaser splurged on the optional $20 sound deadening material. Unfortunately, 'do not disturb' signs and tune-up-free ignition aren't items that most people associate with cars like the Trans Am. It was looking like the masses would be adjourning for pipe smoking by the hearth.

The 1974 model year witnessed the sales slide of performance cars that saw the L75, SD 455 Formula, Trans Am and Chevrolet Camaro Z/28 axed. However, once the gas lines eased and temporary restrictions, like changed school hours to cut on energy consumption, dissipated, a funny thing happened on the way to

the auto market. Buyers went back to large cars and powerful engines, or at least whatever power that remained. As the gas price stabilized to saner levels, demand for traditional domestic cars gathered pace. Manufacturers rushed into the kitchen to prepare the candy that the children needed badly. Apart from renewed interest in intermediates and full-size models, manufacturers were busy tricking out compacts and sub-compacts to satiate the public's appetite.

1975½ Trans Am 455 HO

The powers that be and social forecasters were predicting a bleak future for the automobile and internal combustion engine. Soon everyone would be relying on their trusty bicycle. However, the reality was rather different. Ford reintroduced the 302 into Mustang II for 1975, and ritzy GM H body 262-cube V8 Chevy Monza 2+2 hatchbacks roamed the highways. The world may have needed to tighten its collective belt, but market demand for such fun mobiles just couldn't be ignored. Detroit could hardly resist passing on its true spirit of showmanship to the utilitarian domestic sub-compact.

By '76 MY horsepower was down, but Trans Am sales were up. Firebird's annual total reached 110,775 and Pontiac was sitting pretty! (Courtesy Sheila Hartnagle)

Pontiac tried to exploit this renewed interest in sport and adventure by bringing back the 455 as a mid-model year Firebird option. That's right, just when you thought it was all over, PMD reintroduced the 455 for a paltry 150 bones. What did you get for $150 above the 1975 Trans Am's $4740 base sticker price? The end product was the 1975½ Pontiac Firebird Trans Am 455 HO, no less! The new model represented the first time that the 455 HO tag had been revived since the class of '72. The reunion brought both welcome and unwelcome changes.

The 1975½ Trans Am 455 HO package consisted of the

Magazines loved to point out that the 1975½ Trans Am 455 HO 4-speed derived its engine from the full-size Pontiac Grand Safari wagon. (Courtesy Zachary Leasure)

then unique power team of a 455-cube motor, Borg Warner Super T10 4-speed stick, and a 3.23 final drive ratio. There was a mildly special exhaust terminating in the familiar twin chrome downpipes. Semi-metallic front brake pads were standard with the 455 HO package. By this stage the Safe-T-Track limited slip differential was supposed to be present on all Trans Ams. However, some tested cars revealed that this was not the case.

There was one item that the 1975½ 455 HO option didn't have, and even if you strode into your friendly local Pontiac dealer and dumped all of Fort Knox's gold bullion on the dealership floor, you *still* couldn't have it. There was no custom engine to complete the three-course meal. The motor lying beneath the blocked reverse hood scoop was a 455 HO in name

only. Yes, it did benefit from a special exhaust system, but 150 dead presidents couldn't procure anything more potent than 200 ponies net at 3500rpm, and 330lb/ft of torque at 2000rpm.

Why was this the case? Well, the 455 motor had been plucked from civilian life in Pontiac's regular full-size line-up. That 455 just happened to be the same engine one could tick off for a Grand Safari wagon. Boo, said the motoring magazines, that can't be fair. How could PMD do that to loyal followers? The resurgent interest in sporty motoring had taken many by surprise. Pontiac had hedged its bets in the right direction by retaining the Trans Am's services for 1975, but at such short notice that the Mom and Pop wagon 455 was all that was available.

The special valvetrain, engine machining techniques, custom

manifold, and all the good stuff that went into a SD 455 was plain absent. However, the 1975½ 455 HO motor was a torque-ripe device capable of laying down a nice line of rubber on asphalt. If that was your wish. The added power and torque enjoyed over the L78 400 permitted the skilled, and not so skilled, to relish such delights as power oversteer. Many had found that the contemporary L78 400 engine negatively impacted on the Trans Am's excellent neutral handling. Limits of adhesion were as high as ever, but a lack of firepower meant new 400-cube Trans Ams couldn't be steered on the throttle as easily. So the 455 HO made things better, but not ideal.

The catalytic converter from which GM had shied away and then, in the words of Consumers Union, embraced with passion akin to teenage romance, failed to bring the flawless driveability hoped for.

69

By 1976 this Trans Am 400 was down to 185 horses. However, Firebird wasn't about to mosey on into the sunset. (Courtesy Lynn Drinnin)

On take off and at certain points in the rev band, there were moments of rest punctuated by a sudden return to consciousness. This lack of linear power delivery also made holding a constant line through corners difficult.

Perhaps of greater concern was the omission of a baffled oil pan for the 200bhp 455 motor; something akin to a circus high wire act without a safety net. Trans Ams can generate high cornering forces, and 1975's car was no exception. Couple this ability with the fact that V8 engines can be prone to oil starvation, and trouble was on the cards. High speed turns could see precious engine oil miss the oil pump pick-up points. Use the

Trans Am's natural handling ability to the full and you just might risk internal engine damage.

The 1975½ 455 HO Trans Am had a relatively soft powerplant, and suspension settings. The Trans Am could still assert its handling supremacy amongst domestic cars. However, noises were being made that, even in this area, the Trans Am was getting tamer. Softer suspension settings and the use of GR 70 15in radials brought greater refinement. While it was true that the Trans Am wasn't as single-minded as it was in the days of 60 series bias belted tires, that might not have been such a bad thing. The standardization of RTS for the 1974 Formula and Trans

Am, and absence of bias belted tires was in keeping with the growing popularity of Pontiac's hot Firebirds. Why alienate a multitude of new friends by stubbornly adhering to past practice?

Things weren't all rose tinted in Trans Am land; by 1975 this likeable 455-cube sport compact wasn't exactly a model of space or fuel efficiency. Then again, neither was the Jaguar XJS or Maserati Khamsin that *Road & Track* felt were such a good match in acceleration. That said, imported cars had opened up new viewpoints on gearchange and steering feel. The 4-speed Borg Warner Super T10 manual box was a sturdy device

70

This is a 1977 Formula W72 400 4-speed with the optional W50 Formula Appearance Package. From 1972 Firebirds were built at Norwood only, but in 1978 production resumed at the Van Nuys factory. (Courtesy Walter Ulrich)

The first W50 color scheme was yellow and black, but, by 1977, color combinations had risen to six. The two-tone effect and large 'Formula' door graphic lettering proved popular, and W50 continued until the end of the second generation Firebird's run. (Courtesy Walter Ulrich)

By 1977 the W72 Poncho 400 was the only 6.6-liter V8 engine that could be teamed with four on the floor. Pontiac's L78 400 and Old's L80 403 were around, but they were automatic-only. (Courtesy Walter Ulrich)

capable of dealing with the 455's torque, but the clutch and shifter action was not as easy-going as on the imports. To some extent this was made acceptable by the precision of the Hurst shift linkage. The Trans Am's power steering was accurate and had good feel by domestic standards, but was much lighter than the systems found on high priced European sporty cars. In this respect the semi-metallic front brake pads were a welcome change because they raised pedal pressures. Brake feel and the ability to moderate braking effect without lock-up actually improved.

Defects and compromises aside, the Trans Am was still serving up as much fun as anyone could reasonably expect. It was a ray of sunshine in the cloudy and depressed autoscene, and still much cheaper than a Vette. Take exception to the 100mph speedo, the orange zone on the tach that started at four grand and space saver spare, by all means, but know that the Trans Am was the only show in town worth seeing in 1975. Even in this darkest hour when the nay sayers claimed that there would be

neither gas nor cars in the future, the car lover had some reason for hope. For the mechanical idealist, living to some extent in all decent folk, the L78 400 and L75 455 HO Trans Am still ruled in what remained of pony car land.

The 1977 model year saw another significant restyle for PMD's Bird. The tail was much the same as before, but the nosecone was a different story. The front polyurethane nose was reworked to resemble Pontiac's traditional visage. The 1977 Firebird had grown a mite longer to almost 197in in Trans Am guise. The front had an uncanny resemblance to George Barris' Batmobile creation used in the 1960s *Batman* TV show starring Adam West. The 1977 shape also marked the introduction of what would become a North American market rage – quad headlights. Yes, when it came to cars like the Fox-bodied Mustang or US specification Volvo 264 GLEs, it was hip to be square.

It was only right that quad lamps should figure on a popular, fashion-conscious design like the Firebird. The 1977 and 1978 model

year Firebirds shared the same shape but with slight differences. 1977 Firebirds possessed a honeycomb-style mesh grille. The 1978 models had a diamond pattern mesh grille. The earlier production year Trans Ams had two-piece interior door trim panels with the lower section trimmed in hard molded plastic. 1978 Trans Ams featured a more luxurious, one-piece soft door panel with integrated armrest and flush mounted door latch release lever.

The 1977/78 body style has become one of the best loved Trans Am shapes. The car has a look readily associated with Pontiac's F body. Speaking of family favorites, 1977 was also the year that the aluminum alloy 'Snowflake' rim was introduced. The pattern did indeed resemble a snowflake. Jim Shook was mainly responsible for the design, with some assistance from John Schinella. These new alloy rims took over from the well loved Honeycomb design of the 1971-1976 period. Time moves on and the new Snowflakes perfectly complemented the restyled 1977 Firebird. However, as with other contemporary alloy rim designs, the elaborate pattern made it tough to clean.

Pony cars depend on looks and power to survive. Now that appearances have been studied we can move on to the 1977 power teams. The line-up changes were motivated by economic and legislative factors. The base engine

One of the minor style changes for 1978 was replacement of the Firebird's 1977 honeycomb-style mesh grille with a diamond pattern. John Schinella swayed Bill Mitchell to the idea of a hood bird decal. Mitchell was originally against the concept of a hood bird when the second generation T/A was being prepared. (Courtesy Brett Campbell)

The Year One Burt Reynolds Edition Trans Am is a tribute to the 1977 Smokey & The Bandit T/A. (Courtesy www.yearone.com & Pat Staton)

A 1978 Firebird. By 1977 the base engine for Firebirds and Firebird Esprits was the Buick 231ci V6. (Courtesy Sheila Hartnagle)

was no longer the 250-cube Chevy I6, but the 231ci Buick V6. This engine has come to be known as the 3.8-liter V6 in more recent times and, like the Chevy I6, it featured cast iron construction and an overhead valve layout. During the late 1970s the Buick V6 was starting to make waves in the Turbo Regal and subsequent sporting blown Buicks. Around a decade later it would supply the thrust in the 20th Anniversary turbocharged V6 Trans Am. However, that's getting well ahead of the story. For the present the 231 V6 was just an automotive book end, propping up the Firebird line and earning valuable EPA gas credits for GM.

Second up for the party introductions was a new lightweight Poncho 301 V8. Like the Snowflake rims and quad lamps, the new 301 was a sign of the times. Before the first energy crisis GM had the worst fleet economy average of any of the US automobile manufacturers. Naturally, in the pre-gas crunch days this fact was considered of little importance. However, in subsequent years gas economy

started to appear higher up on car buyers' wish lists, and that included sporty car buyers. Yes, big was considered beautiful again once the gas lines and prices eased, but frugality with petroleum distillate was affecting sales on a scale never experienced before.

Doubters should consider the increasing market share garnered by utilitarian and luxury imports in the post-1974 period. Higher oil prices and America's reliance on imported oil precipitated the passing in Congress of the 1975 Energy Policy and Conservation Act. This legislation forced the nation's autofleet to become more frugal. There would be a predetermined annual national fleet mpg target. A 'gas guzzler' tax would have to be paid on vehicles not meeting the

average. The US Federal Corporate Average Fleet Economy scheme (CAFE) implied an average of 18mpg for 1978, rising progressively to 27.5mpg by 1985. Well, that was the intention anyway.

GM was the first of the big domestic manufacturers to downsize its auto fleet in the search for more mpgs. First off were the new downsized, full-sized family cars for 1977. Next came the intermediates, compacts and sub-compacts, and eventually the 1982 sport compacts. It represented a huge reinvestment in redesigned car lines that were much smaller on the outside, but offered just as much useable internal space. Performance was either maintained or improved upon compared to immediate predecessors. Smaller engines could be used to deliver similar acceleration with much improved gas mileage.

A big part of the second generation Firebird's long and successful run was attributable to its graceful shape. With or without graphics and wings, the Firebird had a sporty spirit. (Courtesy Sheila Hartnagle)

This 1978 L78 Trans Am 400 automatic fits in with the image many associate with the Trans Am. (Courtesy Sheila Hartnagle)

Understandably, these well thought, efficiently designed models were a commercial success. Rivals that abstained from downsizing were forced to play short run musical chairs with model nameplates. There was also some bizarre auto advertising which claimed that pre-downsized models gave the buyer greater value for money through extra girth and added sheet metal inches!

A major part of the efficiency drive at GM was the development of smaller displacement, lighter powerplants, which was where the 301 and 403 V8s came in. Both were based on the familiar post-war, overhead valve, cast iron US V8 style, but with a significant number of new design elements. With the

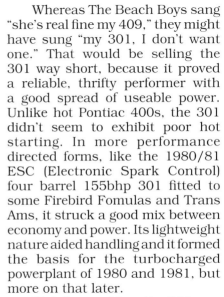

301, Pontiac engineers started with the usual Poncho medium block V8 and sent it to Weight Watchers. The small displacement 301 featured a low deck cylinder head, reduced cylinder wall thickness, half the crankshaft counterweights, and a single level intake manifold. All-up this diet netted a 119lb weight saving when compared to the usual Poncho 350. The special intake manifold and small siamesed intake ports helped keep economy high, but restricted breathing and did performance no favors. Indeed, this motor has had a limited following in the years since due to a negative public perception concerning performance.

Whereas The Beach Boys sang "she's real fine my 409," they might have sung "my 301, I don't want one." That would be selling the 301 way short, because it proved a reliable, thrifty performer with a good spread of useable power. Unlike hot Pontiac 400s, the 301 didn't seem to exhibit poor hot starting. In more performance directed forms, like the 1980/81 ESC (Electronic Spark Control) four barrel 155bhp 301 fitted to some Firebird Fomulas and Trans Ams, it struck a good mix between economy and power. Its lightweight nature aided handling and it formed the basis for the turbocharged powerplant of 1980 and 1981, but more on that later.

Strictly speaking, the 301 was actually 302in in displacement (301.6ci). However, to distinguish it in marketing terms from the Blue Oval's 302, Pontiac billed the new-for-1977 powerplant as the 301. Underscoring the impact of European trends on the local auto scene was marketing's move to label the new motor the '5 litre.' For Formula and Trans Am, much play was made of the 4.9-liter designation. In fact, by now, overseas sporty car influence had

Auto icons can be a base for self-expression and folk art. (Courtesy Sheila Hartnagle)

resulted in the 4.9, 5.0 and 6.6 metric engine size labels becoming more commonplace. Certainly, the 1976 model year was the last time the '455-cube' tag appeared on a Trans Am shaker scoop.

For those who might still be harboring doubts over the 301's worth, I'd like to draw your attention to Herb Adam's late 1970s 'Silverbird' SCCA Trans Am Category II racer. This track star with tenuous links to the contemporary road-going Trans Am, used a 366-cube racing V8, based not on the Chevy 350 but the humble Poncho 301. Ram Air IV heads were used, along with Lucas fuel injection tinkered with by Kinsler. The 301 was based on Pontiac's medium-sized V8 block. Herb Adams felt that the extra material would lend a margin of durability not present on the lither Chevy small block. All V8s are not created equal!

Our second Firebird newbie for 1977 was Oldsmobile's 403 V8. With downsizing and the inevitable end of Old's 455 motor, GM needed a large displacement engine that had enough torque to move around family-sized cars like the Olds 98 with reasonable gas economy. The 403 was the answer; a lightweight engine with a slightly larger block size than the Chevy small block V8. The extra girth was just enough to permit a big bore and short stroke to get displacement out to 6.6 liters. It did the trick in a full-sized car, but it also came in handy for the Firebird line. As with the 301, the 403 was

earning GM important CAFE gas mileage credits. Credits that could be used to maintain the presence of some performance models whilst rival car makers were going through a drought. Speaking of automotive droughts, a few words should be said about California.

Power teams featuring a manual gearbox had not been available in that state since the end of the 1974 model year, because of California's stricter pollution laws, a situation which prevailed until the Chevy 305 4-speed power team was emissions certified in California for the 1981 model year. 1975/76 saw the L78 400 and THM 350 as the only partnership available on Californian delivered Trans Ams. For 1977, 1978 and 1979 Californian Trans Ams were only available with the Olds 403 and THM 350 combination. The 4bbl Olds 350 and 4bbl Olds 403 took care of Firebird business in high altitude areas.

The 135bhp L27 2bbl 301 was the Formula's 49 state base engine for 1977, but wasn't available in California until the 1981 301-powered Turbo Trans Am. The base motor for the 1977 Californian Formula was the 4bbl Olds 350. The contemporary Pontiac 2bbl 350 wasn't emissions certified for California. For a number of years California got the slowest and thirstiest versions due to its stricter pollution laws. In fact, in 1980 the LG4 305, automatic gearbox combination with computer

controlled carb was the only Californian power team available for the Corvette.

If that was the bad news, let's move on to the good. It has something to do with a little order sheet code, named 'W72.'

The W72 400 – there *is* life after the Porsche 930

Some might look at the performance figures of W72 400-powered, second generation Firebirds and conclude that they aren't that special. Older models posted some hot elapsed times, and much younger WS6 Formula/Trans Ams have been able to combine incredible, 1320 foot sprints with mind-blowing top speeds. However, this is to completely miss the point.

Early cars were mostly devoid of pollution controls and supped premium grade leaded petroleum distillate. In addition they had very short final drives and gearing dedicated to the ¼ mile. If creature comforts, a motor that could handle an a/c compressor, or a taller rear end ratio for interstate travel were required, then the search started elsewhere. The glamorous, fire-breathing cars tested by the major car journals had a specification that most would have found hard to live with on a daily basis.

The younger cars benefited from a lengthy gestation period in which engineers established and refined pollution controls. The upshot has been pollution

For an extra 50 bucks your new Trans Am could have the high performance W72 400 engine. This is a 1977 Buccaneer red Trans Am W72 400 4-speed. (Courtesy John Witzke)

controls that hardly detract from performance, and engines capable of extracting maximum energy from lower octane unleaded gas. Younger Formulas and Trans Ams are impressive performers, but performance levels have generally improved across the board for all makes and models over the years. To be honest, it's never been easier to do the quarter mile in under 14 seconds; quite a number of automobiles can achieve this, at least once price is taken out of the equation.

Back in 1976/77, performance in any form was hard to come by and

pollution controls were still in the early stages of development. As late as spring 1973, GM publicly aired its concern that catalytic converters wouldn't make the grade vis-a-vis durability and meeting future emission targets at reasonable cost. The world had experienced one fuel crisis and another was on the way. In addition, 1978 was the first year a Federal CAFE ceiling forced everyone in the auto industry to become good citizens.

What was happening on the domestic performance scene? Well, not much to speak of. There was still the Corvette, as expensive and

exclusive as ever. Beyond the Vette were a number of sporty cars that advertised rather than possessed performance. The aftermarket still made hardware, but that was strictly for non-public road use. A hot car straight from the showroom floor was hard to find.

In spite of everything, interest in sport was increasing. In 1977 the Camaro Z/28 returned to the market but, of even greater importance, was a surprise Firebird engine option. The 1975½ 455 HO package wasn't exactly expensive, but the W72 400 order box could be ticked for a mere

The W72 400 was available on Formulas and Trans Ams over 1977-79. 1979 W72-powered cars made use of 8690 stockpiled motors from the 1978 model year. (Courtesy John Witzke)

$50 if a Trans Am was under consideration. For a measly $50 your new Trans Am could have the closest thing to a custom race-built engine detuned for the road. Perhaps they forgot to tell Pontiac this was 1977 and not 1967? The W72 400 embodied a number of improvements over the 180bhp L78 400. The new engine offered enough extra go to make comparison between the W72 and L78 400s similar to that between night and day.

In April 1977 *Car and Driver* tried to relate what it thought was a W72 400 to the 200bhp 1976 455 engine option. The magazine didn't really know what it was dealing with. On paper, the W72

400 produced 200 horsepower net, making it equivalent to the 1976 L75 455 engine, but paper specs can lie! The output of this special 400 was seriously under-quoted, and accurate estimates put the real net flywheel horsepower figure in the 260-290bhp range. There is simply no other way a W72 400-equipped Formula or Trans Am could record the ¼ mile times that it did. A W72 400 motivated second generation car could exceed 130mph, go from zero to sixty in under 7 seconds, and record times in the low 15s for the quarter mile. However, Dave Wallace from *Hot Rod* magazine recorded a limbo low of 14.61 for the quarter mile in a non-air conditioned, 1979 Trans Am W72 400 4-speed. Still not

impressed? Well, let's look at what the big names on the contemporary US scene could deliver.

Two favorites of the auto press were the US spec Jaguar XJS and Porsche 928. The Jaguar managed zero to sixty and quarter mile times of 8.3 seconds and 16.4 seconds respectively when tested by *Car and Driver* in 1977. The Jaguar had a 5mph advantage in top speed, but was 5 seconds slower from 0-100mph. There was also the small matter of the $21,900 sticker price.

In much the same vein the contemporary US Porsche 928 looked and sounded impressive, but respective 0-60mph and ¼ mile times of 8-8.5 seconds and low 16s were merely adequate,

78

1977 W72 400s had different cams depending on whether a manual or automatic car was to hand. 1978 and 1979 W72 motivated Formulas and Trans Ams made do with the W72 400 using the 'auto' cam. (Courtesy John Witzke)

considering its price. By 1979 a correctly specified L82 Vette could match W72 Trans Am acceleration, but cost nearly four grand more, had just two seats, and no trunk to speak of.

The W72 400 motor was assembled at Pontiac's Michigan engine plant and featured a number of refinements compared to the base L78 400. It had moly filled rings and slotted spring pin main bearing caps, rather than the solid dowel type on the L78 400. Smaller combustion chambered, 6X, number four heads from the Pontiac 2bbl 350 engine helped boost stated compression from 7.6 to 8.1 to one. The 800cfm Q-jet received special primary jets and metering rods, and a harmonic balancer replaced the usual rubber floated weight found on the L78 400.

Under the chrome valve covers were internal oil deflectors and, for the first time on a Firebird since the first generation cars, a specific manual and automatic camshaft. The same intake and exhaust duration figured, but with different timing events. Having a different cam depending upon which transmission was chosen was a real blast from the past. However, this tailor-made motor only existed for the 1977 model year. For 1978 and 1979 only the automatic cam profile would be utilized due to tightening pollution laws.

A unique version of the THM 350 was used for the W72 400 package. There was a special governor, modulator, oil control valve body, smaller 11.75in torque converter and shift points raised from 4200rpm to 4800-4900rpm. The Rally Shifter device was standard, and permitted spirited movement between gears without skipping ratios or engaging neutral by accident. The manual transmission option was taken care of by the Borg Warner Super T10. Final drive ratios for stick shift models started out at 3.23 to one, became 3.42 for 1978, and reverted back to 3.23 for the 1979 model year.

Concerning exhaust systems,

This Ohio-delivered 1979 Trans Am W72 400 4-speed has air conditioning and no T-tops. The car now resides in Arizona so it's just as well it doesn't have those brain-warming, glass T-tops! (Courtesy Jon O'Neall)

1977 saw the – by then familiar – single 2.5in pipe from exhaust manifold to catalytic converter, followed by a single 2.5in pipe into a single crossflow resonator, finishing with dual 2.25in tailpipes. The only change for 1978 and 1979 was that 2.25 dual pipes with dual resonators replaced the 1977 single pipe assembly after the catalytic converter.

Unlike previous Poncho V8s the W72 400 featured a ground cam that was installed retarded. While giving up some low end response, the W72 cam produced a sound idle and a better high end. This specification didn't stop the W72 400 doing its best work in the low to mid-rpm ranges. Even though the engine was redlined at 5000rpm, *Car and Driver* was

able to push its 1979 Trans Am W72 400 4-speed on to a top speed of 132mph where no less than 5400rpm was registered.

Now for some confusing late '70s production changes. From the start of the 1978 model year, the W72 400 and WS6 performance package was a mandatory combination. Subsequently, this forced joint venture was terminated. However, later in the 1978 model year the W72 and WS6 package became a mandatory combination once again, albeit in an informal manner. There were no 1977 or 1978 Firebirds with the L78 400/4-speed power team. Secondly, from mid 1978 the W72 400 could only be purchased with the manual 4-speed transmission – I hope that clarifies matters.

W72 400 specified cars had a 60psi oil pump and, thankfully ,a baffled oil pan. Yes, Pontiac bestowed upon W72 400 cars a feature sadly absent on the 1975½/1976 455 HO Trans Ams. From 1978 there was an even greater chance of engine lubricant being flung into locations where no oil pump pick-up points could help, because of WS6. This suspension

That BW Super T10 was easier to use than the Muncie 4-speed, but don't expect the light shifting of an imported sportscar. Then again, with all that 400-cube torque, you didn't have to shift that much to get from A to B quickly. (Courtesy Jon O'Neall)

Above: Under that familiar body, Year
One has worked in a race car chassis.
Engine choice starts with a 515bhp
injected dry sump 7.0 LS7! (Courtesy
www.yearone.com www.youtube.com/
watch?v=V1UT7heqNt0)

The 1979 10th Anniversary Trans Am
(TATA) coincided with the final model
year in which the W72 400 motor was
offered. This particular TATA has the
W72 400/4-speed power team.
(Courtesy Joe Figurelli)

Note the raised 3D 'Pontiac' lettering on the front bumper, just in front of the driver's side low beam lamp on this 1979 Esprit 301 auto. Firebird Esprits had their quad lamps framed by chrome trim. (Courtesy Lee Rehorn)

hardware upgrade set had its genesis in the Fire Ams Herb Adams created for SCCA Trans Am road racing. Some salient points from the Fire Am filtered through to the WS6 package, WS6 involved upgrading the stock Trans Am suspension. $249 bought 15x8in Snowflake rims, a constant ratio high effort steering box, bigger sway bars, urethane bushings, stabilizer links and metric footprint P225/70R-15 radial tires. Turbo rims appeared during the 1979 model year.

A partially metric tire size, metric T/A 6.6 hood scoop call-outs and increased attention to handling and balance, revealed the extent that domestic performance was being increasingly affected by overseas influence. The higher effort steering gear and 1979 model year introduction of rear disk brakes, option code J65, further underlined this trend. The 1979 model year gave buyers who wanted the WS6 trimmings, without rear disks, the $284 WS7 package. At a time when production line variations were being rationalized, it was Pontiac that was offering greater choice.

To recap; Pontiac offered a showroom stock Trans Am capable of times in the low 15s in the quarter mile for an extra 50 bucks, for a possible 1977 sticker price of $5506. Compare that with the 1976 Lancia Scorpion's (aka Lancia Beta Monte Carlo) $9943 price tag;

nearly ten grand for a car *Road & Track* declared an automotive eunuch, due to the emissionized 1756 cubic centimeter Fiat dual cam four banger, no doubt. Whereas 1806 Lancia Scorpions sold in North America during 1977/78, 72,244 W72-powered Firebirds were produced in the 1977-79 timeframe. Buyers obviously knew a bargain when they saw it. What lay in store for 1980? The writing was on the wall that big changes were on the way.

The listing of the W72 400 option for the 1977, 1978 and 1979 model years was actually a sleight

of hand by Pontiac. For a start it seems no W72 400 blocks were built after November 1977. Secondly, whatever W72 400 motors Pontiac offered in the 1979 model year, were surplus stock from the previous year. 1979 W72 Formulas and Trans Ams actually had a 1978 model year powerplant. Pontiac set aside 8690 W72 400 engines for a rainy year. Thank GM's decision to downsize for allowing Pontiac to offer engines like the regular Pontiac L78 400, Olds 403 and W72 400 in the late 1970s. Without the cross subsidizing effect of new, lighter, fuel efficient models, Pontiac couldn't have held out for as long as it did. One could say that all those two barrel 301s played a

A 1979 Trans Am in Japan. When it came to Trans Am exports during the 1977-79 era, the power team chosen was exclusively Olds 403/THM 350 auto. That is, mostly the tightly controlled Californian spec. However, for 1979 this power team became 50-state in nature, and felt sharper. (Courtesy Keishi Imai)

The 4bbl 301 fitted to this 1979 Redbird automatic was a lively and economical motor. The 301 first appeared in 1977 and was the center of Pontiac's turbo V8 of 1980/81. (Courtesy Dan Rolston)

part in allowing the final W72 400s to be offered.

W72 400 – Pontiac's possible bait & switch?

When *Car and Driver* previewed the new 1977 W72 400 T/A, along with Camaro Z/28 in April 1977, maybe it didn't realise what it had. Then again, maybe it did? There was a lot of performance disparity in the recorded independent magazine testing of the 200/220bhp W72 400 Formula and Trans Am: for the above mentioned report, respective 0-60mph and ¼ mile times of 9.3 and 16.9 seconds. *Motor Trend* tried a like-powered teamed 1979 Formula in October 1978. This report issued forth respective figures of 9.1 and 16.1 seconds for the uprated 220bhp W72 400 Formula.

Road & Track tested a 1978 220-horse T/A with W72 400/4-speed combo, that offered 6.5 and 15.3 seconds for 0-60mph and ¼ mile respectively. *Car and Driver*'s 1979 Trans Am, with the same power team, got respective readings of 6.7 and 15.3 seconds in January 1979. Adding to the statistical tie, the November 1978 issue of *Cars* told of its '78 Formula 400 4-speed, the star of 1978 testing, that ran a limbo low 14.93 seconds at 94 mph. However, Peter Klutt of TV's *Dream Car Garage* sampled a perfect condition 1977 Trans Am W72 400 with T-tops and 4-speed. This Y82 SE mobile was felt to be sluggish and in keeping with the above-mentioned slower times.

It seems that even in the '70s, automakers were submitting specially prepared rides, so as to make a solid impression in national journals. In the '60s, Pontiac PR man Jim Wangers was well known for doing this, via dealer Royal Pontiac. Can you say Bobcat Special? In the '70s, one noticed a similar phenomenon by Ford with its Cobra Jet 351 V8 Gran Torinos, Chevrolet with its post-1970 Corvettes, and Pontiac with the W72 400. Smog tuning had its price.

Little engines – 305/301/301 Turbo

The L78 400 wasn't available in 1979. The Olds 403 was the mainstay Trans Am motor for 1979, with a few W72 400s adding

a sprinkling of flavor. Buyers could order the L37 150bhp 301 4bbl and get a $195 credit. However, records show that the vast majority of buyers chose the Olds 403 motor.

The end was nigh for the 6.6-liter engine, regardless of whether it came from Oldsmobile or Pontiac. CAFE was already demanding an auto fleet average of 19mpg, a figure that would only rise in the years to come. Thrifty as it was, there was just no way a gasoline powerplant displacing over 6 metric liters could have a future in diesel-loving, economy-hungry, 1980s America. The Olds 403 was no longer just a Californian Trans Am engine. The 1979 L80 4bbl Olds

1980 brought Namco's Pac-Man video arcade game, Neil Diamond's The Jazz Singer film, and the 210bhp Turbo Trans Am! (Courtesy Michael Russell)

The Pontiac turbo 301 drew on the turbo system and electronic ignition used by Buick on the Turbo Regal, but used more boost and achieved more consistent performance. (Courtesy Michael Russell)

403 gave new Trans Am buyers a real taste of how performance used to be in the good ol' days.

For 1980/1981 Trans Am engine options were pruned to variations on a 301 theme. California would receive the Chevrolet sourced LG4 305. By 1980 the 49 state 231 and floor-mounted 3-speed manual was the only power team left involving a stick shift. Thoughts of 1979 W72 400/4-speed/4-wheel disk Formulas and Trans Ams were a fading memory. The base Trans Am engine outside California was the 301 4bbl, available in two states of tune: the regular L37 301 was rated at 140bhp and the Electronic Spark Control (ESC) version weighed in at a mean 155bhp.

The ESC 301s had electronic ignition and a real world performance feel greater than the 15bhp advantage the specification sheet suggested. A 170bhp W72 301 package with real dual exhausts was planned, but never made it into production. The W72 option code stuck and this was the box to tick if the 155bhp ESC 301 4bbl engine was required.

On a slightly negative note, in much the same way that Ford brought out the miserly 255 to complement the 302 V8, Pontiac revealed its 2-barrel 265-cube V8. The 265-cube version of the 301 became the Formula's base engine for part of the 1981 model year and helped Pontiac ration out what remained of 301 stocks for the Trans Am. For the remainder of 1981 the Buick 3.8 V6 was the Formula's standard engine.

However, the real news for 1980 lay with the new Turbo Trans Am! The 1960s Chevy Corvair turbo and Oldsmobile's turbo work with the 215ci aluminum V8 represented turbo's early days, but the combination of small engine economy and large engine performance seemed more relevant in the mid to late '70s. Technically, a turbocharged engine would only behave as such for a limited duration of any governmental economy or pollution test. In theory, the turbo's impact on the environment was directly related to the decisions of the driver. North America rediscovered the turbo with the 1978 Buick Turbo Regal. The

The Firebird Formulas and Trans Ams fitted with the blown 301 had this non-hood scoop hood. The power bulge was to clear the motor's air cleaner. This is a 1980 WS6 Turbo Trans Am. (Courtesy Daniel Hillebrand)

If this 1980 WS6 Turbo Trans Am was ordered without the D53 hood bird decal, $120 was saved. The Turbo rims featured only on WS6-equipped Turbo Formulas, Trans Ams and Californian LG4 Trans Am 305s in 1980. The second generation bird had a new style Firebird logo to replace the 'dead chicken' of the first generation era. Pontiac design chief William Porter drew inspiration for the second generation logo from Norm James' Firebird III show car design. This pattern, in turn, was influenced by a big wall mural at the Phoenix AZ airport. Porter conceived the hood bird decal as a bigger version of the second generation Firebird logo. (Courtesy Brent Grove)

1979 Ford Mustang Cobra Turbo was another high profile exponent of forced induction. With both 6.6-liter motors laid to rest, Pontiac turned to the turbocharger for the 1980 model year.

The turbo system of the 1980 Turbo Trans Am owed a great deal to Buick's Turbo Regal. The draw-through setup saw the familiar Rochester Q-jet feed a Garrett AiResearch TB0 305 turbocharger unit through an aluminum plenum chamber. Fresh air was drawn through a 4in duct just above the front air dam. The turbocharged 301 Trans Am had no shaker scoop, functional or otherwise. The non-turbo 301's exhaust crossover was absent from the blown engine's intake manifold. In the interests of keeping things cool, a water jacket surrounded the plenum chamber. It offered warmth to aid cold driveability but, once the coolant attained 217F, a thermostat shut off the flow. Pontiac engineers

This 1980 hood bird decal is composed of five different colors. In mid 1981 that was cut to just two colors, but the decal price was increased to $125. The Screamin' Chicken decal was first thought up by William Porter to visually accommodate the T/A shaker scoop. The bird's feathers were originally influenced by the flame-look motifs on Tiffany blown glass that Porter was collecting. (Courtesy Lee Rehorn)

The Turbo Trans Am was a bit slow in the 0-30mph range, but took off after that. The Turbo Trans Am was just a bit slower than the mid '70s L75 Trans Am 4-speed in terms of 0-60mph, 0-100mph and ¼ mile acceleration. (Courtesy Lee Rehorn)

turned up the boost pressure to 9psi: much higher than on the contemporary Buick Turbo Regal or Ford Mustang Cobra Turbo.

To combat the very real possibility of major engine detonation with this much boost, and relatively low octane US unleaded gasoline, Pontiac turned to retarded ignition timing, a nifty gadget used by Buick on the blown Regal. Ignition timing would be retarded instantly by an electronic black box. An accelerometer-style transducer attached to the intake manifold monitored the vibration associated with detonation, and signalled the E/C module to back off the timing and restore it once gasoline quality picked up. The GM Delco E/C system was handy

on the non-turbo 301, but a real lifesaver on the blown version. Rather than use a primitive blow off valve, the 301 turbo utilized a wastegate activated by intake manifold pressure. The wastegate ensured that boost pressure didn't rise above 9psi.

A fair few internal changes were made to the 301 to make it suitable for forced induction. Within the 301's economy-based architecture, hardware was upgraded in preparation for the turbo. Additional material was added to the block bearing webs, and the surfaces to which the cylinder heads attach. The diameter of bolts securing the main bearing caps rose from ⁷⁄₁₆in to a full ½in. As with the SD 455 engine of

1973/74, the crankshaft received pressure rolling treatment to the journal fillets. Special pistons, rods and head gaskets were also part of the 301 turbo experience. Finally, as with the W72 400 motor, a 60psi oil pump and baffled oil pan were present to safeguard the 301 turbo.

Creating a turbocharged engine is no walk in the park, especially if the finished product is to be handed to a large section of the motoring public. Given that turbocharging places such a strain on durability, it comes as no surprise that the 301 turbo motor should utilize some of the engineering tricks that made the earlier SD 455 and W72 400 engines so special. Perhaps the fair-minded would allow the LU8 301 Turbo to join those illustrious

Bet on Turbo Trans Am to pace the 1980 Indy 500, with stock 301T motor. (Courtesy John Kirkbride)

predecessors as one of the truly great ones.

The 301 turbo got a mixed reception from the motoring press, which was in favor of a turbocharged 301 as such, but couldn't help comparing the newcomer to previous top engines that powered Formulas and Trans Ams. For 0-60mph and ¼ mile work the blown Trans Am, or Formula, was on a par with contemporary US specification, automatic Jaguar XJS V12 or Porsche 928. It was a valid performance comparison because the Pontiac was a comfortable, automatic grand tourer. The two European imports had to cope with the same US economy and pollution laws and were highly regarded by the US motoring press. It would be

logical to conclude that Pontiac's new 301 turbo had done well.

The new turbocharged Trans Am was approximately 1.5 seconds slower to sixty than the final W72 400 4-speed Trans Am. However, some facts should be noted before jumping to conclusions. Firstly, all Formulas and Trans Ams fitted with the 301 turbo were automatic-only cars. Secondly, 1980/81 Federal economy and emissions targets were stricter than in preceding years. Thirdly, all second generation cars fitted with the turbocharged 301 possessed factory-fitted air conditioning. Most of the W72-400-powered Formulas and Trans Ams tested by magazines were stick shift cars without air conditioning. Factor in all of the above and the blown Trans Am

appears in a better light. Being objective, had the W72 400 motor lived on for 1980/81, it would be fair to assume that economy and pollution laws would have tamed the powerplant to some extent. As previously mentioned, the final W72 400s fitted were not so much 1979 model year powerplants as refugees from 1978.

Testers aired a number of concerns about the turbocharged Trans Am that were hard to understand. Even though engine compression was maintained at a relatively high 7.5 to one, the turbo motor couldn't light up the rear tires. This didn't please magazine testers, even though wheelspin doesn't improve elapsed times. They took exception to the fact that

Come 1980, folks were hankering for a '79 Formula 400 4sp, just like this! (Courtesy Jefffrey Brown)

the engine lacked sufficient torque to push the car into oversteer. On the plus side the lightweight turbocharged engine and WS6 suspension hardware created the best neutral handling modern domestic car. Registering 0.82g on the skidpad and going through slalom course cones faster than the almost doubly expensive Corvette, was reality for a turbocharged Trans Am owner.

The turbo package needed to be optimally tuned and have good quality gasoline on hand to perform at its best. Unfortunately, some magazine tests were conducted in Southern California where unleaded high test wasn't available. In addition, whilst the 301 turbo had a larger compressor housing than the unit used on the Buick Turbo Regal, the particular turbocharger used was still too small for the 301. It was well suited to the Turbo Regal's 231-cube V6, but wasn't enough

for a 301ci V8. It's unlikely that a well tuned turbocharged Trans Am would have experienced more than 7.5psi of boost. One thing the new turbo did possess was refinement. The blown motor felt like a larger normally aspirated engine and turbo whine was truly beyond perception.

There was no point in the rev range where one could feel the turbo come into play, and the THM 350's full throttle shift points of between 3800 and 4000rpm just added to the seamless feeling of power. The turbo lag experienced by early Turbo Regals and Ford 'Fox' Mustangs was only noticeable by its absence. As *Car and Driver* said in October 1979, it just felt like a really nice 350 V8. Strangely, while motoring journalists said they wanted the immediate response of the former 6.6-liter V8s, they also intimated that they preferred the all-or-nothing power delivery of European turbo cars like the 1974

BMW 2002 Turbo and 1975 Porsche 930 to the stately refinement of the Turbo Trans Am.

At first there was literally no indication that a turbocharger was helping the little 301 live up to Trans Am tradition. Designers had originally dreamt up a line of turbo boost lights that would face the driver at the base of the Turbo's hood bulge. This was cancelled due to expense and it seems that no turbocharged second generation cars built before February 1980 had turbo boost hood lights. This meant that the majority of magazines testing the new Turbo Trans Am had a car without a turbo boost gauge, a simple dash warning light, or any technical means of measuring the TB0 305's activity.

Eventually, a simplified arrangement of just three lights were incorporated into the leading edge of the hood bulge. They were a $40 option during the 1980 model year, and standard equipment come

This 1980 Trans Am has the Hurst 'Dual Gate' automatic shifter. The Hurst works on the same principle as the Pontiac 'Rally Shifter,' but with a more noticeable second gate. (Courtesy Jerry Derren)

Unfortunately, many turbo 301 cars didn't receive the care and maintenance from their first owners they should have, so often had original motors swapped for 400s and 455s. This 1980 Turbo Trans Am now has a worked L78 400. (Courtesy Michael Russell)

1981. The exterior lights joined the asymmetric hood bulge, clearing the air cleaner, and 'Turbo 4.9'/'Turbo Trans Am' decals as outward signs of the power within. However, surely the new turbo hood bird decal with its head lifted, issuing flames heavenward, was enough to signify to one and all that the Turbo Trans Am had indeed landed?

Initially, the turbo 301 was rated at 210bhp at 4000rpm, and 345lb/ft of torque at 2000rpm. By the 1981 model year, the motor was re-rated at 200bhp and 340lb/ft of torque at the same respective rpms.

1981 also saw the introduction of the computer-controlled Q-jet on Formula and Trans Am models. This was the Computer Command module introduced the previous year on the LG4 305 Californian market automatic 1980 Corvette. It adjusted the air/fuel mix ten times per second. It was thanks to this device that the Turbo Trans Am was finally emissions-certified for California.

A 1980 Barclay brown Formula 301 auto wearing Rally IIs. The dual scoops mean that this Formula 301 is a non-turbo car. (Courtesy Robert Korstad)

So, in the final year for the second generation Firebird, California was reacquainted with a stick shift Trans Am: the LG4 305 and BW Super T10 4-speed power team – the first time since the 1974 model year that a 4-speed manual Trans Am had been permitted in California.

The long absence of the stick shift variety was ironic because Trans Ams, plus other big image performance cars, were popular in California. Early on it was thought that the Turbo Trans Am would only be built in the Californian GM F body plant on Van Nuys Boulevard. However, this model was also constructed at the Ohio Norwood factory. One

This is a 1981 Trans Am 305 4-speed, the first Trans Am 4-speed since 1979, and the first stick shift Trans Am certified for Californian sale since 1974. (Courtesy Michael Raycraft)

thing that never changed was the automatic-only nature of the Turbo Trans Am. The THM 350 was the only gearbox available for the turbo 301. Steve Malone and others at Pontiac discovered that it was impossible to create a turbo 301/4-speed power team capable of both passing the EPA's hydrocarbon test and maintaining acceptable driveability.

In keeping with the domestic auto industry's transition to rationalized production, the LU8 turbo 301 carried air conditioning (C60) and automatic transmission (MX1) as mandatory options. In spite of the convenience equipment the Turbo Trans Am was EPA rated 2mpg higher than 1979's W72 400 4-speed for both city and highway. The turbocharged model's taller 3.08 final drive helped in that respect; indeed, its Q-jet carb,

whether by vacuum pressure in 1980 or computer in 1981, was able to enrich the fuel mix under turbo boost conditions. Owners who have experimented with other carbs have found that the correct enrichment under boost conditions implies over-rich settings across the board.

Consumer Report was once

moved to say that the turbo performance option available on the Corvair must have been the most complex method imaginable for achieving more power. Turbocharging was at odds with usual preferences for straightforward performance through displacement. Perhaps it was just too much of a gamble to

This Trans Am's hood scoop decal alludes to the presence of the LG4 motor. 1981 marked the final year that Pontiac would use the European spelling of 'litre' on the Firebird. (Courtesy Michael Raycraft)

A one-owner 1981 Trans Am 301 automatic. When news of the radical for '82 F body surfaced, many fans rushed to get the final examples of the iconic 2nd gen. (Courtesy Keith Fuerst)

Most magazines tested the Trans Am Turbo, but figure a lower 3700lb non turbo T/A with a/c was good for 0-60mph in 10.5 seconds. Also budget on over 20mpg overall, for the 301 4bbl ESC-powered Trans Am. (Courtesy Keith Fuerst)

By 1981 the 49-state 301 4-barrel had electronic Q-jet, and ESC (Electronic Spark Control) to govern ignition timing. Trans Am put its faith in the microchip to get 155bhp net. There were plans for a W72 190 horse edition for 1979 Grand Am CA. (Courtesy Keith Fuerst)

For 1981, Firebird and Trans Am got GM's Computer Command Control system, plus computer controlled lockup torque converters concerning automatic cars. All to deal with smog law and CAFE! (Courtesy Keith Fuerst)

The 2nd gen's looks were actually functional. Engineer Paul Lamar helped develop the T/A's aero package, while at Aerodynamic Research. This ride is nicknamed Ol' Blue. (Courtesy Keith Fuerst)

1976 marked not only Bicentennial celebrations, but also Pontiac's 50th anniversary. 2057 1976 black and gold Trans Am LEs (Limited Edition) commemorated the latter milestone. (Courtesy Brent Grove)

introduce forced induction on a car that had derived a reputation for rough and ready action? The absence of water-cooled bearings on the Garrett turbo made it wise to let the engine cool off at idle before turning off the ignition. If this wasn't done the turbocharger bearings would fry when the engine was shut down. As with most early turbo setups the blown 301 also lacked an intercooler. Such engine savers arrived later in the eighties.

There's irony in the fact that Firebird and Trans Am sales took off after the first fuel crisis, after what was generally believed to be the death of domestic performance cars. It has already been recounted how the F body's rivals bit the dust as industry executives geared and steered the public towards a brave new world. Naturally, the sudden execution of the majority of your rivals is going to put you in number one position for your market. Many thought this sector was going to die on the vine, but they were wrong! Pale imitation of a glorious past or not, Trans Am sales exploded from 1975 onwards. The Firebird nicely moved into the '80s riding the crest of a wave.

Of course, it's hard to keep a secret and it wasn't long before other players chimed in for an intense session of 'me too' syndrome. They raided their shelves, resurrected, painted and taped, as they boarded the marketing bandwagon in the hope that some of the market

1976 Trans Am LEs could be ordered with or without T-tops, and with a 400 or 455 motor. This particular Trans Am LE is a 455 4-speed T-top car. (Courtesy Brent Grove)

Gold Honeycomb rims were part of the 1976 Trans Am LE's visual package. 1976 was the last year for Pontiac's Honeycomb rim; in 1977 it was replaced by the Snowflake design. (Courtesy Brent Grove)

In 1977 the Trans Am LE was renamed the Trans Am SE. 1978 saw the SE color scheme change to Solar gold halfway through the model year, giving us the Y88 package. (Courtesy Steve Mau)

The Y88 package added $1263 to the Trans Am's price, and Camel tan trim to its interior. This particular car features the W72 400/4-speed power team and WS6. WS6 was a new item for 1978. (Courtesy Steve Mau)

By having W72, WS6 and Y88, this low mileage, one-owner car is very collectible. The W72 400 performed extremely well by late '70s emissions and CAFE-struck American standards. (Courtesy Steve Mau)

segment's good luck would rub off on them. Ford brought out the 139bhp Mustang II Cobra II for you in 1976/77, and who can forget the glamor that was the 1978 King Cobra? Chrysler Corp was dropping names from the past like crazy by launching the Dodge Aspen R/T and Plymouth Volare Road Runner compact twins.

If that trip down memory lane wasn't enough, then the local AMC dealership was worth a visit. The smallest member of the big four decided that all was forgiven and brought back the 'AMX' tag. In 1977/78 the AMX name would be affixed to the tail of a special Hornet. The 1979 model year AMX looked suspiciously like it had something to do with a Gremlin. In spite of the reincarnation it was only an AMX in spirit! Fortunately, Firebird always put substance ahead of paint and tape decoration. The Great Ones still packed hot car hardware.

True Turbo Thrills!

Back in October 1978, *Motor Trend* was well pleased with the performance exhibited by its test '79 Formula W72 400 4-speed with T-tops. This loaded car even had a/c, a weighty accessory at the time. However, so did the 1980 Turbo Trans Am – a model with mandatory auto tranny. If the *Motor Trend* times are accurate, it shows the more tightly emissions-controlled 1980 car in a good light. This 301 Turbo machine registered 8.7 and 16.003 seconds for respective

0-60mph and ¼-mile acceleration, when examined by *Road Test* in February 1981.

The 1981 turbocharged example missed out on T-tops, but still seems to accord with Pontiac

engineers' mission statement of getting 6-liter performance out of a 5-liter V8, using forced induction. Pontiac engineers were offered use of the Chevy 350/auto power team for 1980, pending their 400's

As per the 1973-74 SD455 engine option, choosing a turbo 301 Formula implied the same hood arrangement as a like-engined LU8 Turbo Trans Am. That is, no Formula hoodscoops! (Courtesy Danny Manning)

In 1981 the Turbo Formulas and Trans Ams were the fastest cars GM made: quicker accelerating than Camaro or Vette. A 210 horse 1980 Turbo Formula is shown. (Courtesy Danny Manning)

94

It looked spectacular but Y88 paint problems concerning variability and matching resulted in the black and gold SE color scheme being reintroduced. As with all second generation Trans Ams, that shaker was attached to the engine, not the hood! (Courtesy Steve Mau)

demise. They passed on this, preferring to turbo their own 301 in 1980 and 1981. In the 1981 *Road Test* report, Turbo Trans Am out-accelerated the Camaro Z/28 on test.

1981 Turbo Trans Am was also faster than the 4-speed Corvette *Road & Track* tried in 1981. Chevrolet offered only a 190-horse 350 for Vette that year. With 4-speed stick, *R&T* obtained 0-60mph in 9.2 seconds and the ¼ mile in 17 flat. This made Trans Am GM's performance champ of 1981, and faster than the more expensive Corvette. It also explains GM's policy of Corvette King Performance from 1982, by loading the power team deck. However, in 1981 Pontiac still made The Great Ones!

Special Edition Trans Ams – the Y code cars

The limited edition Trans Am was one special that really lived up to its billing. With Trans Ams flying off the production lines in the tens of thousands, the limited edition Trans Ams really were limited in number.

It all started in 1973 when GM styling giant Bill Mitchell informed John Schinella that a unique Trans Am would be appropriate for Pontiac's 50th anniversary in 1976. Mitchell – influenced by the John Player Special livery used in racing – went for black and gold as the color choice. The first sign of this planning was seen at the 1974 Chicago Car Show.

Following this show car came the official, showroom-available

Y-code cars of the 1976-81 period. These Y-code cars were only appearance packages offering no further advancement over stock performance. 2400 'Limited Edition' black and gold Trans Ams were planned for the 1976 model year. Non-T-top cars were coded Y81 and T-top versions Y82. 1414 of the former and 643 of the latter were eventually sold, giving a total of 2057 cars. Y81 cars cost $450 above the stock Trans Am's base sticker price, and Y82 models sold for a $1100 premium.

So well received were these limited edition cars that they were offered once again for the 1977 model year. From this point on they became 'Special Edition' Trans Ams. For 1978, the

The 1979 Y89 Tenth Anniversary Trans Am celebrated a decade of Trans Ams. This particular TATA has the W72 400/4-speed power team.

Trans Am SE changed to 'Solar' gold for the exterior color. $1263 bought a Camel tan interior, brown pinstriping and gold anodized Snowflakes. The Y88 Solar gold exterior made a refreshing change, but the new combination suffered from paint matching problems.

The Trans Am SE returned to the familiar black and gold exterior combination later in the 1978 model year.

Regarding the T-top option, 1978 heralded the almost total transition to Fisher T-tops from the earlier Hurst design. The earlier

T-top hatches were physically smaller and supply problems were partly responsible for the switch in design used. Of course, most people who like T-tops prefer larger panels to give a greater feeling of fresh air motoring.

T-tops, or targa tops, became more popular as manufacturers pulled the plug on convertible models due to fear about future government safety roll-over tests. The second generation Firebird was the only member of the four model generations not to feature a factory-built convertible. Buyers in the seventies didn't seem to mind. T-tops were very much a product of their time and became closely associated with Pontiac's Firebird for many years. Once again that didn't stop competitors offering T-tops on their sporty cars.

Finally, a word of warning concerning Trans Am SE cars. The particular car at hand may be a fake. The various items that comprised the SE package could be ordered using regular order forms. More than a few dealers tried to steer showroom traffic their way by creating Trans Am SEs of their very own. Obviously, with interest in the Trans Am running sky high, plus dealer allocation of genuine Trans Am SEs rationed, the temptation for forgery was tempting. Given

The TATA had an all-silver leather interior and a long list of standard equipment. 7500 Y89 TATAs were built. The TATA was the 1979 Daytona 500 pace car.

The TATA came with W72 400/4-speed or Olds 403/THM 350 auto combinations. This car has the latter power team but, either way, the TATA was pretty spry. (Courtesy Steve Fairweather)

that the Trans Am was so popular and numerous on dealer lots, it's understandable that a few people would want to distinguish the Trans Ams on *their* lot by adding a little gold!

We now enter something akin to Pontiac's very own tri-year era with the 1979-81 Firebird/Trans Am line, a major front and rear restyle, adopting a new smooth nose section. The rear got a sinister tail-wide black lens, which was an internationally popular style between the mid '70s and mid '80s, and especially on West German cars like the Porsche 930 and 1980 Audi Quattro. Pontiac combined this welcome restyle that nicely updated an ageing design with the long-awaited adoption of a column-mounted headlamp high beam dipswitch. (Previously located in the footwell area as per usual domestic car practice.) The black and gold SE continued to be a part of Trans Am fare and was coded Y84. However, something more exotic was awaiting buyers with three very special limited edition models.

1979 marked the 10th Anniversary of the Trans Am, so naturally there was the 10th Anniversary Trans Am (TATA), coded Y89. 7500 cars were

A larger than normal hood bird decal and two-tone charcoal silver over light silver exterior set apart the TATA from regular Trans Ams. (Courtesy Steve Fairweather)

This 1979 WS6 Trans Am SE W72 400 4-speed is the only one of its kind in Austria, and features air conditioning. (Courtesy Reinhard Lackner)

produced with the Olds 403 as the standard powerplant. There was the possibility, if one wasn't a Californian resident, of a W72 400 4-speed power team subject to a dwindling stockpile. However, the real importance did not lie beneath the hood but concerned the TATA's special accoutrements, of which there were many.

Perhaps first to catch the eye, apart from the exterior silver paintwork, were the new-for-1979 turbine rims. (Remember that the Turbo Trans Am didn't exist yet so they were mostly known as turbine rims.) The rims were designed by John Schinella, built by Appliance Industries, and had a polished silver finish.

TATAs were sequentially numbered and had two-tone silver paint. The top half was resplendent in charcoal silver, the lower half distinguished by light silver. The hood bird decal was present in a larger than usual format that extended onto the fenders. The interior was an absolute delight, if you liked silver. Silver leather seating material was a first for a second generation Firebird, and it had silver door trims and silver trim surrounding the gear shifter. A stock car was replete with WS6 handling pack, air conditioning, power windows, power antenna, power door locks, rear window de-fogger, leather-trimmed adjustable 'Formula' sports steering wheel, 3.23 final drive and halogen quartz lamps. Perhaps the best standard items, all new for the 1979 model year, were the 4-wheel disk brakes.

Schinella and crew left no stone unturned in the search for visual excitement. A computerized sewing machine imported from France was used to create the three interior trim Firebird emblems. The emblems were placed on the door trim panels, with a single, centrally positioned emblem on the rear bench seat. It's hard to imagine such extravagance on today's cars because of cost. Even with the Olds 403 and THM 350 autobox, the Tenth Anniversary Trans Am, or TATA, gave the impression of halcyon days of performance, although the earlier models never did brake or handle quite as well as this $11,065.55

By 1978 the W72 400 powerplant was rated at 220bhp, but its true horsepower level was way higher. 1979 was the end for the big displacement 4-speed Birds. (Courtesy Reinhard Lackner)

One of the few visual changes distinguishing the 1981 Firebirds from 1979 and 1980 models was the addition of the bird logo on the gas filler door. Back then, many tried to update their '79s and '80s by retrofitting the bird on the gas filler door.
(Courtesy Reinhard Lackner)

ride. However, why mention price or vulgar valuations by speculators for short-term economic gain, which only serve to distance these cars from those that truly appreciate them?

Moving on, then, to one of the single, most important events in international motorsport, the Indianapolis 500. The car manufacturer that earns the right to have its automobile pace the field of 33 determined and brave souls, plus successfully completing the task, receives major kudos. An excellent cameo appearance on race day would allay fears that small displacement Turbo Trans Ams weren't up to the traditional Pontiac Trans Am billing. Such an endeavor was embarked upon by Pontiac and satisfactorily completed in full view of millions. It wasn't as easy as it looked. A pace car contender had to meet set targets for acceleration, top speed and general endurance before it would be permitted to pace the field. Auto manufacturers loved the idea of their car pacing the field, but was it technically possible?

The answer must be yes – and no – given the state of domestic performance cars during the latter half of the 1970s. It should come

as no surprise that off-the-shelf auto moxie wasn't easy to happen upon. To make up for the shortfall and avoid the very real possibility of major embarrassment, engineers – sometimes not even belonging to the car maker – feverishly fettled designs so that they could make the grade.

One example was the 1976 Buick Century Pace Car. This

model used a turbocharged version of Buick's 231 V6 before the 1978 Turbo Regal went into production. Over 20psi of boost pressure was also well above what would be found on a road-going turbocharged car.

Move on to 1979 and the new third generation Ford Mustang Cobra was that year's Indianapolis Pace Car. Ford was pushing the

In 1980 the Indy 500 and Daytona 500 were both paced by a Turbo Trans Am. Pontiac created the Y85 1980 Turbo Trans Am Indy 500 Pace Car. In 1981 there was the Y85 1981 Turbo Trans Am Daytona 500 Pace Car. The latter car is pictured.
(Courtesy Mark Melton)

Both Y85 Pace Cars had a similar white exterior color scheme and decal set. Once again, a 1981 Turbo Trans Am Daytona 500 Pace Car is shown. (Courtesy Brent Grove)

2.3-liter turbo, four-cylinder engine as the performance wave of the future. While Ford sold Pace Car replicas with the blown 2.3-liter four-cylinder or 302 V8, only the latter engine was used for Pace Car duty. Ford got Jack Roush to build a custom 250bhp tricked-out 302 motor for the big race. This was at a time when the stock 302 that powered the showroom Mustang Cobra was rated at 140 horses net.

A project car for the great race is one thing, but for a car that can be believed in, a replica with more in common with the Pace Car than a nameplate and decals, turn to the Y85 1980 Turbo Trans Am Indianapolis 500 Pace Car. Apart from removal of the standard air con, shaved tires for high speed running on the oval and a 2.56 gear set, this car was identical to the Turbo Trans Am Pace Car replica that folks could actually purchase. A car with the same performance as a regular WS6-equipped 1980 Turbo

Trans Am. It was good to know that the 5700 delivered replicas were a near identical match for the car veteran racer, Johnnie Parsons Sr, guided around the Brickyard on May 25 1980.

The 1980 Pace Car came with the same convenience features found on the Y89 TATA, but with a cassette deck rather than an 8-track player as standard equipment. John Schinella was concerned that the

Pace Car should stand out from the gray Brickyard track surface. Stark white was chosen as the main exterior color, contrasting with a charcoal silver hood bird decal that embraced the roof section. While 'Turbo' rims and silver mirror glass hatches meant that the new Y85 car was similar to the Y89 TATA, there were important differences.

On the inside white vinyl seating with charcoal, patterned cloth inserts looked very tasteful. The cloth inserts helped to keep the driver in place during spirited driving. This was a problem with the TATA's slippery leather seats.

The 1980 and 1981 Y85 Pace Cars had a white exterior, but the younger car sported black rather than charcoal accents, and had a simpler black hood bird decal. The 1981 Y85 Pace Car also differed in its red and black interior with Recaro seats. (Courtesy Brent Grove)

The 1980 and 1981 Pace Cars both wore Turbo rims, but the younger car had 7.5in-wide rims rather than 8in as the previous year. The Y89 and both Y85 Pace Cars had WS6 as standard equipment. (Courtesy Mark Melton)

Once again the complex Firebird emblems seen on the rear bench and door trims of the TATA were present on the Indy Pace Car. They were also used on the subsequent 1981 Pontiac Firebird Trans Am Daytona 500 Pace Car.

Decal lettering for the Indy Pace Car's doors, plus a 'Pontiac' front windshield decal, could be attached by a dealer. The decals certainly left little doubt that a 1980 Indy Pace Car was at hand. Of course, as per any other 1980 model year passenger vehicle sold in the US, an 85mph speedo was automatically part of the sticker price: rest assured that any 1980 Trans Am, turbo or otherwise, could go faster than 85mph. Red was the chosen color for the dashboard lighting, mirroring what had been done on the 1979 TATA.

1981 saw the Y85 Daytona 500 Pace Car special edition Turbo Trans Am. This newcomer was similar in an overall sense to the 1980 Pace Car, but please note the following points of difference. The 1981 Pace Car was painted stark white once again, but with black rather than gray accents. The Turbo rims were part of the WS6 package fitted to every 1980/81 Pace Car, but rim width was cut from 8in to 7½in. However, the most notable change from the 1980 Indy Pace Car concerned the interior.

The Trans Am had finally received seating that permitted its chassis and WS6 package to be fully exploited without the driver

being flung to the four corners of the car. The cloth interior featured black with vibrant red inserts, and, more importantly, West German Recaro front sport seats. Finally, it had bucket seats with adequate side bolstering and adjustable seatback. These two points alone should elevate the 1981 Turbo Trans Am Daytona 500 Pace Car to being one of the best Trans Ams up to that point in time.

1981 was the third year in a row that the Pontiac Firebird Trans Am had paced the Daytona 500. Pontiac made 2000 1981 Daytona 500 Pace Car replicas, so rarity will guarantee the collectibility of this Trans Am. Indeed, the Y89 TATA and 1980/81 Turbo Trans Am Pace Cars are all collectible cars. The Y89 is a visual delight and the latter two cars have a motorsport connection befitting the Pontiac Firebird Trans Am's tradition. All three cars represent the meeting of form and substance. Unfortunately, these 1979-81 Trans Ams represent one of the last occasions for detailed trimming of a domestic special edition model. The accountants have spoken and the numerous, intricate color and trim variations have been shown the door!

The Firebird was riding a wave of popularity and such indulgences in trim and color variation were

economically viable. Even after the recession sparked off by the second gas crunch, 50,898 Trans Ams found new homes during the 1980 model year. In 1981 that number fell to 33,493. Chalk the decline up to the fact that many were waiting for the all-new 1982 model; that the second generation Firebird was in its 12th production year, or it was highly unlikely the majority of folks had worn out the 117,108 Trans Ams they bought in 1979!

The Skybird, Redbird & Yellowbird: Firebird Esprit W60, W68 & W73 packages

Rising interest in the Trans Am was all well and good, but to make sure that it wasn't all one-way traffic, Pontiac cooked up an appearance package to increase interest in the luxury Firebird Esprit.

The special Esprits took their name from the main color used on the particular special edition. Things kicked off with the 1977 'Skybird' which was coded W60. Originally it was hoped that the fancy Esprit might be called Bluebird, but the Bluebird Body Company of Georgia already had a claim on that title. The Skybird had a two-tone Lombard blue paint job, color-matched grilles, taillight bezels and 15x7in blue Snowflake rims wearing OBW

The W68 Redbird was the second of three Firebird Esprit appearance packages. This 1979 Redbird has the 4bbl 301/ THM 350 auto power team. 15x7in red Snowflake rims round out the package. (Courtesy Dan Rolston)

coded whitewalls. The interior, available in cloth or vinyl, was colored to match, as were the seat belts and Formula sports steering wheel. Bearing in mind that the Skybird was in no way intended to be a sports model, engine options were normal Esprit fare.

In the middle of the 1978 model year Skybird was replaced by the W68 Redbird, so named due to the predominant use of red. Two tone

The W60, W68 and W73 Firebird Esprit appearance packages were as visually arresting as contemporary Firebird Formulas or Trans Ams. Halfway through the 1980 model year the Redbird was replaced by the Yellowbird. (Courtesy David Fillinger)

The final Esprit appearance package was W73 Yellowbird. It flew into the Firebird coop in the mid '80 MY. (Courtesy Stan Rakowski)

During the 1977-80 era the Skybird, Redbird and Yellowbird Esprit packages, were aimed at lady buyers. Pontiac ads featured the cars with exclusively female models. (Courtesy Stan Rakowski)

Yellowbird had the pizazz folks wanted, with a Formula-style steering wheel and Trans Am's Disco Dash! (Courtesy Stan Rakowski)

The Yellowbird came with doeskin vinyl interior, or the pricier hobnail velour seating. This car had the top 4bbl 301 V8, but thrifty types could fly on base 231 V6 or 2bbl 265 V8 power. (Courtesy Stan Rakowski)

Yellowbird's yellow shades were unique to this model. Yellow code 56 for the main exterior color, and code 37 for accents. Today, male and female Firebird fans enjoy Skybird, Redbird and Yellowbird! (Courtesy Stan Rakowski)

This 1978 Macho T/A #160 shows that if you didn't live in California, DKM could have built a nice Poncho 400-powered Macho just for you! (Courtesy Sheila Hartnagle)

Roman red replaced Lombard blue; there was a subsequent change to Francisco red for 1980. Rather than blue stripes the Redbird had gold stripes, and had similar equipment and trim to the Skybird, but some 1979 Redbirds received the gold steering wheel, dash trim and front arrowhead emblem used on the Trans Am SE. Midway through the 1980 model year the W73 Yellowbird took over from the Redbird package.

The Yellowbird also had gold stripes, but had either a Camel tan cloth or vinyl interior. The taillights had yellow horizontal ribs. Most Yellowbirds had the gold Formula steering wheel and Trans Am SE dazzling disco dash trim, plus the option of a rear spoiler. When the Skybird package first hit the sales charts it retailed at $342 for the cloth edition and $315 for the vinyl version. By the time of the Yellowbird's arrival those prices had risen to $550 and $505 respectively. All Skybirds, Redbirds and Yellowbirds had a contrasting cartoon-style bird illustration done in pinstripe matching color on the rear sail panels. Once again, it's unlikely that such attention to detail and creativity with special edition trim packages will ever be seen again.

The aftermarket – welcome to Macho, Turbo and 455 country

With the Trans Am occupying center stage in the late '70s US performance scene, it's understandable how various aftermarket tuner specials might get created. Given Trans Am popularity, some individuals would have hankered for a special touch, something to distinguish their particular set of wheels. What price, then, for exclusivity, especially when Trans Ams were filling the streets?

DKM Inc based in Glendale Arizona fulfilled a number of auto dreams. The company was started by brothers, Dennis and Kyle Mecham, whose father owned one of the biggest Pontiac dealerships in the Western United States. DKM produced a number of special Trans Ams, starting in 1977, and offered a range of packages involving cosmetics, engine and suspension.

DKM would buy in new Trans Ams and take them to various levels of appearance, power and cost. Naturally, being the late 1970s, customizers didn't have free rein and had to work within set federal guidelines, most notably in the area of pollution control. It would also be true to say that performance buyers wanted something more refined and cohesive than the dealer specials of yesteryear. Everyone wanted more power, but allied to a certain level of comfort and convenience. To quote *Car and Driver's* Davis E Davis Jr from December 1980: "The serious enthusiast is no longer as one-dimensional as he was a decade ago." To this end, with the possible exception of the exterior decal set, DKM-modified cars held true to this credo of thoughtful performance.

On the outside, DKM 'Macho' Trans Ams received DKM paint, accents and graphics. 'MACHO T/A' decals were posted as large as life on door panel bases and rear spoiler. A low-key version was available with just paint accents, devoid of Macho T/A script or regular Trans Am decals. Hood birds could be full-size, or a smaller nosecone example like the one used on 1970½-72 Trans Ams. At the end of the day the customer was boss when it came to choice.

As might be expected power gains were achieved without touching engine internals. Hooker or Headman headers, and real duals using two catalytic converters, aided through-flow with the help of a crossover balance tube. Dual catalytic converters were ruled out on stock Camaro Z/28s and Trans Ams because of cost. The familiar Trans Am hood scoop was made functional. DKM also played around with the stock Q-jet and the weights inside the distributor.

The end result was a package that performed better than stock whilst, allegedly, remaining within

Dennis and Kyle Mecham started building special Trans Ams under the 'DKM Inc' banner in 1977. Their father owned one of the biggest Pontiac dealerships in the Western United States. (Courtesy Sheila Hartnagle)

state pollution laws. Keep in mind that Macho Trans Ams were sent to Pontiac dealers all over the country, including California, for which DKM did the above tricks to the Olds 403/THM 350 power team. Indeed, the company adjusted the automatic on this particular Macho version for quicker shifts. Two rather neat Macho touches were a fiberglass lift-off or lift-off/tilt hood, and an oil pressure restorer. The former

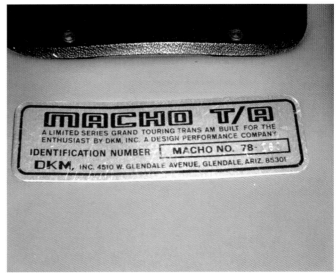

The DKM plaque that guaranteed a genuine, custom Macho T/A built to exacting standards for the auto enthusiast. (Courtesy Sheila Hartnagle)

DKM's Macho Trans Ams were reasonably priced and popular. The mechanical and cosmetic format of the finished vehicle depended on the customer's wishes. (Courtesy Sheila Hartnagle)

improved the weight distribution whilst the latter prevented the motor being damaged from oil starvation. During high speed cornering, a firewall-mounted flask containing one quart of oil under pressure, would rescue the engine by divesting its contents when there was a drop in oil pressure. The genie would return to its lamp once danger had passed. The fiberglass hood and oil pressure regulator were optional. It would seem that the regulator was intended for non-W72 400 motors such as the Olds 403 and Pontiac L78 400, since these engines lacked a baffled oil pan.

Suspension changes involved replacing stock Delco shocks with Koni units set on full soft. Front springs were compressed to lower the ride height by 1½in, but stiffness remained unchanged. Naturally,

DKM worked with the WS6 package once it became available. Later 1978 Machos could be fitted with rear disk brakes, pre-dating Pontiac's 1979 model year issuing of 4-wheel disks. In terms of gearboxes, choice ranged from the usual THM 350 automatic and Borg Warner Super T10 to the close ratio Doug Nash 5-speeder. Hurst shifter linkages featured on the manual gearboxes.

Even more exciting, although on an even smaller production scale, was the Macho Turbo, a similar animal to the regular Macho but with the addition of a Rayjay 301E turbocharger, and up to 7lb of boost pressure for the Poncho 400. The turbo was positioned well down in the engine bay, but a clear indication that something was up to no good was a big, shiny tube attached to the hood scoop/air cleaner. It was this pipe that channeled the forced

air into the 400 motor. As with the 1980 Pontiac Turbo Trans Am a wastegate was used to limit boost pressure.

A boost gauge was cut into the dash or console, and turbo exterior graphics on the tail and front fenders, in place of the normal Trans Am decals, showed this to be no sleeper. A Hurst competition shifter, standard German sports seats and the all-important oil pressure regulator were standard issue. The battery was mounted in the trunk for better weight distribution. Water injection and an ignition retarder were used to ward off detonation. With a blown 400 under the hood, the optional 9in-wide rims available on the normal Macho would have come in handy.

Common to both Macho and Turbo Macho was the availability of a range of auto-sound equipment from Audio Mobile, Concord and others. A few Machos had three dials cut into the console for the audio system. Even a power moonroof was an option. The Recaro LS or Scheel 410S seats were possible choices. All Machos had a 160mph speedo and 8000+rpm tachometers. These were more visually appealing than the standard 100mph units

In 1978 a turbocharged Macho Trans Am using a Poncho 400 and Rayjay 301E turbo became available.1980 saw a new Macho based on the new Turbo Trans Am. This is a 1979 Macho T/A. (Courtesy Sheila Hartnagle)

This customized 1981 Trans Am 305 4-speed features Dupont Chromabase paint with ghost flames. The color changes with the light and viewing angle. (Courtesy Kerri Hebert)

that made it seem like one might fall off the edge of the world if the gas pedal was floored. Chrome, black or interior color-matched roll bars could be arranged for that extra special racetrack aura. The sky was the limit if the buyer was

flush. In fact, that isn't really fair as DKM offerings were reasonably priced, especially when compared to the large amounts demanded by European car emporiums.

In June 1978, when the base sticker price for a Trans Am was

$7331, the non-turbo Macho evaluated by *Motor Trend* listed for $10,156 and the Turbo Macho was somewhere in the $12-13,000 range. Not cheap, but certainly not expensive considering the level of performance and exclusivity assured by Macho Trans Am ownership. A small, brushed aluminum console plaque stated DKM's credo and the car's serial number. The build number was repeated on the car's exterior just behind the front wheelwells. It seems that only eight Turbo Machos were built in 1978, and only a further 22 for the 1979 model year. DKM did make a Macho 301 Turbo, complete with 'Macho Turbo' and '5 litre' exterior decals. Unfortunately, the recession had

A Chevy 350 crate motor has replaced the original LG4 305. The 4bbl Holley 600cfm unit has been zinc-plated and has chrome-plated fuel bowls. A Weiand intake manifold is present. (Courtesy Kerri Hebert)

The car still has its BW Super T10, but is assisted by a Hurst shifter and dressed up with a B&M chrome shift handle. (Courtesy Kerri Hebert)

softened demand for the Macho concept by this stage. No Macho Trans Ams were produced using 1981 model year cars.

In any event, with the demise of the L78 400 at the end of the 1978 model year, and rationing of the W72 400 during 1979, motor options for DKM were limited to the Olds 403 and non-turbo 301 for much of 1979. This motivated DKM to investigate a different powerplant for future projects. Unfortunately, for Pontiac fans, at any rate, this change of pace dictated enlistment of the Chevy small block V8. Still, needs must when the devil drives. Mouse motor or no, the 1979 DKM Tallon Super Tourer was quite a machine, so let's go over and greet this devilish creation.

The starting point was a brand new Pontiac Firebird Trans Am. The difference between this car and earlier DKM automobiles was in the use of the Chevy motor, and the sheer extent of modifications. DKM bought a loaded Trans Am and then stripped it down until only the doors and basic unibody, 4-wheel disks, radiator and rear axle assembly remained. It was now ready to receive a turbocharged Chevy 350 and Doug Nash 5-speeder, amongst other

The interior is trimmed in Plum tweed by Columbia Auto Seat and the owner. By 2+2 standards the second generation Firebird is quite spacious. (Courtesy Kerri Hebert)

108

things such as DKM's usual dual exhaust system, Hurst shifter linkage, 11in L88 clutch, American Specialty aluminum rims 15x9½in front and 15x11in rear, 50 profile BF Goodrich radials, gold anodized Moto-Lite steering wheel and aluminum dash trim! In short, enough trinkets to out-do almost any other F body or Vette owner.

But it didn't stop there! In addition to the already described DKM Macho suspension practice,

Jim Donaldson's American Fiberglass, based in Phoenix, created custom rear quarter panels, flared front fenders and DKM's usual hinged or pinned hood were included. The pinned hood even had a pair of Camaro Z/28 front fender louvers and a bolt-on airdam to give your special Trans Am a wide body look like no other. You could say it was a wide body look to match Pontiac's traditional 'Wide-Track' performance angle!

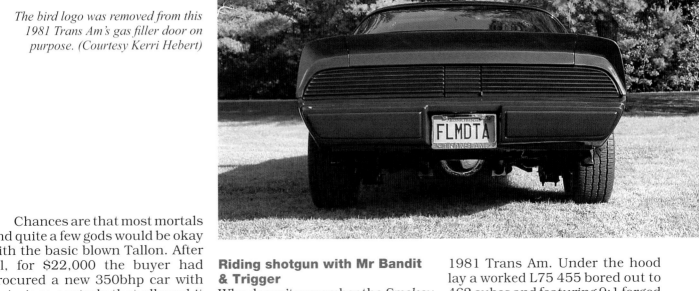

The bird logo was removed from this 1981 Trans Am's gas filler door on purpose. (Courtesy Kerri Hebert)

Chances are that most mortals and quite a few gods would be okay with the basic blown Tallon. After all, for $22,000 the buyer had procured a new 350bhp car with emissions controls that allowed it to be sold and registered in Arizona. However, for all you over-achievers, $29,600 secured even more Trans Am; 457 horsepower and 16in Jongbloed racing rims wearing Pirelli P7 tires, to be precise. Just for you DKM secured a nice mouse motor from the home of IROC Camaro motors, Traco Engineering. The four bolt 350 with steel crankshaft had Carillo aluminum rods, 11 to one comp TRW pistons, a solid lifter cam, and slant plug Turboheads using Crane roller rockers. An 850cfm Holley double-pumper met an Edelbrock Victor manifold, which was ported and gasket-matched by Manning & Brady. The solid lifter mouse motor could be wound out to 7000rpm without breaking sweat.

The 457bhp Tallon that *Hot Rod* magazine tried on for size in March 1979 was destined to live with a wealthy Saudi Arabian owner so, naturally enough, this particular car kept its factory air conditioning. As a final thought, consider the fact that, only a few months after *Hot Rod* tested that white hot Tallon, a 1980 US market BMW 633CSi had a list price of $31,870. With that in mind who could begrudge anyone expending $29,600 on what must be one of the rarest and hottest Trans Ams of all time?

Riding shotgun with Mr Bandit & Trigger

Who doesn't remember the *Smokey & The Bandit* franchise courtesy of Universal Studios and Hal Needham? The series of three motion pictures released in 1977, 1980 and 1983 helped put the Trans Am in the national consciousness. The first film played a big part in making the 1977/78 Firebird shape and black and gold color scheme the only choice for many Trans Am fans. The second movie introduced us to the Turbo Trans Am, and the third film tied in with the downsized third generation car's very early days. A successful Hollywood film bolstered the popularity of Pontiac's performance model and soon everyone wanted a car just like Bandit's. That's probably what Trans Am Specialties of Cherry Hill, New Jersey, had in mind when it created a run of 200 'Bandit 455' Trans Ams after release of the second motion picture.

Naturally, one would expect the car to be black, and it was, but there were a few niceties that may raise an eyebrow. Firstly, the car didn't have a hood bird, but did have the stylized Bandit insignia in no less than eight interior and exterior locations, including the trunk. While the Bandit had a shaker scoop, don't get the idea that this was just another non-turbo 301 or 305 1981 Trans Am. Under the hood lay a worked L75 455 bored out to 462 cubes and featuring 9:1 forged pistons, mild hydraulic lifter cam, aluminum intake manifold and tubular exhaust headers. Mindful that some owners might actually try to exploit the WS6 suspension and 4-wheel disks provided, Trans Am Specialties threw in a baffled oil pan. The Bandit rode on 15x8in Turbo rims and Gabriel Strider shock absorbers.

On the comfort front the Bandit was decked out with all the usual contemporary features such as air conditioning, T-tops, lighted vanity mirror and remote trunk release. However, velour-covered Recaro sport seats, a Blaupunkt 3001 4-speaker auto-sound system and Escort radar detector were also thrown in. It goes without saying that the Bandit also packed a CB radio for those situations where one just had to copy and get out! The car looked remarkably stock from the outside and it took a keen eye to notice that 60 profile Goodyear Eagle GTs had replaced the normal 70 profile tires.

Contrasting with the stock appearance were fiery performance times. Use the heavy Doug Nash 5-speed box to best effect and $30,000 worth of Trans Am may have been persuaded to record times in the low 14s in the quarter and sprint to sixty in 6 seconds.

In Smokey & The Bandit, the hero, Bandit, drove the restyled 1977-shape Trans Am. The film has a lot to do with the reverence shown to 1977/78 Trans Ams today. (Courtesy Mark Haynes)

The view Sheriff Buford T Justice saw most of the time when trying to apprehend Bandit. Trying to catch a 400-cube T/A would definitely involve hot pursuit! (Courtesy Mark Haynes)

Of course, a big hunk of the Bandit's price tag went towards pacifying Universal Studios for the use of the 'Bandit' name on this low volume, Burt Reynolds signature model.

Chuck Posey's New Jersey company continued their work with a Bandit model based on 1982's downsized third generation Firebird Trans Am. There was a further run of 200 serial numbered Bandit Trans Ams. The new lighter car was much more affordable at $16,500 and relied on a Chevrolet 305 / BW Super T10 4-speed power team. The Chevy 4bbl 5.0 featured a Crane Blueprint cam originally designed for 1968's Chevy 327, and offered 30-35 horses more than a stock LG4 305. The 1982 Bandit Trans Am was about handling and balanced performance. The third generation car's WS6 suspension was upgraded with tauter springs, solid bushings and Goodyear NCT P245/60/15 tires on 15x7 Appliance Industries aluminum rims. Custom fiberglass fender wells accommodated the Bird's bigger feet. Trans Am Specialties produced their own fiberglass hood, air dam, flares and wing for the 1982 Bandit Trans Am.

In Rocky II, Rocky Balboa bought a brand new 1979 black and gold T/A from a Philly Pontiac dealer, after going the distance with Apollo Creed. (Courtesy Reinhard Lackner)

Only a stick shift could fit in with the Trans Am's tire-burning image. However, in Smokey & The Bandit II, our hero, Bandit, drove the auto-only 1980 Turbo Trans Am. (Courtesy Reinhard Lackner)

More Firebird silver screen & small screen appearances

When you're hot, you're hot. In the late '70s and early '80s Firebird, especially Trans Am, was THE American performance icon. More so than even Corvette. As such it was featured in many movies and much television. One rare non T/A appearance, was the 1979 Formula used by Miami cop Doug von Horne (Jerry Reed) in 1979's Hot Stuff movie.

After the Formula got blown up, a common occurence in the era, von Horne lamented he only had a couple hundred or more payments left to make on the coupe! George Barris customized a couple of wide body '79 Firebirds: the 'tasteful' Travolta *Fever* mobile, and a yellow cousin car. The latter featured in Steve Martin's 1979 comedy *The Jerk*. 1979 *Playboy* Playmate of the year, Dorothy Stratten, modeled with both cars.

In the 1980 movie *Borderline*, starring Charles Bronson, people-smuggler Hotchkiss (Ed Harris) drove a new Turbo Trans Am. A '79 Olds 403-engined T/A was featured in a combine harvester farm field chase in Steve McQueen's last movie, *The Hunter* (1980). Although McQueen was playing real-life good guy bounty hunter Ralph 'Papa' Thorson (who couldn't work a shift), the automatic car was passed off as a 4-speed model.

Why didn't McQueen have his familiar Mustang? At this hour, Mustang only had enough machismo to be used by Farrah Fawcett Majors and Cheryl Ladd, in the form of a '76 Mustang Cobra II in Charlie's Angels. In addition, the Mustang's post-1973 economy ways meant it was off the public radar for hot cars.

1981 saw Turbo Trans Am take the lead role in Canadian sci-fi flick, *Firebird 2015 A.D.* A post-apocalyptic *Mad Max Road Warrior*-style tale – also starring Darren McGavin and Doug McClure. That year, a '79 Trans Am cop car got harassed by a Lamborghini Countach in *The Cannonball Run* movie. In 1983's *Blue Thunder*, actor Roy Scheider's hero chopper pilot drove a '79 Trans Am. His character's nemesis had a silver late C3 Vette.

On the small screen, James Garner's famous L.A. gumshoe Jim Rockford, drove a tan Firebird Esprit in *The Rockford Files* (1974-1980). Trailer-home-living and answer-machine-using Rockford updated his tan Bird from 1974 to 1976 and 1977 shapes. The show didn't switch to the 1979 shape 2nd gen Bird. This was probably because doing so would have meant downsizing from the usual Olds 350 to a smaller LG3 305 2bbl V8. This would have made stuntwork harder.

Herb Adams' Fire Am (Firebird American)

We turn closer to home for the next two Firebird/Trans Am spin-offs – Herb Adams' Fire Am or 'Firebird American,' and Pontiac's Trans Am Type K Sport Wagon.

As stated earlier, the Fire Am's suspension was the starting point for Pontiac's subsequent WS6 package. In 1977 Pontiac asked Adams to create the ultimate Trans Am, with two caveats: any alterations had to be done on a regular assembly line, and the car had to retain a measure of street civility.

The Fire Am was already under development in 1976 when Pontiac came up with the idea of an 8-car celebrity race. It seems the SCCA threw cold water on the exercise by demanding too much money and the race never became a reality.

Herb Adams went on to offer the public a Fire Am conversion kit through his company, Very Special Equipment (VSE). State and Federal regulations meant that the VSE package had to be owner-installed. Some or all of the hot-up items could be built in depending on how far the buyer wished to go. Overall, the Fire Am was closer to the performance specials of a decade earlier than contemporary modified Trans Ams produced by DKM and Trans Am Specialties. The Fire Am's character didn't lend itself to everyday use, in contrast to the grand tourer concept that was becoming increasingly popular; after all, who doesn't want to drive their Trans Am everyday?

Left: In 1977 the second biggest money-making film at the box office, was Smokey & The Bandit. No Luke Skywalker, just Bandit and Snowman trucking bootleg Coors beer across the state line! (Courtesy Richard Beer)

Below: The Trans Am's iconic shaker hoodscoop. It moved when one blipped the throttle, because it was attached to the V8 motor. The scoop ran from 1970½ to 1981 model years, and was made functional on this 1978 T/A, by owner Richard Beer. (Courtesy Richard Beer)

Above: Trans Am owner and Smokey & The Bandit fan Richard Beer with Burt Reynolds! (Courtesy Richard Beer)

Such was the lure of Smokey & The Bandit that the original owner of this 1978 Y88 Solar Gold Trans Am SE converted the car to the familiar black and gold color scheme of a Y84 Trans Am SE. The car's original L78 400 was also replaced by a worked W72 400, to cope with Sheriff Buford's hot pursuit! (Courtesy Richard Beer)

The Poncho 400 V8 was a great all-purpose performance/economy motor. This 1980 Turbo Trans Am was converted to a warm 1976 L78 400, when the original 301T flew the coop! (Courtesy Michael Russell)

112

Above: The shaker's 'T/A 6.6' decal callout implied a W72 400 underhood. Pontiac stockpiled 8690 of these special 220hp 400s, for 1979 Formulas and Trans Ams. (Courtesy Paul Kenney)

Above: A black and gold 1979 Trans Am was used in a combine harvester farm car chase, in Steve McQueen's final movie, The Hunter (1980). However, an automatic L80 403 T/A featured, not the W72 400 example shown here. (Courtesy Paul Kenney www.youtube.com/watch?v=s0bjDgS5soA)

Right: W72 400-powered cars implied a M21 BW T10 4-speed stick; no automatics. Evidenced by the two extra central circular dash vents, this Trans Am had optional a/c. This Bird was cool, in more ways than one! (Courtesy Paul Kenney)

Below: With '79 MY being the curtain close call for big-engined Birds, Car and Driver suggested buying two 6.6 liter cars. One for regular use, and the other for storage and asset appreciation. The last of the fast cars? It seemed that way. (Courtesy Paul Kenney)

A 1977 Fire Am, still wearing its cool supersonic hood bird decal. The Fire Am started with the 1976 bodyshape and had a heavy duty feel. (Courtesy Jimmy T Means)

Under the hood, bearing an unusual bird decal resembling the Concorde supersonic jet, lay a functional shaker scoop attached to a Poncho 400 devoid of pollution controls. Engine internals were untouched but 180 degree headers and 3in, single pipe exhaust with slide-in muffler helped the stick shift Fire Am zoom to sixty in 7 seconds flat. The quest for better weight distribution saw the battery get repositioned to the trunk. To safeguard the motor from oil starvation during serious handling, dry sump lubrication was included by VSE.

Fire Am suspension hardware consisted of semi soft Koni shocks, steel suspension bushings, larger sway bars, shorter front coils, repositioned front subframe and lowered rear ride height Fender wells were altered all round for sufficient tire clearance. The Fire Am did get full metallic brake pads and linings, but, unlike later WS6 packages, 4-wheel disks were absent. Even so, the sight of the Fire Am hunkered down on 60 profile tires, Corbeau racing seats/safety harness and interior roll bar sure did shout road racer!

Suspension tuning from the Book of Adams

Racer indeed, because Herb Adams had a racing background. The former Poncho R&D engineer was a SCCA/IMSA road race veteran, who had left Pontiac in 1973, to go solo with VSE. Adams had definite ideas on optimal race car set up: soft front springs/shocks, a hefty front swaybar for roll stiffness, and adjust the rear swaybar to fine tune the whole shebang. Adam's suspension credo was expressed in the suspension packages offered by VSE for 2nd gen Firebird (Fire Am) and Camaro (Cheverra). VSE's comprehensive instruction booklet, well illustrated, overviewed Stage I (street), Stage II (autocross) and Stage III (race). In March 1979 *Hot Rod*'s Dave Wallace said the VSE demo car would turn doubters into believers.

The 'Cutting Corners' article recounted a 1973 Firebird 400 4-speed with 3.08 final drive ratio, and VSE's Stage 1 job. It handled like a dream. Gone was the usual F body's skittish behaviour over imperfect surfaces. The Fire Am would hold its line through a corner, no steering corrections needed. Banished were F body's traditional early understeer and ultimate roll oversteer. The recipe for Swiss-like neutrality was beaucoup rigidity!

Normally, F body was a partial monocoque, a front third subframe, attached to a rear two-thirds unibody. In January 1979 *Car and Driver* said it was like having

The start of the Fire Am legend. This 1976 type coupe was going to feature in an 8-car Pontiac-initiated celebrity race, before the SCCA demanded too much cash. (Courtesy Jeffrey Brown)

The mere act of adding headers, 3in exhaust and dumping pollution controls, was enough to drop the 400ci-powered car's 0-60 mph time to 7 seconds flat. (Courtesy Jeffrey Brown)

Legendary ex-Pontiac engineer and subsequent VSE founder Herb Adams, with the Fire Ams he was famous for, at the 2015 Trans Am Nationals. (Courtesy Jeffrey Brown)

a windshield hinge! The journal added that Adams' work prevented a Chubby Checker shake, rattle and roll fest on rough roads. VSE brought a couple of V-braces tying subframe to firewall, saving a claimed ¼in of flex. The firm also framed the rear passenger compartment with a custom steel rollbar.

Apart from VSE subframe connectors welding frame to unibody, stock mounting blocks were removed to lower the whole deal 1in. VSE also had its own body-lowering mounts. A lower center of gravity meant better handling. Adams also believed in the old 'Wide Track Pontiac' slogan. Appliance Wheel Company built him a set of 15x8in zero offset rims. These were

half the price of Pontiac's like spec Snowflakes. VSE preferred these black center steel rims, and covered 'em with Goodyear GT radials sized P255R60-15. This necessitated a little inner fender panel work to clear. Even then, there would be some wheel well contact on full lock.

P265 rubber could fit a 2nd gen F body with a lot more panel work. VSE proclaimed that placing the battery in the right rear trunk location was like moving the motor back 10in. Adam's suspension genius ran to special front and rear swaybars, along with a higher front spring hanger location for less roll oversteer and tail squat. There was no room to do this mod on a 1st gen. The smaller wheel wells also limited tire size.

The VSE booklet guided the novice through spring cutting or heating to save money, basic sheetmetal work and bending the accelerator linkage to allow heel and toeing. VSE staff claimed that the cost in time and money, including purchase of the abovementioned 6-year-old 1973 Firebird 400, ran to 42 hours and 4 grand concerning their Stage I conversion. If one was a handy mechanic type, and didn't mind driving around potholes, this was the deal of the century! Henceforth, the Firebird nose was 2in closer to the road, and the coupe always followed its nose.

VSE arranged its kits so work progress could be built on, allowing one to continue daily driver

The 1976-1980 VSE fettled Fire Ams, represented the ultimate handling 2nd gen Firebirds. A tight chassis from the genius of Herb Adams. (Courtesy Jeffrey Brown)

Herb Adams and VSE continued road circuit handling work into the 3rd gen F body era. Handy qualities in SCCA (Sports Car Club of America) category racing. (Courtesy Jeffrey Brown)

service. Stage II brought solid steel bushings, and a brake cooling kit with metallic brake shoes and pads. VSE also had a deep baffled oil pan. Camaro and WS6 1978-79 T/A owners needn't have worried, but regular Firebird owners feared 350/400 oil starvation in hard cornering. Adams' Stage III race car went one better with dry sump lubrication for its mildly worked SD 455 mill, fed by Holley 850 CFM double pumper.

Adams proved this 1979 Fire Am was streetable, by driving it to magazines for testing and races to compete. Those races were the 1979 and 1980 24 Hours of Daytona! Even so, the car 'sported' power windows within its fiberglass replica doors, AM-FM radio and factory heater, plus fresh air system. For the '79 enduro, this Fire Am even had a B&M shifted THM 400 autobox.

The spec included a Ford 9in full floater differential permitting 2.50 rear end, and 160mph at 5000rpm. Hurst/Airheart rear disk brakes, slowed the 3500lb bolide, and VSE HD spindles/hubs kept axles safely attached. New for 1980 Goodyear Wingfoots were better than the previous GTs. This rubber was fitted to 10in-wide rims, necessitating the VSE Stage III Wheel Flare & Fender kit.

Previously, fed regs meant one had to fit VSE kits obtained from Adams' Californian concern. However, from 1980, under agreement between VSE and Cars & Concepts Inc. (Michigan),

completed cars could be purchased. C&C would build the Fire Ams, and inform buyers which Poncho dealers could supply their work. The Pontiac warranty and emissions clearance were intact, because C&C didn't touch the motor. Supply your own 455 V8, and 160mph was there for the taking – in spite of that new fed mandated 1980 85mph speedo!

Hi there Silverbird!

The Appliance Wheel Company-sponsored SCCA Trans Am Category II 1978 Herb Adams' Silverbird could certainly top 85 mph – 200 mph even. Adams was on the 1967 development team that did the first 1969 Trans Am. He was also involved at the same time with the I6 PFST (Pontiac Firebird Sprint Turismo) – always earnest about the importance of handling. Ten years later, former Pontiac alumni were on Silverbird too. Tom Nell, that developed the 301 derived 366ci V8, was on the Poncho team with Adams and Skip McCully, that turned the 455 into the SD 455.

Paul Lamar, who oversaw Silverbird's bodyshape, was also behind the aero package of the 2nd gen Trans Am, while at Aerodynamic Research. According to the rulebook, the racer only needed the same suspension/chassis type as a stock Trans Am. A stock T/A's 4-speed featured a single plate Borg & Beck clutch. Manualwise, a Fire Am could have a Doug Nash 4+1 5-speeder, but Silverbird featured a 3-plate Indy-

style Lakewood clutch. Silverbird went with a racer backbone type frame, front and rear tubular subframes and Herb Adams' own custom front end. Some body production panels had to be used, but overall the racer's link to the road car was tenuous, as in most modern motorsport. With regard to being ahead of the era, Herb Adams' focus on handling is also in keeping with today's high performance cars. Herb Adams, Fire Am and Silverbird – all ahead of their time!

The Pontiac Trans Am Type K Sport Wagon

It's only partly right to say that the Type K model belonged to Pontiac, because the Type K's story started elsewhere. It was a design staff project driven by designer, Jerry Brochstein, who worked under Dave Holls in GM's Multi-Purpose Studio.

The very first car had a fiberglass body and glass designed by Libby Owens Ford. This creation made its first appearance at the 1977 Chicago Auto Show, resplendent in silver metal-flake. The short tail, or Kammback, was the reason for the Type K's name.

It was at this point that Pontiac saw the possibility of further development using the Trans Am as a base. John Schinella's Pontiac II Studio group went about designing a follow-up, utilizing the restyled 1977/78 bodyshape as the foundation for the Trans Am Type K Sport Wagon. It's interesting to see that half a decade after the Volvo

The lack of a factory, second generation Firebird ragtop meant cars like this NCE 1979 Olds 403-powered Trans Am convertible were in demand. (Courtesy Svein Arne Holmedal)

1800 ES said goodbye, the sport wagon concept still had a following. Pontiac engineers lowered the front ride height, and chose the stiffest rear springs possible to keep the new bodystyle – with its greater rear mass – balanced. The Type K drove in a very similar manner to a regular Trans Am.

Pininfarina was approached with the idea of building the Type K, with a proposed sticker price of $18,500. Two steel prototypes were constructed in Italy using gullwing windows fabricated in West Germany. One car was silver and the other gold. Both cars had hood scoops, Snowflake rims and hood bird decals, and both did show car duty once returned from their Roman holiday. Both got the '79 Firebird facelift, and appeared on the show circuit and *The Rockford Files* (silver wagon) that year.

Unfortunately, Pininfarina

couldn't build the cars for the target retail price; even the Fisher Body Company was 30 per cent over budget on the escapade. This left three Type K cars in limbo. The very first car produced was sent to GM's basement and the two steel bodied Pininfarina-produced cars had temporary residence status for critique and evaluation, after which they had to be either exported or scrapped. After all, while they looked like Trans Am wagons, they were still not US-built. As it happened the gold car was crushed and the silver car lived on as part of the Pontiac Historical Collection.

If the model had been given the green light it would have arrived as a 1980 model year car. That means the Type K wouldn't have had either the Olds 403 or Pontiac's 400. Then there was the economic recession and fuel economy targets. As British Leyland North America discovered when introducing the

luxury V8 hatchback Rover 3500 for 1980, now was not the time for extravagance.

The people may have liked the look of the Type K, but general economic belt tightening might have resulted in a commercial flop. Pontiac had enough to do introducing the 1980 Turbo Trans Am without having to deal with the Type K. One can also imagine that the Type K's extra weight would have dulled the 301 turbo/THM 350 power team. The Type K would certainly have been too much vehicle to haul for the non-turbo 301 and Chevy LG4 305 powerplant options.

Some may have said that the 1980 Type K didn't have the go to match its show. Sometimes it's better to let sleeping dogs lie. However, in the mid '80s, Pontiac revived the Type K using the third gen T/A. Unfortunately, once again, the model didn't make it past the prototype stage.

American Clout and National Coach Engineering (NCE) were behind custom ragtop conversions of Firebird Formulas, Trans Ams and Chevy Camaro Z/28s. NCE's work was showcased in the opening Hawaii-set episodes, of TV's Charlie's Angels' final 1980-81 season. (Courtesy Svein Arne Holmedal)

Headless Firebirds – Second Generation Convertibles

One ray of auto hope that did get to see the light of day was the second generation convertible. American Clout of San Jose California was behind Formula and Trans Am rag tops. American Clout was linked to Autowest, a company that sold such custom convertibles to Budget Rent-A-Car and car dealers. The convertible conversion was available on the Firebird Formula, Trans Am, and the Chevy Camaro Z/28. All cars were loaded with air conditioning, power windows and cruise control, and came with a 1980 base sticker price of around $16,500.

Coachwork and installation were performed by National Coach Engineering of Michigan. The handbuilt top was dressed in sail cloth, and the car reclaimed some structural rigidity through the use of steel box section longitudinals that connected front and rear subframes. It was felt that the front windshield area required no reinforcement. Safety may not have been compromised but that didn't stop annoying scuttle shake from raising its head. Early production examples exhibited some rough edges when it came to design and finish of the non-power top. However, with the sudden decline in availability of pillarless and ragtop factory cars, the admiring glances and compliments afforded by American Clout convertible ownership were something special.

Visit Veloce on the web – www.velocebooks.com
Special offers • Details of all current books • Gift vouchers • New books

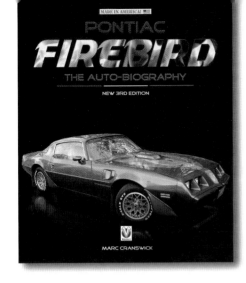

8

Firebird Lite – the third generation; a new kind of Firebird for the '80s

Climate change – life at GM

To better understand the third generation Firebird it may be helpful to examine life at GM. Just how is a corporation supposed to behave when it's the largest automaker in the world? For GM it was business as usual; GM was in the family-sized car business and that's exactly what it was concentrating on. Growing interest in small cars and imports was all well and good, but there was more money to be made on big cars. GM was happy to leave small cars to someone else. However, even giants can't ignore change.

Between 1962 and 1972, GM's share of the domestic market dropped from 51.9 per cent to 44.2 per cent. The first world oil crisis at the end of 1973 made things even worse because GM's fleet had the worst average gas mileage of the domestic car makers: just 12mpg. The distain shown in John Z DeLorean's book *On A Clear Day You Can See General Motors*, and by a GM executive's 1970 statement that: "There's something wrong with people who like small cars," had to change. GM did start to alter course and pay greater attention to outside influences.

In 1972 an internal 'energy task force' was formed, and this group's work paved the way for a changed outlook at GM. The Chevrolet Chevette and Cadillac

Say hello to RAIF (Ram Air Induction Firebird), a modified 1987 LB8 V6 Firebird. RAIF features a Sun Coast Ram Air hood, and the usual flip-up third generation Firebird headlamps have been eliminated.
(Courtesy Shannon Haag)

Fourth generation Firebird reversing mirrors feature, along with side body trim from a 1992 Camaro Z/28. The 17in Niche Serpent rims wear B F Goodrich Scorcher tires. (Courtesy Shannon Haag)

SeVille were fast-tracked for a 1976 model year debut. The first wave of downsizing was set for 1977 and it concerned GM's full-size car line. The intermediates followed in 1978, and the front drive GM 'X' cars arrived for the 1980 model year. GM left the hot selling second generation F body alone while the plethora of new model lines settled down. The 1982 model year saw the release of the all-new 1982 F body.

The Chevmobile

The practice of inter-GM divisional engine sharing had become commonplace by the late '70s, but old habits die hard. An Oldsmobile Delta 88 owner got a shock when he discovered that his new Olds had a Chevy 350, not an Olds 350. Chevy 350s were finding their way under the hoods of Buicks and Pontiacs, too, despite being billed as powered by Buick and Pontiac 350s respectively. It wasn't such a big deal with the Buicks and Pontiacs because both companies hadn't advanced the line that their particular butter and egg 350 motors were superior to rivals in advertising, but Oldsmobile did. Ever since the Rocket V8 came out in 1949 Oldsmobile had extolled the special durability and efficiency of its unique Rocket V8s.

By the mid 1970s it was debatable whether there was any significant performance advantage between regular, everyday 350 V8 motors offered by Buick, Oldsmobile,

Pontiac and Chevrolet. However, the public continued to buy V8-powered Oldsmobiles on the strength of the Rocket's reputation. Apart from the inconvenience of arriving at a dealer to find that the oil filter and belts in stock wouldn't fit your new Olds, quite a few had been misled by the great engine swap. A legal case ensued and subsequent adverts for GM cars carried the caveat that your new car may contain an engine made by another GM division. The early 1980s marked the end of divisional distinctions. From now on a new engine, whether it was an Olds 307 V8 or Chevy 305 V8, was simply referred to as a GM family powerplant.

We still build excitement

Despite a move to rationalized production and shared hardware, Pontiac was still pushing the envelope. The suggestion to use a transaxle on the new 1982 F body, as per the 1961 Tempest, was rejected, but it had something else in the works: a 2-seater, mid-engined, plastic-paneled vehicle.

Project Pegasus was released as the 1984 Pontiac Fiero. In spite

of two cuts in project funding, and the use of a 'commuter car' banner to pacify GM management, Hulki Aldikacti's team brought the P car to series production. The Fiero was the first volume produced, mid-engined, 2-seater US car. A mill and drill production technique helped sheet molded compound (SMC) and reaction injection molded urethane (RIM) panels attach to the steel space frame. The use of SMC and RIM exterior panels on an underlying steel structure was repeated on the fourth generation F body, the Fiero was an important lead-up in that respect.

Unfortunately, GM struggled to achieve good initial reliability and component quality on the various new model lines it released in the late 1970s and early 1980s. The Fiero's image was tarnished by early problems, which was a pity because early sales were very strong at 136,840 units for the first year. Four-cylinder engine fires related to defective connecting rods, and block casting woes, were apparent. A GM Saginaw foundry manager admitted that 10% to 40% of Iron Duke connecting rods were

The Chevy LB8 2.8 V6 multi-point injected engine has been treated to a black painted engine bay, which highlights the polished or Candy apple red painted pieces. Cool flex red hoses and Pontiac Fiero aluminum valve covers finish off one very special Chevy V6. (Courtesy Shannon Haag)

substandard. A sleek, redesigned Fiero with Oldsmobile 'Quad 4' motor for 1990 didn't materialize. It was a sad end for a model that could have eventually rivaled the Corvette.

Design in detail

Work on the third generation F body started in 1975, and a number of proposals were put forward for the form the new car should take. There were advocates for front drive, rear drive and even a mid-engined layout. The first fuel crisis and rising popularity of cars like the Toyota Celica and VW Scirocco made it harder to decide whether the F body should stay traditional, or go in a different direction. Pontiac was credited for selling GM management on the idea of retaining rear drive.

It's possible that the decision to stay with a rear drive/front engined layout was related to the third generation F body project being delayed due to workloads on the downsized era of family oriented models, such as the GM X and J cars. By the mid 1970s, the Ford Mustang, the GM F body's main rival, had changed significantly to become the sub-compact Mustang II. The possibility of a future front drive, turbocharged four-cylinder Mustang III may have swayed GM thinking towards a similar type of car. Changing to a front drive four-cylinder or V6 format would have neatly incorporated the F body into GM's growing transition to front drive.

There was a danger that moving away from a rear drive/V8 front engined layout would alienate existing F body fans. The second generation F body sold strongly in the 1975-81 period, and its success mirrored the popularity of GM's new downsized model lines of the late 1970s. 2.84 million second generation F body owners can't be wrong! Ford's rear drive 1979 Fox-bodied Mustang III, and its retention of a V8 option, also fueled thinking that there was still commercial life in the F body's traditional layout.

The new 1982 Firebird brought a number of alterations and refinements to the familiar F body. The separate front subframe was

The third generation Firebirds were hatchbacks, with the convenience of split folding rear seats. (Courtesy Shannon Haag)

The third generation Firebird maintained the traditional rear drive pony car layout. This is a 1982 Trans Am LG4 automatic.
(Courtesy Carl Marshall)

history; the new Firebird now made use of complete unit construction. Computer modeling produced a stiffer – if not lighter – bodyshell. The Firebird had evolved into a hatchback. The redesign was as much about improving refinement as reducing weight. The cross member that supported the engine and front suspension was bolted directly to the underbody chassis rails. The omission of vibration damping rubber mounts implied a stiffer body, better able to absorb road shock.

For the front suspension engineers mounted the coil springs separately from the shock absorbers. The coil springs were positioned between the front suspension's lower lateral links and the engine/suspension cross member. The new wave of smaller, lighter car designs had less space to accommodate suspension hardware. As with the Ford Fairmont, an altered MacPherson strut front suspension was used on the new F body. The F body's sleek front made it difficult to fit bulkier suspension hardware. A live axle was used once again, but the multi leaf springs of old were deep sixed. The live axle was now located by two trailing arms, a large torque arm connecting the differential with the transmission and regular coil springs with a Panhard rod behind the axle.

As before Pontiac retuned various aspects of the F body's suspension to better suit the character of Firebird models. Once again, Firebirds and Camaros would have their own feel. Pontiac used the labels 'level I,' 'level II' and 'level III' to distinguish between Firebird suspension settings. Such terms were coming into use at GM divisions during the 1980s. Level I would be found on the base Firebird. The Firebird S/E and Trans Am came with level II as standard. Level II was a fair approximation of the optional F41 handling package offered by Chevrolet. Level III was represented by Pontiac's WS6 package, and, as before, WS6 encompassed more than just suspension.

WS6 was optional on the Firebird S/E and Trans Am, costing $417 and $387 on the respective models. 15x7in finned Turbo cast aluminum rims with 'bowling ball' covers wore Goodyear

The former leaf springs were ditched, but the live rear axle was still part of the Firebird's rear suspension. Pontiac tried to influence GM management towards a transaxle, but bad vibes from the 1961 Tempest experience still existed.
(Courtesy Carl Marshall)

Eagle GT 215/65R15 tires. WS6 implied 4-wheel 10.5in ventilated disk brakes, and front/rear sway bars measuring 32mm and 21mm respectively. WS6-equipped cars had quick ratio 12.7:1 Saginaw power steering and a limited slip differential.

Ride like the wind

With a pony car it's difficult to say whether a new model adheres to the concept of form following function. However, while the new Firebird perpetuated the long hood/short deck look, form was tempered by function.

The new Trans Am measured 189.8in and rode on a 101in wheelbase. That's a drop of nearly 10in in length and a 7in reduction in wheelbase compared to the 1981 Trans Am. Despite being physically smaller there was no loss of interior space and luggage capacity was considerably improved. With the rear seats folded down useable luggage space was $14.9ft^3$.

Being slow to adopt downsizing

1981 was the last year for Pontiac's V8. Rationalized production and reduced model variation decreed we would be living in a Chevy small block world from now on. (Courtesy Carl Marshall)

123

The Chevy Citation V6, introduced with the 1980 front drive GM X car, was used by the third generation Firebird. The new downsized F body was the first rear drive application of the Chevy 2.8 V6. (Courtesy Tammi Lee)

formally, and anxious to improve its fleet economy average in the late 1970s, Ford discovered the importance of aerodynamics in eking out extra EPA mpg. Improving economy by launching a smaller and lighter new model was a relatively expensive way to improve economy. That doesn't mean aerodynamics can be used instead of downsizing, or that creating an aerodynamically efficient shape is cheap and easy. The 1982 Trans Am was probably the sleekest shape on wheels, but it takes more than a sharply raked windshield to get efficiency. Successful design is in the detail and the sleek new look wasn't a product of chance.

John Schinella was chief designer of the new Firebird and head of the Pontiac II Studio group. Schinella and Pontiac II Studio completed all aerodynamic detail work for the 1982 Trans Am at Lockheed's wind tunnel located in Marietta, Georgia. The studies took place in December 1978. The Firebird's basic shape had been established by that point and the study was to determine the optimal form of the nose section, airdam and other details.

There was greater sharing of exterior sheet metal with the third generation F body. Even though certain parts of the second generation Camaro and Firebird looked similar, they had just 25 per cent interchangeability. With the third generation cars this increased to over 65 per cent with doors and body sides in common. That said, the Camaro and Firebird seemed as distinctive as ever. Traditional tinkering with the front/rear facias, rims and trim reflected each division's different views. Aerodynamics was one area that Pontiac used to differentiate the Firebird. It was reminiscent of how Pontiac used simple styling cues to distinguish the first generation Firebird from the Camaro 15 years earlier.

The 1982 Trans Am's front facia was the fourth proposal put forward. Also note that the openings for the front turn signals didn't disturb airflow. The facia's design moves air over the gap. There was also much experimentation concerning the Trans Am's rear spoiler, which was indeed functional. Add together the effect of the front facia, flush-wheel covers and rear spoiler and the 1982 Trans Am's 0.315 drag coefficient was the result. The Firebird's flip-up headlights and rear spoiler contributed 0.030 and 0.004 respectively towards the final Cx value; little drops do make an ocean. If a Cx of 0.315 doesn't sound impressive when compared to contemporary European designs, it was because GM took its readings using the EPA

Aerodynamic studies took on greater importance with the search for more CAFE mpgs. These 'bowling ball' covers reduced the Bird's drag factor.

This is a 1982 Firebird S/E 5.0 automatic with WS6. The high demand for the WS6 handling pack caught Pontiac off guard and there was a shortage in 1982. (Courtesy Chris McCombe)

Aviation provided the inspiration for the Firebird's new cockpit-like driving environment. The automatic in this 1982 Firebird S/E 5.0 is the GM THM 200C 3-speed unit. (Courtesy Chris McCombe)

The LQ9 2.5-liter, four-cylinder Iron Duke had electronic fuel injection and was the base motor for the new third generation Firebird. Purchasers of 1982 Firebird S/Es got a $125 credit by specifying the Iron Duke. (Courtesy Bill Rittichier)

Pontiac was entrusted with four-cylinder engine development in the GM family at the time. A 'Super Duty' engine preparation booklet of upgrade parts was made available for the Iron Duke. This took output into the 140-160bhp vicinity. (Courtesy Bill Rittichier)

nose-up attitude. The 1983 Audi 5000's Cx 0.30 was recorded using the DIN nose-down attitude which produces more favorable results.

The interior of the Firebird continued the jet fighter impression given by the exterior. The dashboard possessed an aircraft aura with exposed Allen head screws and large circular gauges in the Bird's new cockpit. Two key interior changes consisted of the adoption of a European-style handbrake located between the front seats and a seatback adjustable for rake, both as standard equipment. The elimination of the foot operated parkbrake added to the sporty feel of the new car. Previously, the 1981 Turbo Trans Am Daytona 500 Pace Car was the only Firebird that featured adjustable seatbacks, so this was one alteration that was long overdue. Six-way power seats were optional on the new Firebird. One curious omission on the new model was the lack of a glovebox. Higher level Firebirds had a leather pouch placed where the glovebox would usually be.

Three's company in the new aviary

The new Firebird line consisted of three versions. Matters started simply with the base Firebird and next up came the Firebird S/E. The Firebird S/E was no relation to the Trans Am SE of the late 1970s, but an amalgamation of the previous Firebird Esprit and Formula versions. In short, a low-key, luxury/sports Firebird for the new decade. After all, Pontiac was envisioning a move away from the Firebird's flamboyant past.

The Firebird's new image would rest on its high tech and understatement, so some of the visual hallmarks from the past were bidden farewell. There would be no Esprit, Formula, or hood scoops in this smooth new world. For a time it also seemed that there would be no Trans Am and Screamin' Chicken, either. Pontiac had plans to rename the Trans Am simply T/A; not that this would have stopped the SCCA from demanding its royalty. 97 per cent of 1981 Trans Ams were specified with the hood bird decal, so Pontiac figured that the Screamin' Chicken should stay on as well.

All this gave the impression that your new 1982 Trans Am could have the familiar decorative hood bird. However, this time around the chicken was shrunk so that it rested on top of the – also optional – asymmetric power bulge hood. The 1982 Trans Am had a monochromatic appearance similar to the 1982 Ford Mustang GT 5.0. The Trans Am's body graphics of old were conspicuous by their absence. At least the Firebird logo seen between the taillights of 1981

So iconic was the Firebird in the '70s and '80s sporty car genre, that a 2nd gen Firebird (please note the Esprit chrome headlight surrounds) appeared on the sleeve art of the Bump 'n' Jump Atari 2600 console game port. So one drove Firebird in the adventure! (Courtesy Telegames www.telegames.co.uk)

CARTRIDGE FOR ATARI 2600

Bump 'n' Jump

FOR USE WITH ATARI® 2600™ TV GAME

Firebirds survived the move to the new Firebird.

Although officially GM family engines powered the new Firebird, in truth the range consisted of one Pontiac and two Chevrolet power plants. The base engine was the cast iron overhead valve Pontiac Iron Duke, basically half of Pontiac's 1977-81 4.9-liter economy V8. In the 1982 Firebird the Iron Duke had electronic throttle body fuel injection (TBI), using one centrally located injector to supply all four cylinders. The 2.5-liter four-cylinder produced 90bhp at 4000rpm and, when teamed with the standard 4-speed manual, was EPA rated at 24mpg for city driving.

A 102bhp Chevy 2.8-liter V6 was the standard engine on the Firebird S/E. The Iron Duke was a $125 delete option. Both the Iron Duke and the cast iron ohv Chevy V6-powered GM's X cars. At the top of the Firebird line was another Chevy motor, the familiar 305 V8 used on the Firebird line-up in 1981. This 5-liter engine was available in two states of tune. Firstly, there was the 8.6 to one compression 145bhp edition using a single Q-jet carb. This LG4 motor was optional on the Firebird S/E and standard equipment on the Trans Am. Secondly, there was the new LU5 Crossfire 5-liter V8.

The LU5 was similar to the L83 motor Chevrolet had created for the 1982 Corvette. The main difference was that the LU5 had the economy focused Chevy 305 at its center rather than the regular Chevy 350 mouse motor. The Crossfire name came from the mounting of two throttle body fuel injection units on the intake manifold cover, supplying the air/fuel mix through tuned runners in the intake manifold to the cylinders on the opposite side of the V8. Two injectors were delivering fuel to eight cylinders, it was doubling up on the single point injection found on engines like the Iron Duke. The electronic fuel injection was by Rochester and the engine management computer could adjust the air/fuel mix up to 80 times per second. This compared with ten times per second with the electronic Q-jet on the LG4 motor.

The engine management computer considered various inputs

such as vehicle speed and coolant temperature, with the aid of engine bay sensors. The same computer also governed ignition timing. By the mid '70s electronic fuel injection was, or soon would be, an integral part of the emission control system. The Crossfire injection worked with air injection, exhaust gas recirculation and a 3-way catalytic converter to deliver 20 more horses, better driveability and economy than the LG4 5-liter V8. The LU5's higher 9.5 to one compression ratio was made possible through the use of a knock sensor. To underline the importance placed upon gas mileage, the Crossfire system used the TB401 throttle bodies from Cadillac's 1978 range. These units flowed a mere 255cfm each. The LU5 produced 165bhp at 4200rpm, 200rpm higher than the LG4. Maximum torque was identical at 240lb/ft, but at 2400rpm rather than the LG4's more tractable 1600rpm.

Despite the LU5's engine sophistication, Chevrolet was having a hard time dealing with pollution laws and CAFE. The automatic-only LU5-powered Trans Am was EPA rated at 18mpg overall, just avoiding the gas-guzzler tax. To have created a stick shift LU5 Trans Am would have worsened the EPA economy rating. As shown by the 1980 Turbo Trans Am, heavy stick shift cars are difficult to drive smoothly enough to pass the hydrocarbon part of emissions certification. A stick shift car capable of meeting pollution laws would have had poor driveability and fuel economy. Even the automatic LU5 Trans Am couldn't be sold in California. That state's stricter emissions requirements implied that the automatic/LG4 combination was the hottest power team permissible.

Visit Veloce on the web – www.velocebooks.com
Special offers • Details of all current books • Gift vouchers • New books

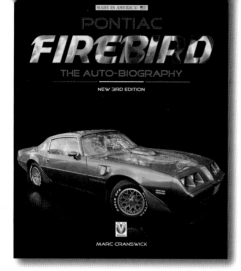

9

More power, more trim, more of everything – the third generation spreads its wings and evolves

The early days

The 1982 Firebird notched up an impressive 116,362 sales, but the transition from the '70s to the '80s wasn't easy. The relationship between the Camaro and Firebird had altered. In the 1970s the Trans Am dominated the pony car scene, and was even pressuring the Vette. The Camaro Z/28 disappeared during the mid '70s and, when it returned in 1977, met stiff opposition from the 6.6-liter Formula/Trans Am. However, rationalized production and engine sharing seemed to play into mighty Chevrolet's hands. Chevrolet's size and budget, plus the firmer policy placing the Vette as the performance king of GM, made it hard for Pontiac to maintain the performance dominance it enjoyed in the 1975-81 period.

The role reversal was symbolized by the different suspension settings used by new WS6-equipped Firebird S/Es and Trans Ams compared to the Camaro Z/28. Previously, Formulas and Trans Ams specified with WS6 employed a take-no-prisoners approach to sports suspension. The 1977-81 Camaro Z/28 took a moderate line entailing some understeer so as not to upset Mr Mainstream. Now Pontiac's WS6 package involved more compliance, with softer rear springs. The result was often less spectacular on the skidpad, but more useful in real world driving that encompassed imperfect road surfaces. The new Camaro Z/28 went into 'go kart' mode, very firm and direct.

According to Pontiac the LU5/automatic combination produced swifter results than the LG4/4-speed

The 1982 Collector's Edition Corvette was the swan song for the 1968-82 C3 'Makovette.' The car's L83 motor had Crossfire electronic fuel injection, a system available on the 1982 Chevy Camaro Z/28 and Pontiac's Trans Am. (Courtesy Noel Carboni)

128

Over the period 1982-84 Crossfire injection was available on the Vette and GM F body. However, unlike the 205bhp 350ci V8 in this 1984 C4 Corvette, the F body Crossfire LU5 engine used only the Chevy 305. (Courtesy Ted Crow)

manual power team, so a 1982 Crossfire Trans Am with WS6 was the meanest new factory Firebird on the street. *Motor Trend's* January 1982 report on the Crossfire Trans Am put its zero to sixty time at 8.89 seconds. This squared nicely with the manufacturer's claim of 9 seconds. The quarter mile time recorded by *Motor Trend* was 16.75 seconds, with a terminal speed of 80.5mph. *Road & Track's* September 1982 test gave a top speed of 106mph. Not the most inspiring of results, but there were other matters to consider.

The 1982 Crossfire Trans Am was EPA rated at 15mpg and 24mpg respectively for city and highway driving. In real world motoring the well appointed 1982 Crossfire Trans Am went twice as far on a gallon of gas compared to a 1970s 400-cube Trans Am. The LU5-powered Trans Am turned in performance figures similar to a 1975-78 L78 Trans Am.

Then there was the latest model's ability to combine a 0.80g skidpad figure with improved ride comfort. The 1980/81 WS6 Trans Am had similar skid pad and slalom speed figures, but didn't ride as comfortably as the new Bird.

The new Trans Am was a refined grand tourer. The fuel injected motor was easier to live with than those used in previous models in terms of starting and general running. Rochester electronic fuel injection implied first time starting and the ability to drive away immediately without stumbling, regardless of weather conditions. The 10in reduction in the Firebird's length was also more in keeping with contemporary motoring.

By the 1980s the average owner placed greater importance on comfort and convenience features. Power seats, mirrors and reclining seats were a welcome addition to Trans Am motoring.

Various factors worked against the new Crossfire Trans Am. The auto-only policy for top powerplants took the edge off performance. In spite of a 500lb downsizing diet the new 5-liter Trans Am couldn't rely on the torque of the 6.6 and 7.5-liter motors of old to mask the autobox. It should also be noted that the Chevy 305 and Crossfire injection were never intended to be the last word in performance. As with the Pontiac 301 and Olds 403, the Chevy 305 was conceived as an economy motor; a derivation of the familiar Chevy 350 with specialized internal architecture directed at economy and weight saving. It was very effective at moving around downsized Chevy Caprices, but not

The new 1984 C4 Corvette joined the 1982 F body in GM's era of downsizing. Greater attention was paid to weight saving and aerodynamics with these new designs. (Courtesy Ted Crow)

The ultimate in the new 1982 Firebird range, the WS6-equipped Trans Am Crossfire. The Crossfire LU5 motor was just for the Trans Am, and was only available with automatic transmission.

so suited to boring out to get more displacement and performance. Similarly, the Crossfire injection and intake manifold was a performance and economy compromise.

Third generation F body and 1982/84 Vette owners seeking more performance discovered that the stock Rochester fuel injection system was limited in the amount of fuel it could deliver to accompany more displacement, cam and other modifications. The Crossfire intake manifold had limited port size, plus the inside of the Crossfire manifold runners were rough sand casted items with large peaks caused by casting seams that impeded breathing. Combine these factors with the LU5's restrained camshaft and it's not surprising that the motor started to wheeze by 4500rpm, and was all out of puff by 5000rpm.

These things didn't stop the new Trans Am from being enjoyed as a normal, everyday sporty car. Acceleration was adequate for passing, gas mileage was acceptable and handling was never in doubt. The new Trans Am contrasted with the Trans Am perception created by the big motored cars of yore, with engines that could be hopped up with carb and ignition timing adjustments. The LU8 and LU5 engines came with optimal performance, economy and pollution control straight from the factory. These powerplants were designed as a unit and traditional tinkering risked making the cars slower.

The 1982 Trans Am was as good as CAFE, pollution laws and its position in the GM performance hierarchy allowed it to be. There were plans to continue and develop the Poncho 4.9-liter turbo motor of the 1980/81 era. Proposed changes involved the adoption of fuel injection and a GM designed turbocharger better suited to the Poncho V8's displacement. The official line from GM was that engine performance didn't live up to its spec sheet promise. In addition, there were reliability issues concerning

This is the 1982 Trans Am's Crossfire LU5 165bhp powerplant. Crossfire injection implies one throttle body fuel injection unit supplying gasoline for each side of the V8. In short, two injectors in 'Crossfire' arrangement.

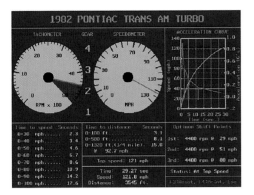

The image shows a computer display for the **1982 PONTIAC TRANS AM TURBO** with tachometer, gear, speedometer, and acceleration curve gauges, along with performance data tables for time to speed, time to distance, and optimum shift points.

Figures showing what the proposed 1982 Turbo Trans Am 4.9 might have been like. Pontiac had hoped to produce the new Trans Am with a revised version of the turbo 301 V8 using a GM turbo and fuel injection. (Courtesy Lee Rehorn)

the turbo system. Then again, Buick was allowed to continue with its turbo V6 program.

It seems possible that any reliability problems with the Pontiac 4.9 turbo could have been worked out with further development. Of greater concern was the possibility of a $14k 1982 4.9-liter turbo Trans Am outpacing both the LU5 Chevrolet Camaro Z/28 and the L83 motivated $22,537.59 1982 Collector's Edition Corvette. Even if the 1982 Poncho 4.9 turbo equaled its 1981 200bhp rating, it's obvious that the 4.9 turbo/3-speed auto combination would have produced strong performance in the lighter 1982 Trans Am. Unfortunately, such things weren't meant to be.

More fun

The third generation Firebird entered uncertain times. Recession aftermath, fuel economy targets and even the possibility of a future

As the 1980s progressed the public wanted performance from affordable, and not so affordable cars. Ford's Fox-bodied Mustang was a rival to the third generation GM F body. A 1984 SVO 2.3 turbo Mustang is shown. (Courtesy Don Hardy)

where Trans Ams would sup grain alcohol constituted Gasohol.

Then there was the quiet nature of the new Firebird, a car intended for an audience that had allegedly grown out of graphics, excess horsepower and body add-ons. It wasn't long before the pendulum of change swung the other way and buyers craved excitement. A better economy and an easing gasoline price meant buyers were willing to spend out on something wild.

The interest in gas economy that made the front drive 1982 AMC Alliance an initial success, was moving back to rear drive, horsepower and extravagance.

There were moves to put more fun in the Firebird, starting with the 1983 model year. The LG4 gained five horses through cold air induction, applicable if the power bulge hood was ordered. The Crossfire Trans Am was re-rated at 175bhp, to match the 175bhp 1983 Ford Mustang GT 5.0. Plus the Trans Am hood decal became a no-cost option. However, the real news for 1983 came in the form of two special high output engine packages.

The 1983 Firebird S/E was now available with the high output version of the Chevy 2.8 V6, the engine seen in the sporty Chevrolet Citation X11. Ticking option code

The L69 5.0 HO was a 4bbl V8 that made a mid '83 MY entry, and re-energized Trans Am performance. At first, L69 305 could only pair with the BW T5 stick. (Courtesy Francois Martinez)

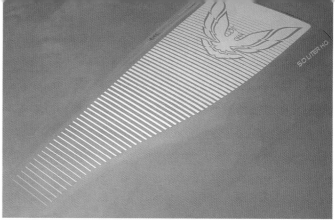

The hoodbird decal lived on, in shrunken form, through 1982-84. Pontiac had stopped using the Euro 'litre' spelling. (Courtesy Francois Martinez)

LL1 gave the owner a higher lift camshaft, 3mm larger intake and exhaust valves, low restriction exhaust and a compression ratio raised from 8.4 to 8.9 to one. The Firebird S/E V6 HO had 135bhp, and, when combined with the relatively new Borg Warner T5 5-speed manual, produced a lively car that made up for earlier third generation V6 Firebirds.

The Chevy V6 had become regarded as a strong, smooth performer in GM's X cars, but it made a slightly deflated entry into F body land. The third generation F body was the first rear drive application of the Chevy V6 and struts placed between the gearbox and engine block were necessary to stave off engine/transmission flex. The V6 lost ten horses in F body translation due to the use of an engine driven cooling fan. The 60 degree Citation V6 wasn't happy in the F body – until now! The Firebird S/E V6 HO was a zesty alternative to the asthmatic LG4 also available on the Firebird S/E.

The second funster was the mid 1983 model year L69 Firebird Trans Am HO. The L69 was a development of the 305 engine, and took its higher lift camshaft from the Corvette. A freer exhaust, advanced timing and cold air induction combined with a 9.5 to one compression ratio. The result was 190bhp at 4800rpm and a torque figure of 240lb/ft at 3200rpm. *Road & Track* found that the new L69 Trans Am HO could reach sixty from standstill in 7.9 seconds and achieve a 16.1 second quarter mile.

The L69 motor was exclusive to the Trans Am and implied WS6 and the BW T5 5-speeder as mandatory options. In light of the increased firepower the F body's longitudinal torque arm locating the rear live axle didn't resemble its usual weight-saving Swiss cheese form. A 3.73 final drive replaced the Crossfire Trans Am's 3.23 gear set. A shorter final drive made the most of the L69's improved breathing. Economy and noise levels weren't adversely affected thanks to the BW T5's overdrive 0.73 fifth gear. The L69 Trans Am HO used a 7¾in Australian sourced differential.

The WS6 pack had limited availability during the 1982 model year. It's been said that there was only a ten-day window when WS6 and the LU5 engine were both in stock at the factory. Pontiac underestimated interest in both the Trans Am and WS6. WS6's early factory departure meant that WS7 was pressed into action. As with the 1979-81 Firebird Formula/Trans Am, WS7 implied everything contained in WS6, except rear disk brakes. WS6 supply was much improved for 1983. As in 1982 WS6 could be ordered on the Firebird S/E, and complemented the new 1983 Firebird S/E V6 HO character very well.

Changes in gearbox options helped with the 1983 Firebird fun

With 5-speed, handbrake and sub 190in length, Formula was so European! (Courtesy Marc Cranswick)

One had to wait for a 1984 Trans Am L69 5.0, like this car, to order the W62 Aero Package and automatic transmission. In July 1984, Hot Rod magazine blamed W62, for the L69 Trans Am's propensity to overheat. (Francois Martinez)

L69 305 V8 first hit F body with Camaro in April 1983, later in '83 MY on Firebird Trans Am. The only Bird to get L69. L69 T/A closed with 26 units made in '86 MY. (Francois Martinez)

Like Ford with Foxstang, GM went back to 4-barrel fun in 1983. A non a/c L69 machine sans fast glass meant low 15s, like that fabled W72 400 4-speed! (Francois Martinez)

the only gearbox available with the L69 engine, and the only manual transmission that could be specified with the LL1 V6. It's hard to imagine these HO motors any other way.

1983 also witnessed arrival of the GM THM 700R4 4-speed automatic, with torque converter lock-up on the fourth overdrive ratio. The THM 700 R4 made for quieter cruising and improved gas mileage. Both the THM 200C 3-speed auto and 4-speed manual continued to be offered alongside the new 1983 gearboxes. The Crossfire Trans Am continued in automatic only form in 1983 with the THM 700R4 as standard equipment. However, its role as the ultimate Trans Am had been taken over by the more powerful 4bbl carb-fed L69 Trans Am HO.

The Crossfire Trans Am and THM 200C gearbox were both discontinued at the end of the 1983 model year. But the multi adjustable Lear Siegler 'Conteur' seat was introduced in that year. Lear Siegler had created the seat for Chevrolet and it was a 1982 Camaro exclusive. The Conteur bucket seats were now available on the Firebird under the B20 Luxury Trim Group in cloth or leather.

In 1984 came the first formal offering of the W62 Aero Package on a regular, non-limited edition Trans Am. The Aero Package's genesis was in the wind tunnel tests conducted by Pontiac II Studio on the 1982 Trans Am. Designers found that sealing off the front facia air intakes, combined with a lower air dam and rocker panel extensions, would lower the drag coefficient. Insufficient time to ensure that GM cooling system requirements were met meant the aerodynamic tricks weren't introduced on the 1982 Trans Am.

factor. The BW T5 5-speed box had already been in use on AMC models in 1982, the 1983 model year saw the BW T5 join the Firebird range. This gearbox also made a 1983 debut on the rival 1983 Mustang GT 5.0. The 4-speed manual box available on 1982 Firebirds was heavy and had a stiff linkage. The BW T5 had a light clutch, easy shift and better spaced ratios. It was no longer necessary to be Charles Atlas to shift the stick. The BW T5 was the perfect accompaniment to the L69 5.0 V8 and LL1 2.8 V6 high output engines. The BW T5 was

The new 1982 Trans Am starred in the hit 1980s television show Knight Rider in which it was KITT, the talking car. (Courtesy Mark Scrivani)

KITT could achieve a number of feats, and often communicated with character Michael Knight, played by David Hasselhoff. KITT's interior had an even greater jet fighter feel than the standard car! (Courtesy Mark Scrivani)

The Aero Package consisted of blanked-off front facia air intakes and a revised lower air dam. Panels behind the air dam were redesigned and this was combined with the lower air dam to pick up more cooling air. A Trans Am equipped with W62 was a bottom breather. Rocker panel side skirts and rear facia side extensions rounded out the changes. Attractive lower body fade-out stripe graphics harmoniously blended the bodykit items into the overall shape. It was possible to order a new 1984 L69 Trans Am HO with the Aero Package and the THM 700R4 automatic. New deep dish, feather-shaped 15x7in 'Hi-Tech' turbo rims were a no-cost Trans Am option.

Horsepower revisited

The 1982 Mustang GT 5.0 and the 1983½ L69/5-speed F body power team were the early developments in the re-emergence of pony car competition and the search for horsepower. Could Motor City executives in the '70s have foreseen affordable V8-powered road rockets in the '80s? Probably not, but cheaper gas and buoyant buyer interest in V8 fun mobiles was unexpected, too.

1985 marked the arrival of the auto only 205bhp Trans Am LB9 TPI 5.0 (Tuned Port Injection). 1985 brought the first restyle for the third generation Firebird, including the Trans Am's new dual louver hood. (Courtesy Maki Shibata)

The LG4 was now up to 155bhp but the real news for 1985 was tuned port injection (TPI). In the 1982-84 period the only type of fuel injection available on the Chevy 5.0 and 5.7 fitted to the Camaro, Firebird and Corvette was throttle body injection (TBI). From the start of the 1985 model year the F body and Vette received Bosch-Rochester TPI.

TPI introduced the sort of fuel injection usually seen on imported cars. There was one fuel injector per cylinder, with fuel injected into the inlet manifold and onto the open intake valve under high pressure. Such an arrangement was present on the US spec 1977 Datsun 280

Z and VW Beetle, both using Bosch L-jetronic electronic injection. The Jaguar XJS' Lucas electronic fuel injection was another example. Multi injector indirect fuel injection was seen on the 1963 Daimler-Benz 600, which had a mechanical injection system by Bosch.

Then there was the 1967 Triumph TR5 PI's Lucas mechanical injection. 1980s cars like the third generation F body and C4 Vette combined established multi point injection and long intake passages with a more refined fuel metering system.

The first computer-controlled fuel injection was Bosch D-jetronic,

TPI took over from Crossfire injection on the Vette and F body. The system had one injector per cylinder, and greater performance potential than the economy focused Crossfire injection. (Courtesy Maki Shibata)

an intake manifold pressure-sensing system fitted to the 1969 VW 411E. 1973 Bosch L-jetronic metered fuel based on the amount of air aspirated. Such electronic systems were necessitated by tightening US pollution laws. Previously, fuel injection – like the 1957 Corvette's Ramjet system – was mechanical and purely for accurate fuel metering and performance. Now fuel injection's superior accuracy was used to improve performance and economy, and emissions compliance.

The trouble with injection systems working on air flow was that air mass was measured indirectly by taking temperature and pressure readings. In addition, their air flow measuring vane meters impeded engine breathing and lacked adjustment speed. Later designs, such as that fitted to the 1985 TPI 5.0 Trans Am, measured air mass directly. A Mass Air Flow (MAF) sensor compared the electrical power required to maintain the temperature of a heated wire against a calibration map. It was a quicker method to measure air density, and didn't block the intake manifold as much as the older vanemeter.

The LB9 TPI 5.0 took the Firebird into the 'power chip' era.

The LB9 engine management computer contained an electrically programable, read-only memory chip (EPROM). This 32K chip contained the calibration maps necessary for the electronic fuel injection to operate. It was possible to replace the memory chip with another chip containing different performance calibrations for fuel flow, fuel cut-off, and ignition timing.

In 1986 the LB9 EPROM was upgraded to 128K, and increased again to 256K for the 1990-92 period. Another important change occurred in 1990: the switch to speed density TPI. Further automotive advances permitted more detailed readings of air mass than a hot-wire anamometer. Air density could now be measured from intake air temperature and pressure. Such readings could also be used to adjust ignition timing. So it was that GM replaced MAF with a manifold air pressure sensor (MAP). 1992 was the final year for TPI.

All this theory implies a smog engine without the feel of a smog engine. As with the LU5 and L69, the LB9 TPI was available on the Trans Am only. It was also only available with the THM 700R4 autobox. The official reason was

This 1985 Trans Am has the standard Y99 suspension, which was 1984's WS6 without the rear disks. 1985's WS6 involved the 16in Hi-Tech rims seen on 1984's 15th Anniversary Trans Am. (Courtesy Maki Shibata)

This modified 1986 Trans Am LG4 was the 1997 Trans Am Nationals Grand Champion. Today, it has a ZZ3 aluminum head motor and THM 700R4 automatic with B&M high stall, 2500rpm torque converter. Here, it's at a special occasion Pontiac display – which includes the Pontiac Type K wagon – at the National Corvette Museum. (Courtesy Eddie Barra)

that the BW T5 couldn't handle the LB9's torque. The 190bhp L69 Trans Am HO continued to be available with both the BW T5 manual and THM 700R4 automatic. The only version of the Chevy 2.8 V6 still available now featured multi port injection like the LB9. The new version of the Chevy V6 was called LB8. 1985 saw a number of Firebird revisions replacing the subtlety of the 1982-84 years with old style flamboyance.

The optional Screamin' Chicken hood decal was reinflated to ¾ hood size. The 1985 Trans Am hood had dual louvers and the Aero Package was redesigned and made standard equipment. The aerodynamic add-ons now had a softer, more integrated look. Fog lights were mounted at the lower extreme ends of the new front air dam. The revised lower front air dam looked like it had front brake cooling ducts. Indeed, the Firebird line received a mild front and rear restyle for 1985. Most noticeable was the new rounded taillight lense, black on the Trans Am.

On the inside smoothed out dash surfaces replaced the hard edged jet fighter contouring and

Allen head screws. A graph paper pattern adorned the dash instrument faces, heat/vent/a/c panel surround and the area around the power window and mirror switches behind the shifter. The new look resembled the 1982-84 Porsche 944 dash instruments' shape and surrounding surface. 1987 would see the option of a new electronic instrument panel for the Trans Am.

To match the aggressive exterior was a more serious-minded WS6 package. The Trans Am's standard Y99 Rally Tuned Suspension for 1985 was 1984's WS6 package without the rear disk brakes. N24 finned Turbo cast aluminum rims with bowling ball covers were no longer available. Standard Trans Am choices lay with either 15x7in deep dish Hi-Tech turbo or 15x7in diamond spoke rims. $664 WS6

implied 16x8in Hi Tech turbo rims with Goodyear 245/50VR-16 Gatorbacks, 34mm front/25mm rear sway bars and gas pressurized shock absorbers. This was the first year a regular, non-limited edition Trans Am was available with 16in rims.

The more assertive WS6 package, which combined sure-footed handling with a compliant ride, was essential given the competition from the Camaro Z/28. Recent Z/28s had improved ride comfort whilst maintaining cornering power. The changed appearance and WS6 equipment made the 1985 Trans Am look like it meant business. The new LB9 TPI motor helped attain cruising altitude sooner, but couldn't be teamed with the BW T5 stick shift. Sure, the unco-operative 4-speed manual had been cut from the team

It's all 24k gold- or triple chrome-plated. The starter motor, motor mounts and front sway bar, are all 24k gold-plated. The radiator support is a one-piece, all-mirrored, stainless steel custom design. The overflow and washer fluid tank are mirrored stainless steel. Chromed cool flex hosing with 24k gold collars complete the cooling system. All that glitters is indeed gold! (Courtesy Eddie Barra)

Parts catalogue listings, plus engine i.d. codes for auto and manual LB9s, suggest a few 5-speed LB9 cars might have predated the formal '87 MY intro of this power team. The Formula and GTA were other '87 MY newbies. (Courtesy Dany Potter & Brett Hack)

at the end of 1984, but the LB9's auto-only nature was hindering the Firebird's flight path.

1986 brought a tinge of sadness for sports fans; the end of the performance 4-barrel carb. Yes, it's true, even though Pontiac and Ford re-enlisted a tuned 4bbl carb 5-liter V8 to spice up 1983 offerings, such old fashioned charm was about to vanish. Ford axed the Holley 600cfm drinking 302 at the end of the 1985 model year, and Pontiac effectively did the same. 1986 was the year the LB9 TPI 5.0 possibly became available with the BW T5, albeit in infamous, downrated 190bhp 'peanut' cam form. The L69 Trans Am HO was available in 1986, but only 26 were ordered.

The L69 HO V8 had durability issues. When magazines tested the L69 Trans Am HO it was remarked how such cars were susceptible to overheating during ¼ mile testing. The problem could be associated with the fact that a large number

of L69 Trans Am HOs were ordered with the W62 Aero Package. There were concerns that the Aero Package limited the amount of cooling air the Trans Am radiator received. It was tempting to exploit L69 engine performance when the car's cooling system shortcomings would have been encountered, with a negative domino effect on L69 longevity.

With the 1986 LB9 downrated to match the L69's 190bhp, there seemed little compensation in the

fact that the LB9 TPI might now be matched to a 5-speed manual box. WS6 now featured a hollow front, 36mm sway bar and 24mm rear sway bar. The LG4 available in the Firebird and Firebird S/E was rated at 150bhp, with the Trans Am LG4 producing 160bhp.

1986 was a year of goodbyes with the Firebird S/E, Iron Duke engine and Screamin' Chicken hood decal joining the L69 in departing the Firebird range. In 1987 the LB8 2.8 V6 became the new Firebird base engine, and bigger changes were in store.

Widening the Firebird's appeal – the Formula, L98 & GTA

In 1987 Pontiac introduced different Firebird versions to better cover the market. The Ford Mustang III had

This Firebird Formula came with the LG4/THM 700R4 combination, but could also have the LB9 TPI 5.0 or the L98 TPI 5.7. (Courtesy Dany Potter & Brett Hack)

All third generation Formulas had WS6, implying 16x8in Hi-Tech rims and 4-wheel disks. However, some buyers wanted the 'sleeper' look, and chose the WX1 two-tone lower accent paint delete option. (Courtesy John Zofko)

carved out a niche in the affordable performance sector, if you can call 224,410 1986 unit sales a niche. As the '80s progressed, 'bang for buck' increasingly seemed to occupy car buyers' thoughts, and the Mustang III made the most of this development. The simplified 1987 Mustang LX 5.0 was an example of the concept that less seemed to yield more. Pontiac realized it didn't really have a performance Firebird in the $12k vicinity and tried to make amends.

After a five year absence the Firebird Formula returned in 1987, but in a new role. Instead of

the luxo/performance Trans Am without wings car of old, the new Formula entered the scene as a lean, mean streetfighter; a vehicle that could deliver punch without emptying the wallet. A sign of the transformation? The 1987 Firebird Formula had a base price of $11,844 with WS6 standard, whereas the 1987 Trans Am weighed in at $13,259, and only came with Y99 suspension as standard equipment.

The new Formula was a package with possibilities. The Formula's standard exterior graphics were reminiscent of the Formula W50 appearance package of 1976-81.

There was two-tone paint and 'Formula' door decals. The 1982-84 Trans Am hood bulge was revived and combined with a Firebird rear spoiler. WS6 suspension with 36mm front/24mm rear sway bars, 4-wheel disks, 16x8in Hi-Tech turbo rims with 245/50VR-16 Goodyear Eagle tires, and 12.7:1 ratio steering, was standard. Regular Firebird sheet metal cut weight and costs. Luxury options and a full range of V8s greeted the new Formula buyer.

The Formula came with a 155bhp LG4 5.0 V8 and 5-speed. It was also possible to combine the

138

The 5.0 and 5.7 TPI motors had punch, but 1987 Firebirds had smaller, more restrictive air intake systems than their Chevy counterparts. The 1988 Firebirds received a larger and freer induction setup. (Courtesy John Zofko)

205bhp LB9 5.0 TPI with a 5-speed, or choose the new L98 5.7 TPI/4-speed auto combination. The LB9 and 5-speed power team seemed the most appropriate for the Formula's new no-frills, enthusiast-aimed nature. However, it was the L98 motor sourced from the Corvette that was the 1987 headliner.

1987 was the first time the Vette 5.7 TPI engine appeared in the F body, but there were some alterations during the translation. The Vette's aluminum heads and stainless steel headers were replaced with more plebeian cast iron heads and exhaust manifold.

Unlike the Vette, the L98 was strictly auto-only when it came to the F body.

The new L98 5.7 TPI made 210bhp at 4000rpm and 315lb/ft at 3200rpm in the 1987 Firebird range. It was available in the Firebird Formula, but was more at home in the new 1987 Firebird Trans Am GTA. GTA stood for Gran Turismo Americano. The new GTA reflected Pontiac's desire to push the Trans Am upscale and away from the Mustang GT/Camaro Z/28 rat race. There was no way Pontiac was going to outsell big budget Chevrolet in the F body family. It made sense to target a more affluent and discerning buyer with the GTA. The only market place to go for the Trans Am was up. With a fully equipped GTA commanding close to $20k, the Trans Am was certainly flying high!

The high zoot 1987 GTA came with 5.7 TPI/4-speed auto, WS6, engine oil cooler, Pontiac's new articulated seats and a monochromatic exterior. The 16x8in gold center, cross-lace

The third generation Formula pared down the pounds using Firebird sheet metal, less convenience equipment, and plainer trim. However, this luxurious LB9-powered Formula shows that one could really option up, if desired. (Courtesy John Zofko)

The 1988 Firebird Formula came with the 170bhp LO3 TBI 5.0 as standard, but this 1988 car features the TPI 5.0/THM 700R4 power team. In 1988 a serpentine belt system was introduced for all V8s. (Courtesy Jessica Taylor)

This 1989 Firebird Formula automatic has the base LO3 TBI 5.0. 1989 marked the fitting of narrower, more discreet Formula side stripe graphics. Three-point rear seat belts became available for the first time. (Courtesy James Slane)

The second generation Firebird Formulas were luxurious, discreet Trans Ams without wings. 1987-92 era Formulas were lean street fighters! This 1989 LO3 TBI Formula is in Poland. (Courtesy Marcin Fedyna)

any doubt that they were flying in the top Firebird.

Trouble for the Firebird came from competition inside and outside GM. The Firebird Formula was a move in the right direction when it came to budget performance, but it was under pressure. A 1987 Ford Mustang GT 5.0 had a base price of $11,324. The 1987 Firebird Formula listed for $11,844. To give the Formula an engine comparable to the Mustang's 5.0 would push the

aluminum wheels were hard to miss. Some magazines were able to match the manufacturer claimed 0-60mph 6.4 second time, and the ¼ mile figure of 14.7 seconds. Naturally, GTAs came with the Aero Package, and 'GTA' fender script and nose emblem left no-one in

They weren't all Formulas and Trans Ams. This 1987 LB8 V6 Firebird auto with 15in, diamond-spoke, aluminum rims is proof of that. 1987 was the first year the Chevy V6 became the third generation Firebird's base engine. It was also the last year of Firebird assembly at the Ohio Norwood plant. (Courtesy Chris Beckwith)

In 1988 and 1989 the GTA was available with the AA8 notchback option. This particular L98-powered 1988 GTA notchback is pretty special because it came with T-tops.
(Courtesy Fredrik Persson)

price up to $12,589. Even with the 5.0 TPI/5-speed the Formula was slower than the Ford.

Motor Trend found a 5-speed 1987 Formula TPI could do 0-60mph and the ¼ mile in 7.7 and 16.09 seconds respectively. *Road & Track* recorded equivalent times of 7.1 and 15.5 seconds for the $18,358 1987 GTA 5.7 automatic. *Road & Track* discovered that the 1987 Mustang GT 5.0 could deliver respective figures of 6.7 and 15.3 seconds. Buyers were seeking out the most performance for the money, and it didn't help that the cheaper Mustang LX 5.0 was even quicker than the Mustang GT 5.0.

Things were no easier for the Firebird closer to home. The Chevy 5.0 and 5.7 TPI motors made slightly more horsepower when fitted to the Camaro. The Firebird's sleeker beak housed smaller and more restrictive air intake hardware. Then there was the Camaro's slight weight advantage that compounded the performance gap. To make matters worse,

The loaded GTA took the Trans Am further into the upmarket sports/luxury arena of the auto connoisseur. The car shown is a UK 1988 GTA automatic. (Courtesy Chris Hall)

Firebird and Camaro suspension setups had never been more similar. The divergence that existed when the third generation F body started out in 1982, had almost disappeared as GM reorganized division life along more rationalized lines.

It was getting harder for the Firebird to state its case. Things had certainly changed since the Firebird's 1970s heyday when Camaro and Mustang lurked in the shadows. As legendary GM boss, Alfred P Sloan Jr, said: "The perpetuation of leadership is sometimes more difficult than attainment of that leadership in the first place."

Fortunately, a car's worth hinges on more than performance data, weight and sway bar diameter. The Firebird Formula was a surprise find. It wasn't as light as the Mustang LX or even the GT, but it had a light feel that encouraged spirited progress. The Formula's selective approach to performance gave a high fun factor.

The Vette-sourced L98 V8 was the standard GTA motor, but, with the GTA, only automatic transmission was available. 1988 saw availability of the TPI 5.0/5-speed power team for the GTA. (Courtesy Frankie Rider II)

The red L98 1988 GTA is a regular hatchback, but the black L98 1988 GTA has the AA8 notchback option. Pontiac production records prove that 625 notchbacks were constructed. (Courtesy Frankie Rider II)

The GTA's luxury knew no bounds, and even included Pontiac's new articulated front seats. From the 1988 model year the third generation Firebird was produced at the Van Nuys factory only. (Courtesy Chris Hall)

Motor magazine testers felt that the TPI 5.0/5-speed power team best suited the Firebird Formula's light, sporty feel. This 1989 Formula features that very engine/gearbox combination. (Courtesy Steve Hovis)

American Sunroof Corporation (ASC) performed the convertible conversions on the Firebird and Firebird Trans Am, but not on the Firebird Formula. This 1992 Trans Am 5.0 TPI convertible is in Australia. (Courtesy Geoff Swavley)

144

In 1988, one-time sober journal Road & Track declared that GTA provided Ferrari 412 performance and looks, at one fifth the price. Pontiac's performance image had invited Maranello comparisons since the '60s GTO! (Courtesy Steve www.tripletransam.com)

U52 Electronic Instrument Cluster – From disco dash to Tron!

The Firebird has always changed with the times. In the '60s, it allowed Pontiac to join the pony crowd. In the '70s, it cruised to the top of the CB radio/trucker genre, overshadowing Corvette and 'Camaro who?' in the process. By the late '70s, things were getting exotic, with many casting an eye towards mid-engined, wedge-profile sportscars.

Many watched TV detective Magnum P.I., and wanted his red Ferrari 308 GTS. With that in mind, Firebird's third coming supplied a sleek Ferrari-like profile, pop-up headlamps, red paint and a possible V8 in a rear-drive format. The '80s were also an era of high tech. Interest in videogames and computing was going through the roof, when the new C4 Corvette was being developed. Hence the new 1984 Vette's standard GM Delco LCD electronic display dash instruments. These electronic numbers, imperial or metric at the flick of a switch, were also seen on mid '80s GM Opel Kadett GTE and Monza GSE. It made a 1987 Firebird range debut. Optional on

Pontiac claimed the uprated '88 225 horse GTA was good for 0-60mph in 6.5 seconds. 1987 debut year GTAs, like this car, had 210bhp. (Courtesy Steve www.tripletransam.com)

As per mid '80s Opels like Kadett and Monza, GM's Delco division provided a digital display for Firebird in 1987-88, optional on the Trans Am and new GTA. (Courtesy Steve www.tripletransam.com/ gta_int.html)

Trans Am and GTA, costing $275 in 1988; a pricey gee gaw that went with the ultra upscale GTA, likened by some to a budget Ferrari 412 grand tourer. The downside was a display of numbers and bar graphs that had to be read, rather than glanced at. Some owners had reliable displays, but some said the displays were slow to work if the car had sat for a spell. However, for a spectacular night show, and that authentic Knight Rider K.I.T.T. experience, U52 was worth every cent. If only that upscale 3rd gen could talk like K.I.T.T.

1988 saw the return to the Firebird line of the 5.0 TBI engine. This was the first time the concept had been dusted off since 1983's LU5. The 1988 170bhp LO3 5.0 TBI replaced the LG4. For the first time in Firebird history a 4bbl V8 wasn't in the options list. The LB9 TPI continued in 190bhp auto and 215bhp manual forms. The 1988 GTA was available with the TPI 5-liter V8, making it possible to get a stick shift GTA for the first time.

In 1988 the GTA also became available with a fiberglass rear hatch: a GTA notchback was born! The GTA notchback had a slimmer appearance from behind and a rear ¾ look that resembled a large Porsche 916. It's thought that the 5.7 V8 was never fitted to GTA notchbacks with T-tops due to the 5.7's torque, but such cars were produced. A shortage of 5.7-liter engines was a more likely reason for the limited appearance of notchbacks specified in such a manner.

Observing Pontiac production records reveals that 625 notchbacks were built. The AA8 notchback package included a special D80 deck spoiler, and, by checking the number of such spoilers fitted [WS4(Trans Am)+Y84(GTA)], the 625 total becomes apparent. There were 624 1988 GTA notchbacks and a solitary 1989 GTA notchback. Interestingly, a Pontiac Dealer Car Distribution Bulletin, dated August 30 1988, reported the cancellation of the AA8 notchback option, suggesting that the single 1989 GTA notchback was built before that date.

A paint problem with the notchback's decklid was apparent. Paint peeling was caused by polymer and fixative gases escaping after the decklid material had cured. The 1980s heralded a general period of problems with the paint on GM-built automobiles. The official line was that Federal law caused GM to use environmentally friendly solvents that didn't give as even coverage and flow as would have been liked. The orange peel and paint flaking seen on C4 Vettes and third generation F bodies have been linked to this solvent issue.

The U52 digital dash polarized popular opinion. Objectively the readouts had to be read, rather than glanced at as per analogue equivalents. This could make track life harder. (Courtesy Steve www. tripletransam.com/gta_dig.html)

At 275 bucks in 1988, the U52 LCD dash afforded one the Knight Rider K.I.T.T. experience that many knew and loved! (Courtesy Steve www.tripletransam.com/ gta_dig.html)

The interior of a regular Firebird convertible. All third generation Firebird convertibles came with the Aero Package and were based on the restyled 1991 Firebird body shape. Earlier ASC did a semi-official small run of third generation convertibles for PMD that included 50 5.7 TPI cars. (Courtesy Steve)

A new, four spoke steering wheel resembled the design of the wheel on the 1986 Porsche 944. The new design brought the chance of steering wheel-mounted stereo controls. A serpentine belt system was now fitted to all V8 engines and the 85mph speedo was absent from the entire Firebird line-up. 1988 Firebirds were only built at the LA Van Nuys factory; Firebird production at Norwood ceased with the 1987 models. 1988 also marked the appearance of the super firm 1LE suspension option for the Trans Am.

All 1988 TPI-powered cars received larger, less restrictive air intake apparatus, and the GTA 5.7 was now up to 225bhp. In 1989 the $155 N10 dual cat package became available on 5-speed 5.0 TPI and 5.7 TPI-powered models. The catalytic converter entered Firebird life back in the 1975 model year, but the efficiency of dual cats had been ruled out until now due to cost. In 1991 N10 became a mandatory option on 5.7-liter cars. At that point N10 became absorbed into the GU6 Performance Enhancement Group that included 4-wheel disks, engine oil cooler and performance axle ratio.

Three-point rear seatbelts were another 1989 model year Firebird first. Firebirds fitted with 4-wheel disks received improved rear disks and calipers. The Pass Key anti-theft system was now standard on the entire Firebird range. The engine management computer wouldn't fire the fuel injectors until the correct signal from the vehicle anti-theft system (VATS) module was given.

Also in 1989 the Firebird Formula received a narrower decorative strip. Motoring magazines weren't over-enamored with the Formula's exterior graphics, a sentiment shared by some owners, who removed decals from their car's exterior. This was in direct contrast to the time when the second generation Formula's W50 graphic package was in vogue. The increasing interest in 'sleeper' performance was shown by the WX1 two-tone lower accent paint delete option that ran from 1986-90 and gave a $150 credit to more reserved Firebird buyers.

1989 marked the arrival of the $450 W68 Sport Appearance Package for regular Firebirds fitted with the 5.0 TBI engine. The package bestowed the look of a Trans Am with Aero Package front and rear facia extensions, fog lamps and moldings.

In 1990 the 135bhp Chevy 2.8 V6 was replaced with a 140bhp 3.1-liter version. The 5.0 TPI now made 225bhp when specified with manual transmission/N10, and the 5.7 TPI motor was now 235 horses strong with N10. A standard driver's side airbag across the Firebird range meant the omission of steering wheel-mounted stereo controls. 1990 was a truncated model year and, in mid 1990, the restyled 1991 Firebirds were released. Front and rear facias were altered with some influence from the Banshee show car. The rounded front incorporating Pontiac's traditional split grille gave a new, powerful, charged aura after the sharp edged look of earlier third generation Firebirds.

There was also the mid-model year arrival of the first official Firebird convertible since the 1969 model year. The convertible conversion was done by American Sunroof Corporation (ASC) and involved the regular Firebird and Trans Am. There were no Formula convertibles. All ragtops had the revised Aero Package. In the case of the Trans Am convertible the dual hood louvers and extractors were actually functional. At least 50 3rd gen convertibles had the 5.7 TPI engine.

To rationalize specification choices various additional option groups were created over 1991/92. The GU6 Performance

This 1992 GTA has the LB9/THM 700R4 power team, plus the SLP 50bhp hop-up kit for TPI cars. This dealer installed kit started in 1989. Note the Dark Jade gray metallic exterior. This was a special Firebird 25th Anniversary color. (Courtesy Alex Claytor)

Enhancement Group was mandatory on 5-speed 5.0 TPI and 5.7 TPI-engined cars. GU6 was recoded R6P for 1992, but still cost $444, even though it was now associated with a 5bhp TPI boost (230/240bhp). The W68 Sport Appearance Package continued until the end of third generation Firebird production.

Since the restyle for 1991 the Formula had a new monotone paint job; it seems GM had listened to those making noises in favor of low-key performance. The aggressive 1LE sports suspension option continued to be available during 1988-92. In 1991 and 1992 1LE was an option on the Formula, too.

Visit Veloce on the web – www.velocebooks.com
Special offers • Details of all current books • Gift vouchers • New books

10

Classic third generation Firebirds – special edition Firebirds and unique models

The first special edition, third generation Firebird was the 1982-84 Special Edition Recaro Trans Am. It was an Appearance Package that centered on the use of Recaro sports seats, and was listed as Y84. It was compensation for the Lear Siegler Conteur seat being unavailable on 1982 Firebirds.

A 1983 Special Edition Recaro Trans Am. With Recaro, one didn't need Lear Siegler! (Courtesy Richard A Clapp)

This is a Swedish 1984 Special Edition Recaro Trans Am. By the 1984 model year the Y84 package cost $1621 and included 15x7in Aero-Tech rims. As ever, WS6 was standard. (Courtesy Bo Hagstroem)

The 1982-84 Y84 Special Edition Recaro Trans Am was an appearance package that initially made up for the unavailability of the Lear Siegler Conteur seat in the 1982 Firebird range. (Courtesy Bo Hagstroem)

149

The Firebird Trans Am paced the 1983 Daytona 500; 2500 Pace Car replicas were built. Note the standard Aero Package that included full aerodynamic bowling ball wheel covers. (Courtesy Ron Marlin)

1500 1984 15th Anniversary Trans Ams were built. They featured a white and blue color scheme reminiscent of that very first Cameo white 1969 1/2 Trans Am with blue decals. (Courtesy J & Liz Vartanian-Gibb)

The Recaro Trans Am had a black exterior with gold accents, and the Recaro name appeared on the door handles in gold lettering. T-tops and WS6 or WS7 were standard and the same Trans Am V8 options applied. Gold N24 finned Turbo Cast rims were also part of the package. 1984 was the last year for the Y84 Special Edition Recaro Trans Am. In 1984 the Recaro Trans Am had gold 15x7 deep dish Aero-Tech turbo rims and the Aero Package.

In 1983 the Trans Am was chosen to pace the 1983 Daytona 500. 2500 1983 Trans Am Daytona 500 Pace Car replicas were built and sold to the public. The cars had a two-tone white over charcoal paint scheme with matching hood bird graphic and general decals. There were 'Official Pace Car Daytona 500' door decals, 'NASCAR' rear quarter panel decals and big 'PONTIAC' front and rear windshield decals. '25th Anniversary Daytona 500' emblems were placed on the front fenders above the usual Trans Am tag.

The 15th Anniversary Trans Am became the first Firebird to have 16in aluminum rims. The 15th Anniversary Trans Am's WS6 package also made use of Goodyear's 'Gatorback' tires used on the C4 1984 Corvette. (Courtesy J & Liz Vartanian-Gibb)

The 1983 Trans Am Daytona 500 Pace Car was the first Firebird to receive what became known as the W62 Aero Package. WS6 was standard equipment, as were leather Recaro seats with suede inserts. Dash instruments were backlit in red, and a special dash plaque and 'Daytona 500' floor mats completed a pretty picture. Power teams consisted of the LG4/BW T5 manual or LU5/THM 700R4 automatic and T-tops were optional. 520 LG4-powered stick shift and 1980 Crossfire LU5 automatic replicas were produced.

1984 saw the release of the commemorative 15th Anniversary Trans Am. Only 1500 were produced with trim and chassis as areas of special interest. The exterior was white with contrasting blue decals and 15th Anniversary badging. Trans Am decals adorned the front/ rear facias and doors. A matching blue and white hood bird graphic was added to the hood bulge. The interior was a combination of white leather and various shades of gray. White leather was used for the steering wheel, shifter, glovebox pouch, handbrake, and on the Recaro seats that had gray suede inserts. All 15th Anniversary Trans

White leather Recaro seats with suede inserts kept driver and passengers in place, whilst the new WS6 suspension was given a workout.
(Courtesy J & Liz Vartanian-Gibb)

Goodyear Eagle GT tires; in other words, the 16in unidirectional 'Gatorbacks' seen on the then new 1984 C4 Vette.

The legendary Buick Grand National represented all of Buick's work on the blown V6, and the ultimate Turbo Regal. A 1987 Grand National is shown.
(Courtesy Ed Chapman)

Ams came with T-tops and the W62 Aero Package.

The 15th Anniversary Trans Am had a special version of WS6, elements of which appeared in 1985's WS6 package. Apart from WS6's usual 12.7:1 steering ratio and 4-wheel disks, rear sway bar thickness was increased from 23mm to 25mm. The 15th Anniversary Trans Am also became the first Trans Am to use 16in rims. Matching white 16x8in Hi-Tech turbo rims wore P245/50 VR16

Pontiac Firebird project manager, Tom Goad, admitted that they didn't get the necessary time to dial in the suspension to the Gatorbacks, so ultimate grip wasn't as good as it might have been. Such issues were resolved with 1985's WS6. Power teams were limited to the L69 HO 5-liter/BW T5 manual or THM 700R4 automatic. The 15th Anniversary package cost $3499 and the 15th Anniversary Trans Am is certainly a collectible automobile that is appreciating in value.

The 20th Anniversary Turbo Trans Am paced the 73rd

15th Anniversary Trans Am power teams involved the L69 HO 5.0 and the BW T5 manual, or – as in this case – the THM 700R4 automatic.
(Courtesy J & Liz Vartanian-Gibb)

The 20th Anniversary Turbo Trans Am used a version of Buick's 3.8 turbo V6 of Grand National fame. It was quick enough to pace the 1989 Indy 500, and outpace the regular 1989 Vette! (Courtesy J & Liz Vartanian-Gibb)

Indianapolis 500 of 1989. The 1989 20th Anniversary Turbo Trans Am used a version of Buick's 3.8-liter V6 turbo usually associated with the hot Buick Grand National. This cast iron, overhead valve V6 with Garrett T3 turbo, intercooler and sequential fuel injection was the culmination of years of work. Years of work that started with the Buick Century that paced the 1976 Indy 500, and finished with the end of rear drive Regal production in 1987. Buick had introduced North America to the potential of turbo V6 power.

Pontiac enlisted a similar version to the Grand National's turbo V6 to motivate its 20th Anniversary commemorative Trans Am. However, transverse cylinder heads were used because stock Grand National heads would have created a clearance problem between the exhaust manifold and the Firebird's front frame rail. The

other main change was the use of a cross-drilled crank.

The only transmission available on the 20th Anniversary Turbo Trans Am was the Regal THM 200R4 4-speed automatic. A manual box was proposed but the 3.8 V6 turbo's prodigious torque created durability concerns. *Road & Track* averaged testing times for two prototypes in different climatic extremes to give 0-60mph in 5.3

seconds, and 13.9 seconds for the ¼ mile at 95.5mph.

Naturally, the 20th Anniversary Turbo Trans Am was able to pace the Indy 500 with no modifications whatsoever. As such the three 20th Anniversary cars submitted for pace car duty were randomly selected from the 1550 production 20th Anniversary Turbo Trans Ams. All 20th Anniversary Turbo Trans Ams used to pace the race, and for events connected to the race, had T-tops, even though this was an option. Of the three cars used for pacing the race one resides in the Indianapolis Motor Speedway Museum and one is kept in Pontiac's collection. The third was presented to 1989 Indy 500 race winner Emerson Fittipaldi! Triple

The automatic only 20th Anniversary Turbo Trans Am was quite loaded and had a base sticker price of $29,839. The Buick Turbo Regal's THM 200R4 automatic was used. (Courtesy J & Liz Vartanian-Gibb)

For a time Pontiac considered making all 20th Anniversary Turbo Trans Ams with the AA8 notchback. However, a need for 1550 notchback decklids, and the paint peeling problems experienced on 1988 GTA notchbacks prompted a rethink. (Courtesy Tom Lomino)

Indy 500 champ, Bobby Unser, drove the 20th Anniversary Turbo Trans Am that paced the great race.

The 20th Anniversary Turbo Trans Am had a white exterior and camel interior. The GTA's usual 'GTA' insignia on the nose and sail panels was replaced by '20th Anniversary' script. Turbo Trans Am tags took over from the usual 'GTA' fender script. All cars were delivered to the dealer with a set of official Indy 500 Pace Car decals for the doors and windshield. Formally speaking, it was up to the customer whether these decals were affixed to the car.

The 20th Anniversary Turbo Trans Am was very much a low volume, specialized car compared to the 1980/81 turbocharged Formula/Trans Am. The older model was more about taking turbocharged performance to a mainstream audience.

The 20th Anniversary Turbo Trans Am was conceived by Pontiac's Bill Owen. The project was outsourced to PAS Inc, an engineering company run by Jeff Beitzel. The V6 turbo motor was constructed at its 'City of Industry' Californian plant. The engines were then sent to Van Nuys and completed cars were transported back to PAS for final inspection. In addition to the 1550 production 20th Anniversary Turbo Trans Ams, five pilot cars were constructed. The pilot cars did not have a white exterior and at least two were sold to the public. One 20th Anniversary Turbo Trans Am convertible was built by ASC for Jeff Beitzel.

The blown 3.8-liter V6 had 8:1 compression and a turbocharger limited to a maximum 16.5psi boost. In light of the 20th Anniversary Turbo Trans Am's 3346lb curb weight and performance, it's commonly felt that the engine's 250bhp rating is very conservative. An IMSA Showroom Stock Competition-style

Like the Grand National, the 20th Anniversary Turbo Trans Am was a low volume model. It wouldn't have been prudent to produce an engine in such a high state of tune for a wider audience. (Courtesy J & Liz Vartanian-Gibb)

Some magazine testers commented that most people would have been satisfied with a normal V8-powered 1989 GTA, like the car shown. It would avoid sleepless nights over the state of the TT/A's blown V6. (Courtesy Jesse McCarty)

baffle in the fuel tank surrounded the fuel pump and helped maintain a steady fuel supply to the pump during sharp turns. The 20th Anniversary Turbo Trans Am braking hardware was taken from the 1LE suspension/performance package.

By the early '80s Pontiac was taking care of four-cylinder business at GM with the Iron Duke 2.5-liter 4 banger. Pontiac created a number of high performance Super Duty items for the Iron Duke that were listed in a Super Duty engine preparation booklet. There was a Super Duty engine block, crank and cylinder head. As a natural extension of this groundwork Pontiac Engineering designed a 1983 Super Duty Firebird. This four-cylinder hell raiser was built to IMSA Kelly Girl racing series specs and embodied

Super Duty Iron Duke items, plus Pontiac-approved engine, chassis and bodywork accessories.

The 2.7-liter Super Duke was enriched with a Hooker Industries competition header, Edelbrock polished 2-piece valve cover, Pro Flow racing air cleaner and intake manifold. The list of companies making parts for the Super Duke motor read like a Who's Who of the aftermarket industry. Arias Racing Pistons, Crane Cams and Armstrong Racing Equipment dry sump lubrication. The dry sump reservoir was located behind the passenger seat and two blowers were placed behind the roll bar's main hoop. The rear axle and BW T5 oil coolers were situated under the blowers.

The Super Duty Firebird had a visually arresting, 13-piece fiberglass bodykit by Diversified Glass Products costing around $1400, and Center Line 16in racing rims with Goodyear Gatorbacks. The Diversified Glass panels featured a double power bulge third generation Firebird hood. Center Line offered 16x10in rims all round; for street use the front rims were 16x9in. The smaller front rims avoided having to relocate the front steering knuckles.

An MSD Extra Duty Ignition System by Autotronic Controls Corporation helped the 2.7-liter motor produce 272bhp at 7600rpm. With that kind of power and racing aspirations, it's little wonder that a full roll cage was tied in at all suspension mounting points, and

all body seams were fully welded. Using a standard 1983 rear axle and 4.11 gears, top speed equaled 151.4mph: a nice, symbolic tie-in with the Iron Duke's normal 151-cube displacement. Not that there was anything normal about a 2700lb, four-cylinder Firebird that could do the ¼ mile in 13.2 seconds with a trap speed of over 100mph. Downsizing never looked so good!

After a hiatus in 1981, Dennis Mecham was working on the Firebird once again. This time both the company and the car's name changed to reflect Mecham's involvement in the SCCA's Trans Am series. It came as no surprise that the 1982 Mecham Racing Motor Sports Edition Trans Am (MR MSE) had the same appearance as the Trans Am MR campaigned on the racetrack. The new car had a

The 1982 MR MSE Trans Am. Mecham Racing won the 1982 SCCA Trans Am championship with the racing version of this production car. (Courtesy Keith Hanner)

154

SLP Firehawk #007 resides in Switzerland. The Firehawk is still the fastest accelerating Firebird of all time. SLP founder Ed Hamburger owns the pre-production Firehawk. (Courtesy Bernard Rudaz)

white exterior and tri-color USA stripe decals. The big 'Aero Tail' rear wing came from the track car and the 15x7.5in turbine rims, wearing Firestone HPR P255/55R 15in radials, were by Modern.

The initial MR MSE car was based on a WS6-equipped, 1982 Trans Am, so MR worked with all the good stuff from Pontiac. Adjustable Koni front and rear shocks, an extra front cross member brace and 20 per cent stiffer springs produced more assured handling, but not a harsher ride. Urethane items replaced stock bushings. Droop limiter straps attached to the rear axle side locators were intended to prevent the shorter, stiffer springs dropping out.

A MR MSE is a sporty car so it's expected that Mecham would work with those engine options available with a stick, such as the LG4 and L69 305 V8s. Thus, the initial MR MSE Trans Am had the Borg Warner Super T10 4-speed and LG4 motor. Power aid for the 145bhp LG4 came courtesy of a 'Git Kit' designed by Huffaker Engineering. Did the hop-up kit breach emissions laws? Did it improve LG4 lifestyle? Yes and yes; the packaged kit located in the trunk boosted horsepower to 215bhp.

The Trans Am was no longer emissions certified, which was bad, but, according to *Hot Rod*, the new car achieved a 15.62 second ¼ mile, which was good! The elixer of goodness was an open element air cleaner, 600cfm Holley 4-barrel, Edelbrock Performer intake manifold and Mallory dual-

point YL distributor coil and wire set, plus Champion sparkplugs. It was possible to have Tri-Y headers going into a dual 2in diameter exhaust with free flow mufflers.

As per the older DKM Macho series, the new car was gadget heaven. However, a less loaded, red-colored MR MSE Trans Am was already in the works. MR MSE Trans Ams continued the tradition of quality, custom ordered Trans Ams. Also some LU5-powered MR MSE automatic Trans Ams were fabricated. Unfortunately, MR matters drew to a close with the 1985 Macho Trans Am.

Emissions certification may have caused a MR migrane, but that didn't apply to SLP Inc. SLP stood for Street Legal Performance, a company founded by Ed Hamburger

All 25 third generation Firehawks built were extensively road tested by Ed Hamburger prior to delivery. The car's starting price? How about $39,995! (Courtesy Bernard Rudaz)

that lived up to its name. This was a major departure from previous operations. SLP Inc. made a 50bhp hop-up kit from 1989 for TPI V8s that could be fitted by Pontiac dealers. The kit was available until the end of the third generation Firebird's run. The 1992 Formula Firehawk was the fastest street legal Firebird until the 1997 Pontiac Hurst Firebird by Lingenfelter. The latter car was based on the fourth generation Firebird and only equaled the acceleration times of the third generation-based 1992 Formula Firehawk.

What were the performance figures? 0-60mph in 4.6 seconds and the ¼ mile in 13.2 seconds made the Formula Firehawk the equal of the Lotus-enhanced Corvette ZR1. The Formula Firehawk also carried a standard warranty, could get 25mpg on the highway and was emissions certified. Tick option code 'B4U' on a Firebird Formula order form and a car would wing its way to the SLP production facility. B4U implied a red hardtop with an L98 V8, 1LE and a starting price of $39,995.

SLP's 'T-RAM' intake manifold, worth 45bhp by itself, sat on a worked Chevy 350 engine. A 4-bolt main block was combined with a forged steel crank, 1053 alloy forged steel 'Pink' connecting rods, lightweight, high silicon cast LT1 aluminum pistons, steel billet hydraulic roller cam, aluminum cylinder heads, SS valves, Tri-Y headers and dual catalytic converters. Firehawk figures started with 350bhp at 5500rpm and 390lb/ft at 4400rpm.

Connected to the potent V8 was a ZF 6-speed manual gearbox. Ronal produced the 17x9.5in rims and Firestone Firehawk SZ P275/40 ZR 17in tires were included. The standard Firehawk brake/suspension was represented by 1LE, something that originated in the GM Canada Motorsports F body racing series (Player's Club).

However, for an additional $8995, the Competition 'R' Option

Package took matters a step further. Competition 'R' meant 1LE Koni shocks, stiffer bushings/springs and Vette rotors were replaced with even more serious equipment. There was more aggressive suspension, roll bar, Recaros, 5-point harness, aluminum hood and no back seat! The 13in Brembo cross-drilled disks were the same units as on the Ferrari F40.

Production of the Firehawk commenced in late 1991, and all third generation Firehawks were promoted as 1992 model year cars. 25 Firehawks were constructed with the final car, #27, based on a Trans Am convertible. Out of the 27 cars ordered #18 and #23 were cancelled, and four cars didn't have a red exterior. Some customers wanted a Firehawk with features available outside those supplied by B4U, so their base car wasn't a red hardtop. The final third generation Firehawk did have a red exterior, and the final three cars had aluminum Rodeck block V8s rated at over 375bhp.

SLP's 'T-Ram' intake manifold was used on all third generation-based Firehawks. The Firehawk motor had 4-bolt mains, forged steel crank, aluminum heads and LT1 pistons. In short, a minimum of 350 ponies. (Courtesy Joe Durk)

Only some third generation Firehawks have the yellow 'Firehawk' door decal. SLP and tire manufacturer Firestone had a legal tussle over the right to use the 'Firehawk' name. Despite the relatively high price SLP charged for the third generation-based Firehawk, the operation wasn't profitable; it would take the arrival of the fourth generation LT1-based Firehawk to turn SLP's fortunes around.

The more affordable fourth generation cars increased production volume and commercial viability. It was also very fortunate that SLP and Firestone had resolved their legal dispute by 1993 and SLP was able to use the 'Firehawk' logo from that point on.

Another third generation Firebird-based aftermarket special was a little less elaborate than SLP's third generation creation. From 1987 until the end of the third generation Firebird's run, the Custom Center of Tennessee, also known as Choo Choo Customs, was behind the 1987-92 Firebird Bandit II. This was an appearance package that mostly utilized regular Firebird 5.0 V8s as a base. The car was sold through Pontiac dealers in the tri-state area.

In addition to a fake, second generation-style Trans Am shaker hood scoop, hood bird decal and aftermarket rims, there were 'Bandit II' decals and special side spoilers. The Firebird Bandit II featured interior 'Bandit II' and 'The Custom Center' insignia, plus a few more trim touches. Each Firebird Bandit II had a dash plaque stating its build number. In 1991, The Custom Center started using W68-equipped Firebird 5.0s to create its Firebird Bandit II.

In the lead-up to the 20th Anniversary Trans Am, Pontiac experimented with a number of possibilities. A higher output 360bhp version of Buick's 3.8-liter turbo V6 was tried in a 6-speed Trans Am with Dana 44 rear end and 3.92 gears. There was also a 605bhp twin Garrett T3 turbo L98 5.7-liter V8 Trans Am with three GNX pumps, two intercoolers and – probably – a partridge in a pear tree!

Once again, a ZF 6-speed manual and Dana 44 differential were entrusted to cope with the horsepower onslaught. This special red and black Trans Am GTA was the Firefox. Three years later history repeated itself with Firefox II.

Pontiac worked in conjunction with a Michigan engineering company called TDM Technologies to come up with the Firefox sequel. This jade green mean machine was based on a 1991 Trans Am and had a special TPI 5.7 and Vette sourced ZF 6-speed stick. The engine had

Starting with car #002, Firehawks featured a modified console area to accommodate the shifter of the ZF 6-speed gearbox. At the time Firebirds were only available with a 5-speed stick. Ronal was responsible for the 17in aluminum rims. (Courtesy Joe Durk)

Arrival of the fourth generation-based model saw Firehawk production step up from 25 cars in 1992 to 201 cars in 1993. This is a 1993 Firehawk. (Courtesy Mal Swain)

Bartz aluminum heads, bigger valves, intake manifold runner diameter was increased from 1.375in to 1.750in, larger capacity fuel injectors, roller tip rocker arms, special valve timing and Edelbrock headers, for 328bhp at 4500rpm and 395lb/ft at 3500rpm.

Aluminum independent rear suspension proposed for the 20th Anniversary Turbo Trans Am made it onto Firefox II. The independent rear suspension made necessary a smaller trunk-mounted fuel cell and special muffler. 17x9in BBS 3-piece rims resembling those on

contemporary GTAs were used, as, too, were ZR rated P275/40 17in Goodyear Eagle tires.

The end result was 0-60 in 5.2 seconds, the ¼ mile in 13.5 seconds and a skidpad figure of 0.93g, according to a December 1991 *Motor Trend* report. Pontiac's manager of special vehicle engineering, Tom Goad, was hopeful that some Firefox II elements would make it onto the fourth generation Firebirds.

The Custom Center of Tennessee was behind the 1987-92 Firebird Bandit II, a fun special that featured yesteryear's Trans Am hood bird and shaker scoop. This is a 1991 Firebird Bandit II. (Courtesy Bud Ashworth)

According to ASC records 330 Firebird-based convertibles were produced for Pontiac dealers in 1989 MY, of which this '89 Formula 5.7-liter was one. (Courtesy John Zofko)

According to ASC records 330 Firebird-based convertibles were produced for Pontiac dealers in 1989 MY, of which this '89 Formula 5.7-liter was one. (Courtesy John Zofko)

Firebird & the aftermarket – 1980s. Off with its head! – 3rd gen Firebird convertibles

Sometimes there are jobs only a specialist can do. ASC had an initial foray with the GM F body in 1986, signing up Chevy dealers to do Camaro convertibles on request for $4390. In 1987, ASC became the GM approved company for doing 'factory' Camaro ragtops. That same year, ASC started a semi-official run of Firebird convertibles, that continued through to the formal reintroduction of the Firebird convertible in mid 1991 MY. The formal 3rd gen Firebird convertible was also by ASC, as was the 4th gen Firebird ragtop.

GM sources have revealed that production/design of the convertibles in-house was considered in the mid '80s, but rejected. Incorporating convertible production would have conflicted with existing plant/tooling layout, so it was easier to farm out the work. This shows that a convertible 3rd gen wasn't seriously considered when said GM F body generation was being planned.

ASC continues its convertible engineering operations in North America and overseas. It has been closely associated with 3rd and 4th gen Firebird ragtops, but so too

Originally, it was thought the Chevy 350 motor wasn't T-top available, because the 3rd gen's structure wasn't rigid enough. ASC built in enough strength for the 350, plus full convertible! (Courtesy John Zofko)

A 1989 20th Anniversary Turbo Trans Am convertible, an example of ASC's work that used the famous blown Buick 3.8-liter V6. (Courtesy Lenny Toylman)

Note the winged tire logo with flags of the Indianapolis Motor Speedway on the 20th Anniversary Turbo T/A's lower front fender. The '89 20th Anniversary Turbo T/A paced the 1989 Indy 500 in T-top form. (Courtesy Lenny Toylman)

The actual 20th Anniversary Turbo T/A base car was constructed between the F body Van Nuys factory and Jeff Beitzel's PAS Inc. 'City of Industry' plant (also in California). One 20th Anniversary Turbo T/A conv. was built by ASC for Jeff Beitzel. (Courtesy Lenny Toylman)

two seats, but not its trunk. Built into the rear decklid was an access lid with chrome hinges and gas struts taken from the Firebird's former hatch. The lid opened to a trunk no smaller than that on a normal Bird. Refinement could be counted on, thanks to a spring-assisted/counterbalanced hardtop, covered in handcrafted blue, black, buckskin or white vinyl. To make sure the fiberglass body parts color matched the rest of the steel Firebird, said fiberglass was color impregnated with 'Gel Coat.' This ensured cameleon-like blending with the stock red, white, black or beige Firebird/Trans Am base car.

The other part of Auto-Form's refinement lay in what one couldn't see: welding work to get back the rigidity lost due to the missing top. Heavy gauge steel channel bars were used at the sides, along with a structural crossmember brace bolted in place. There were steel

have other companies. In the early to mid '80s, prior to ASC getting the official nod from GM, a number of concerns made hay of the new 3rd gen F body's popularity, and applied a can opener to the Bird's roof. Auto-Form Corporation of Indiana had a relationship with GM from 1983 to 1986 concerning convertible conversions for Firebird and Camaro, similar to that enjoyed by ASC and Pontiac dealers during 1987-89 for Firebird alone.

Apart from ASC ragtops, Auto-Form's convertibles are the second most numerous decapitated 3rd gens out there. This was a company that did quality work: with specific reference to Firebird, this involved a 2-seater roadster conversion, with raised fiberglass headrest aero fairings that were somewhat reminiscent of the '60s TV Batmobile. The special rear fiberglass decklid seamlessly integrated – and held a few surprises.

The Auto-Form roadster may have caused the Firebird to lose

This 1992 Trans Am convertible sports the 305 H.O./THM 700R4 power team, and is one of just 35 Jamaican yellow cars. (Courtesy John Kirkbride)

160

A desirable 1984 Auto-Form Trans Am convertible with L69 hi po 305 4bbl motor and N24 finned Turbo Cast alloy rims. (Courtesy Auto-Form)

Auto-Form changed the 3rd gen Bird from a 4-seater hatchback to a 2-seater roadster. Gel-Coat colored fiberglass body parts blended with the F body's usual steel panels. (Courtesy Auto-Form)

A STEP BEYOND

The racy Firebird look is enhanced by Auto-Form's clean-lined sculptured deck and vinyl-covered hardtop.

5.0 LITER H.O.

You needn't sacrifice storage space to enjoy a convertible. Auto-Form installs an easy access door and retains the original trunk.

Sleek, clean colorful styling.

From the color-coordinated vinyl top to the sculptured rear deck, the Auto-Form convertible reflects superb automotive styling.

The interior and tops are color-coordinated with Firebird fabrics to blend beautifully with the original color schemes. (Tops are available in Blue, Black, Buckskin and White.)

On the outside, a rich padded roof gives you the appeal of a ragtop with a sharp European roadster look.

The entire vinyl top is fabricated at Auto-Form, where skilled upholstery craftsmen give it a smooth and exact fit with a custom appearance.

All fiberglass components are color impregnated with Gel coat to match exterior Firebird colors. (Red, White, Black and Beige.)

161

Auto-Form dealt with certain dealerships, and their work added rigidity restoring reinforcements, plus $5500 to the final tab. (Courtesy Auto-Form)

Leaking tops, wind whistles and scuttle shake were some of the convertible maladies that expert craftsmen tried to prevent. (Courtesy Auto-Form)

It looked like a neat factory job, and Auto-Form was one quality purveyor satisfying the demand for ragtops, in the absence of factory provision. (Courtesy Auto-Form)

A look, a feeling.
A promise of the extraordinary.
A step beyond.

Drive a Pontiac Firebird and you drive a dependable sports car. Drive a Firebird with an Auto-Form convertible and you drive excitement. Flair. Exhilaration. You go a step beyond.

Structural integrity.

Through careful engineering, Auto-Form has achieved what other manufacturers have only attempted: a convertible conversion that retains the Firebird's original uni-body and chassis strength.

This means you can finally have all the enjoyment of a convertible, together with the handling ease you expect from a Pontiac Firebird.

To reinforce the chassis, for example, Auto-Form welds heavy-gauge steel channel bars to each side, attached to the rocker sills and floor pan.

To ensure that the body has proper diagonal strength, Auto-Form installs an X-member of heavy-gauge formed steel, and welds a steel cage assembly to the door pillars and floor pan.

Then, a chrome-plated steel reinforcement header is added to the door pillars and windshield frame.

The result of Auto-Form engineering is total structural integrity.

And the driving pleasure for which the Firebird was designed.

A steel cage assembly is welded to the door pillars and floor pan to provide cross-sectional strength and support.

Heavy-gauge steel angle brackets give extra support to the hardtop roof.

Quality control inspector.

The convertible hardtop is equipped with a spring-assisted counterbalance for easy raising and lowering.

The Firebird uni-body is strengthened and reinforced by an X-member made of heavy-gauge steel channel bars.

The original design and color integrity is maintained throughout your Auto-Form convertible. Even the original seating fabric is converted for use on the headliner.

Strict quality control.

Auto-Form convertibles are quality checked at every step of the conversion process — from the welding of structural parts, to final assembly.

Fiberglass components are formed from high-precision molds to ensure a consistently proper fit. They are carefully monitored before assembly for color and thickness.

All vinyl material undergoes rigid inspection. The convertible top is thoroughly checked for quality of upholstery work and appearance.

Before any vehicle leaves our plant, it is given a careful final inspection, including road testing.

At Auto-Form we have but one objective: to offer you the very finest convertible made anywhere.

auto FORM corp

Auto-Form Corporation
P.O. Box 359
Bremen, Indiana 46506
1-219-546-5222
1-800-348-3708

Auto-Form Southwest Corporation
103 North Kickapoo Street
Shawnee, Oklahoma 74801
1-405-275-5093

Auto-Form reserves the right to make changes in materials or specifications at any time. Patent Pending.

During the early to mid '80s, John Greenwood's company did GM F body as well as Corvette convertible conversions. A Greenwood Firebird convertible is pictured. (Courtesy John Greenwood & Wayne Ellwood)

As per other '80s 3rd gen convertible specialists, Greenwood covered Camaro too. Note the 'Greenwood' front spoiler decal on this Camaro Z/28. (Courtesy John Greenwood & Wayne Ellwood)

reinforcements around the door pillars and floorpan, with a chrome-plated steel reinforcement header for the door pillars/windshield frame area.

Auto-Form's work required two weeks, and it wouldn't accept used cars. Auto-Form got new Birds from the factory and worked with certain dealers. The cars were sent to either its Bremen Indiana, or Shawnee Oklahoma facilities. Once completed, the new convertibles were then sent to the dealers, along with a $5500 surcharge. Around 600 GM F body convertibles were constructed by Auto-Form during 1983-86.

Corvette tuner and specialist John Greenwood also entered the F body conversion business during 1983 MY. Greenwood's 'Spirit of C3 IMSA Corvettes were colorful high flyers. In 1973, he set a top speed

Ferrari 308 GT-esque wedge styling and the Valerie Bertinelli hairstyle add to the '80s appeal of a Greenwood Firebird ragtop! (Courtesy John Greenwood & Wayne Ellwood)

Greenwood offered convertible conversions on Camaro, Corvette and Firebird at a time when GM did not. Greenwood's canvas tops used Mercedes SL-like material, and cars featured Konis for the sports suspension. (Courtesy John Greenwood & Wayne Ellwood)

Camaro Convertible

STANDARD FEATURES

- Power operated convertible top system
- Reinforced chassis and inner body
- Reinforced windshield header
- Polished aluminum header windshield cap
- Stainless steel latch system
- Stainless exterior fasteners
- Undercoat protection
- Inner body anti-rust coat at all weld junctions
- Utilization of original window weather seals and tracks
- Haartz cloth fabric sport top
- Padded bow pads (color coordinated)
- Padded rear side panels
- Color coordinated vinyls
- Top switch integrated into dash
- Electrical wire loom system with integrated fuse network
- Matching vinyl boot

- Soft vinyl top well
- Electrically accuated trunk.
- Complete factory installed trunk interior.
- Nylon shoulder washers at all pivot points
- Owner's manual
- 12 month unlimited mile written warranty
- Water spray tested
- 29 quality control checkpoints
- Integrated quality assurance program
- Complete nationwide delivery system
- Complete nationwide engineering/service support and parts program

OPTIONAL

Leather Seats

Matrix3's convertible conversions for GM F body involved a power Haartz cloth top, and the option of leather seats. The latter a rarity in this F body era. Matrix3 work was deliverable nationwide out of a facility in Costa Mesa, California or Jacksonville, Florida. (Courtesy Matrix3)

record of 211mph for the Mulsanne Straight at Le Mans. Three years later, Greenwood took his 'Spirit of Le Mans '76' C3 to the 24-hour race – appropriately liveried in red, white and blue given the Bicentennial. A decade later, and into the C4 era, Greenwood's downsized GM ragtops covered both Firebird and Camaro. At the Longwood, Florida operation the roof was removed, body structural reinforcements added, and a new convertible top was crafted using a heavy Mercedes SL-like canvas.

Greenwood's Corvette and F body convertible conversions used unique parts. They weren't taken from other car lines. Unlike Auto-Form's conversion, the Greenwood convertibles had a soft top that sat on the rear deck, instead of the fold-away type. The suspension was retuned, to allow for the loss of structural rigidity, using Konis, a Greenwood favorite.

Why all the convertible attention from outsiders? Feared federal safety rollover testing in the '70s scared off car makers from doing ragtops for years. There was no

After a decade of dominance by Firebird, Camaro was back in the F body ascendancy. The Chevy increasingly featured in third party PR material. Matrix3 did a high quality upscale F body conversion, unusual in that it brought a powered top. The 12 month unlimited warranty showed they meant business. (Courtesy Matrix3)

When ASC formally covered Firebird convertible business for Pontiac during 1991-92, its conversions involved just the base Firebird and Trans Am; not the Formula. (Courtesy John Kirkbride)

factory 2nd gen F body convertible, the C3 Vette ragtop was terminated at the end of '75 MY, and the '76 Cadillac Eldorado was GM's final factory convertible of the era.

Safety never stopped the public's love for open air motoring, one 72-year-old gentleman from Nebraska bought six '76 Caddy Eldo ragtops! So it was that while GM and others went crazy for T-tops, specialists offered real ragtops. Therefore we next visit Matrix3, purveyors of third gen convertibles next in popularity after ASC and Auto-Form. This company had factories in Costa Mesa, CA and Jacksonville, FL, producing F body ragtops from 1983 to 1987.

Apart from the expected body reinforcements and strengthened windshield header, the Matrix3 convertible distinguished itself as an upmarket conversion. As with Auto-Form, there were copious quality checks, plus Matrix3's convertible had a power top which sat neatly under a vinyl boot when resting. The Camaros and Firebirds had a polished aluminum windshield header cap with Haartz cloth for the soft top. There was the option of leather seats, a rare find on the F body at a time when the B20 Luxury Trim Group Lear-Siegler adjustable bucket seats with leather retailed for $945-$1294 (1983 MY).

Evel's Ragtop
As with other operations, Matrix3 was taking the F body upmarket, increasing the value-added margin

as it delivered the cars nationwide. For 1983, the F body gained even more glamor when American Custom Coachworks started to do 3rd gen F body convertible conversions. Jan Meyer's operation commenced in 1953, in the '60s, it gained exclusive rights for handling the revived Stutz marque, with the first car going to Elvis. Purveyors of limos to the stars, by the late '70s ACC was America's biggest custom coach builder, with the bulk of its work involving convertible conversions. Such work necessitated a 6-week wait, and a completed F body ragtop was in the vicinity of $20k. The company continues in Beverly Hills, California, but since 2003 has become American Limousine Sales and deals exclusively with limos.

The Firebird also had a specific connection to Stutz. Stutz was reborn as 1968's Stutz Motor Car of America Inc. The new Stutz built exclusive rides for a well-heeled clientele which included members of The Rat Pack and Evel Knievel. Indeed, Knievel and the Stutz Blackhawk both featured in the daredevil's 1977 cinematic motion picture debut *Viva Knievel*. The Stutz also served as a pimpmobile extraordinaire, when driven by Michael Keaton's character in the 1982 movie *Night Shift*.

Stutz was the winning hand in the game of automotive one-upmanship, for those that considered Excaliburs too passe. Stutz Motor Car of America Inc. billed itself as

the purveyors of 'The World's Most Expensive Car.' They were pricey and pretty exclusive: just 617 were made by the time the final factory-produced cars rolled out in '95 MY. However, prior to that, Firebird was in the house.

Stutz cars were based on GM platforms, and used said corporation's engines and hardware. Pontiacs were often a starting point, with the Grand Prix and Bonneville serving as base cars at various times. For '87 MY, Stutz switched from Bonneville to Firebird, because the former had gone front drive and Stutz needed rear-drive platforms to work with. This made the GM F body a perfect fit, and the Firebird served as the new basis for the Stutz Bearcat convertible during 1987-92.

That Miami Vice Tojan GT Coupe
How does one distinguish the popular 3rd gen Firebird, and overcome the Vette's shortcomings? Get a Tojan GT Coupe, that's how. Nice as it was, there used to be a 3rd gen on every street corner. Even the local pizza delivery kid had one, for crying out loud! In addition, Chevy's plastic fantastic still only had two seats. Just enough room for an overnight toothbrush, but not the toothpaste …

The 3rd gen 'Boid' was like the working class guy's Magnum P.I. Ferrari 308 GTS, a Corvette with a backseat if you will. However, to impress the neighbors, take a

Tojan GT offered an exclusive, and practical, 3rd gen Firebird-based alternative to Corvette. It bore a resemblance to the car from the 1986 movie The Wraith. It even appeared on TV's Miami Vice! (Courtesy Whelan Pontiac-Buick)

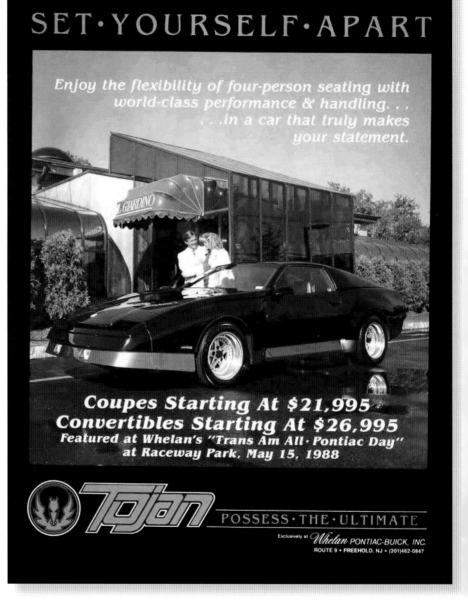

trip down to New Jersey's Whelan Pontiac-Buick, or other selected Poncho dealers across the land. Like the ad said: 'four-person seating,' 'world-class performance and handling,' from a car that makes a statement? Yes, a Tojan GT reached the nightclubs a Vette dare not venture into, and one had the option of a ragtop too!

GM commissioned the Firebird-based Tojan GT and Carralo. Knudsen 'Bunkie' Automotive built around 150 units of each between 1985 and 1991. One could have the usual options: 305 TPI/5-speed power team, digital dash and such. Plus some fine touches along the lines of burl woodgrain dash and Gotti aluminum wheels. The Tojan GT appeared in TV's *Miami Vice* and many were shipped overseas. All this glamor from $21,995 (1988 MY), with a paltry 5-grand surcharge for the ragtop. Yup, with Tojan GT one went far. Possess the ultimate indeed!

Visit Veloce on the web – www.velocebooks.com
Special offers • Details of all current books • Gift vouchers • New books

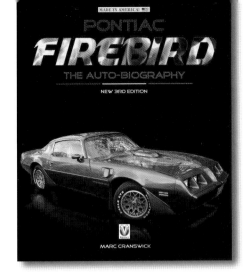

11

Carrying on the Firebird tradition – the fourth generation cars

Having the right stuff

The 1993 fourth generation F body was practically all new, involving a major reworking of the third generation platform. The previous modified MacPherson strut front suspension was replaced with a short/long arm setup. The result was a tidy, coil-over spring layout with the suspension arms separated from the spring assembly, not unlike racing car practice. The familiar live axle rear suspension continued, with a guiding hand from dual lower trailing links and Panhard rod.

So it could be said that Pontiac had partially introduced the suspension ideas it had been playing around with on the Firefox experimental cars. Pontiac had hoped to include independent rear suspension, but this was ruled out due to cost. Gas-charged DeCarbon shocks were used all round.

The fourth generation car was the first Firebird to use rack and pinion rather than recirculating ball steering. Another of the Firebird innovations was the extensive use of plastic exterior body panels. The new Firebird took a leaf out of the Pontiac Fiero's book and made good use of special plastic panels for durability and ease of restyling. As per the Fiero sheet molded compound (SMC) panels were used for areas requiring rigidity, such as doors, roof and hatch. Reaction injection molded urethane (RIM) panels were used for areas subject to frequent contact such as front fenders and facias. The only steel panels attached to the unibody were the rear fenders and hood.

Inspiration for the Firebird's

The fourth generation Firebird made a 1993 model year debut. Production was now at the Ste. Therese factory in Quebec, Canada. The car featured is a Japanese-delivered 1993 Trans Am. (Courtesy Keishi Imai)

The new dash was certainly on the curvy side compared to the 1980s block-style, third generation Firebird design. This particular Trans Am has the optional GM 4L60 4-speed automatic, but the Trans Am's standard transmission was the M29 close ratio BW T56 6-speed manual. (Courtesy Keishi Imai)

styling once again came from the 1988 Banshee show car. Jack Folden was in charge of Pontiac II Studio Group and the use of plastic panels helped the team incorporate elements of the Banshee's complex form. The latest Firebird had a fresh, futuristic, organic look that distanced it from the sharp edged, flying wedge appearance of the third generation models.

The interior was also transformed. The third generation large, kitchen counter top-like dash was replaced with a hooded instrument pod and centrally grouped console heating, air conditioning and stereo controls. The arched instrument display found on contemporary Corvettes was certainly present, albeit with easier to read analog gauges. The new layout was functional and had the welcome inclusion of a real glovebox, a feature not seen since 1981.

The new fourth generation Firebird made great use of Fiero-style plastic exterior panels. Only the rear fenders and hood were steel. (Courtesy Keishi Imai)

The traditional long hood, short rear deck appearance was hard to ignore. In fact, the fourth generation Firebird Trans Am matched the 197in length of the 1979-81 Trans Am! Fortunately, the new car's weight was in line with that of the downsized third generation model; if anything, it was a touch lighter. Another feature that was hard to walk past was the steeply raked, 68 degree front windshield. The new Firebird certainly had the look of sport.

A rationalized new range
The Firebird family now consisted of the base Firebird, Firebird Formula and Firebird Trans Am. The Formula had body-colored reversing mirrors and contoured taillights with neutral density lenses. The Trans Am enjoyed special front and rear facias with fog lamps at the front. There was a Trans Am-specific rear spoiler and rocker panel bodykit.

Tire and rim specifications also differentiated each version. The normal Firebird rode on 16x7.5in rims with P215/60R16 tires. The Formula and Trans Am both had 16x8in rims, but different tire sizes. Standard issue Formula footwear was P235/55R16s, and, as with the normal Firebird, they were Goodyear GAs with a 108mph speed rating. The Trans Am came with P245/50ZR16 Eagle GS-C tires. The Goodyear GS-Cs took over from the Goodyear Gatorbacks worn by

The 1993-97 LT1-powered Formulas and Trans Ams took Firebird performance to new heights. Cars like this 1997 Trans Am were decidedly quicker than their L98-powered predecessors. (Courtesy Ron Bigham)

various members of the Firebird flock between 1984 and 1992. The Goodyear GS-Cs were optional on the latest Formula.

Chassis differences between the initial Firebird versions were straightforward. The base Firebird had front and rear sway bars measuring 30mm and 17mm respectively. On the Formula and Trans Am the front bar was identical but the rear bar was 19mm. Quicker 14.4 ratio steering on the Formula and Trans Am replaced the slower 16.9 ratio on the regular Firebird. All fourth generation Firebirds came with GM Delco ABS brakes, plus driver and passenger front airbags. However, the Firebird's disk/drum setup was replaced with 10.9in front and 11.4in rear ventilated disks on the higher flying Formula and Trans Am. A wise choice, considering the amount of thrust the V8 Firebird was producing.

The Corvette-sourced LT1 V8 gave the fourth generation Formulas and Trans Ams aluminum heads, and near Vette performance at a much lower price. (Courtesy Keishi Imai)

The base Firebird had a development of the familiar Chevy V6 that started life as a 2.8-liter motor in GM's X cars. For the fourth generation F body the Chevy V6 grew from 3.1 to 3.4 liters. The 3.4-liter V6 was now pumping out 160 horses at 4600rpm and 200lb/ft of torque at 3600rpm. A value-packed powerplant to kick-off the new Firebird range, and EPA rated at 19mpg city and 28mpg highway.

However, for those that could stand the decibels – and stomach the insurance premiums – there was more excitement in store: the 1993 Formula and Trans Am came with a version of the Chevrolet Corvette's LT1 5.7-liter V8.

Under-hood packaging, cost and model hierarchy meant the Formula and Trans Am had more restrictive exhaust manifolds, a single catalytic converter and one stainless steel muffler. The Vette doubled the cat and muffler tally to achieve an efficiency gain. The F body's LT1 sloshed ordinary, mineral-based oil rather than the more rarefied, fully synthetic lubricant specified for the C4 Vette. The F body's LT1 didn't share the Chevy Caprice LT1's cast iron heads. However, both LT1 versions

The LT1, 5.7/BW T56 6-speed combination was standard with each and every 1993-97 Formula/Trans Am. Self-restraint was certainly called for! (Courtesy Ron Bigham)

had 2-bolt mains, rather than the Vette LT1's 4-bolt mains.

The sum of the above equaled Firebird power and torque figures of 275bhp at 5000rpm and 325lb/ft at 2400rpm. The equivalent figures for the LT1-powered Corvette were 300bhp and 330lb/ft. Specifying the $110 G92 performance rear axle ratio changed the rear gears from 2.73:1 to 3.23:1, and brought onboard an engine oil cooler to mop the LT1's brow.

The other big news, apart from the LT1's adoption, concerned shifting. The regular Firebird's standard transmission was a 5-speed stick shift, and the optional GM 4L60 4-speed auto was also available on the racy Formula and Trans Am. However, the standard transmission for the V8-powered racers was a Borg Warner T56 6-speed manual, a version of the box that first appeared in the Dodge Viper. The Formula came with the M28 wide ratio BW T56, implying a 3.36:1 first gear. The Trans Am had the closer ratio M29 version with 2.97:1 for first. The BW T56's fourth was a direct one-to-one top gear, and fifth and sixth were overdrive ratios, with the latter being a super tall 0.62:1.

Even with the performance rear axle ratio, 60mph in 6th registered a mere 1650rpm. The 1993 V8-powered cars with stock 2.73:1 final drive were EPA rated at 17mpg city/25mpg highway. The Firebird's 6-speed box didn't have the Vette's 1-4 skip shift economy gadget, for the 1993 model year at any rate. Even so, fuel economy figures showed that the LT1-imbued ability to defy time and space made a smaller dent in world fossil fuel supply than expected.

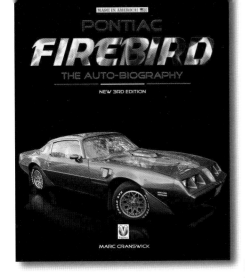

12

Power to the people – rediscovering horsepower in the '90s

1994 saw the 4L60 autobox replaced by the electronic 4L60-E. It was a worthwhile buy because stick shift 1994 V8 Firebirds received the awkward 1-4 skip shift CAFE helper.
(Courtesy Stefan Tradgardh)

Life on Woodward Avenue was never this good

The fourth generation Firebird brought a level of performance to pony car circles that had never existed before in terms of availability or completeness. *Car and Driver's* Patrick Bedard summed up the 1960s ratio of so-called 'secretary' pony cars to hot versions in February 1993: "We looked right past them in traffic, searching for the relatively few that were packing the go-fast options."

In the sport compact and intermediate glory days a fair proportion of plain Tempests complemented GTOs on the street,

and GTOs tested by magazines were often in a state of tune no ordinary buyer could get hold of. Then again, the past is always remembered with greater fondness.

Fast forward to 1993 and the Firebird hardware on offer was beyond '60s belief. Two of the three Firebird versions came with fuel injected V8s that would have been rated at 300bhp gross or more in the old days, plus 6-speed stick shifts. It was guaranteed ¼ mile times in the low to mid-14s and top speeds over 150mph or your money back!

The LT1 V8 revved more freely and packed more punch than the outgoing L98 V8. Who would have

As shown by this 1994 3.4 V6 Firebird, T-tops were still part of Firebird life the fourth time around, and were available from the start of fourth generation production. (Courtesy Ronny Stobbaerts)

believed the LT1's 1960s-style, 10.3:1 premium fuel compression ratio, using nothing finer than humble 91 octane unleaded? The improvements didn't rest with extra power: forget about the past where pony cars had more horsepower than brakes; since the mid '70s the Firebird had progressively moved to match go with whoa. The latest fourth generation Firebird with 4-wheel disks and ABS had the ingredients to stop repeatedly in controlled fashion from high speed.

Handling and ride comfort were other areas of gain. The new cars offered astounding levels of grip and improved behaviour in slippery conditions. The Firebird still employed live axle rear suspension, but refinement and links location meant a better level of compliance and axle tramp avoidance than had been the case with pony cars to date. Improved ride comfort wasn't

an open invite to suspension slop; early versions of the new Formula and Trans Am with 245 section tires were in the 0.85g skidpad register range and capable of 60mph slalom speeds.

The Firebird's 6-speed gearbox wasn't as light in action as that found on four-cylinder Japanese performance cars, but it was easy to use and much lighter than anything from the 4-speed Muncie and subsequent BW Super T10 eras. The BW T56 even had a lighter feel than the ZF 6-speed box found

in contemporary Vettes. The new Firebird structure also had a stouter feel than earlier models. The rigid 22 Hertz body structure gave a feeling of heft and quality.

Interior fit and finish wasn't perfect, but, overall, things were securely tied down and the quota of squeaks and rattles noticeably diminished.

The price for a 275bhp, 150mph-plus V8 super coupe? Try $17,995 for a 6-speed Formula V8. Add the $110 G92 performance rear axle/engine oil cooler and $144 QLC P245/50ZR16 tire set, and perhaps the $895 C60 custom air conditioning, and you had a complete road burner for all occasions without having to break into Fort Knox.

Faults encompassed the raked windshield and thick A and C pillars necessary to maintain roof strength in possible roll-over accidents. The thick pillars were necessary, given

Advantages of selecting a 1994 V8 Firebird automatic were the chance to get the new, optional NW9 electronic traction control, and avoid the 1-4 skip shift gadget introduced on 1994 V8 stick shift models. (Courtesy Scott)

Only automatic fourth generation Trans Ams were exported to continental Europe. The loss in acceleration compared to the 6-speed was minimal, and the automatic V8 cars were rated only 1mpg less for CAFE. (Courtesy Stefan Tradgardh)

the low roof and angle of the front and rear windshields, but impeded outward vision. The sleek nature of the front windshield and expansive dash created unwelcome reflections that hindered driving. To facilitate parking owners flipped up the front headlamps and raised the rear radio antenna as points of reference because it was very difficult to judge the Firebird's extremities.

To some extent such shortcomings, and the car's high cowl and low seating position, reflected the fact that the third generation F body platform had been carried over. Such problems aside, the new Firebirds offered a new level of performance and greater value for mainstream buyers: performance that combined ¼ mile acceleration of the late '60s with Ferrari high top speeds with matched handling and braking. As for convenience features and ease of driving, there was nothing moving in the 1960s that could touch the latest Formula and Trans Am. Did I mention that the new car's air conditioning had CFC-free R134a refrigerant as well? Game, set and match to the new Firebird!

Efficiency improvements

1994 witnessed some welcome – and some not so welcome

The 3.4-liter Chevy V6 Firebird was a spirited and thrifty performer, with more affordable insurance premiums. (Courtesy Ronny Stobbaerts)

– technical refinements. The optional automatic transmission became the 4L60-E, a computer-controlled version of the previous year's 4-speed auto with a dual mode shift program. For the V6

Firebird this involved driver-selected normal and second gear start modes, the latter a useful traction-maintaining measure in slippery conditions. On the V8-powered automatic Firebirds

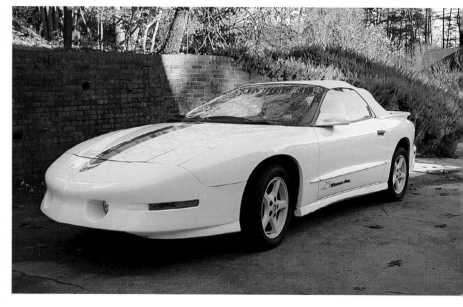

The 25th Anniversary Trans Am was available in T-top and ragtop forms. It was chosen to pace the 1994 Daytona 500. (Courtesy Bob & Edie Mohalley)

were normal and performance modes. Performance mode had a greater propensity to downshift and higher rpm before changing up with part throttle acceleration. In flat-out driving it didn't matter if the car was in performance mode or not because the automatic gearbox changed at optimal rpm in both scenarios.

Both the 4L60 and 4L60-E were okay automatics, but somehow the smooth, ready shifting of the THM 400/350 days had been lost. One thing gained was the Corvette ZF 6-speed 1-4 skip shift facility. V8 Firebirds with the BW T56 manual transmission had the economy 1-4 skip shift from 1994 onwards due to CAFE. Light throttle applications in first gear would be followed by an electro-mechanical shift from first straight to fourth if vehicle speed was 15mph or less. The skip shift facility improved the V8 Firebird's EPA rating by 1mpg. Efficiency on 1994 LT1-powered Firebirds was improved through the adoption of sequential fuel injection, where fuel injector solenoids open only when necessary. Running in the opposite direction to economy, the optional performance axle ratio was shortened from 3.23:1 to 3.42:1 in 1994.

1994 V8 Firebird automatics could be ordered with the newly optional NW9 electronic traction control, costing $450. The computer-controlled system worked in conjunction with the GM Delco ABS brakes. If slippage was sensed

the rear brakes would be applied or engine power reduced. Traction control could be switched off via a console-mounted switch. In 1995 traction control became available on 6-speed Firebirds, too.

Ghosts from a Firebird past

New Firebird versions were introduced in 1994. The already high spec Trans Am was joined by the really loaded Trans Am GT: no additional performance, just additional equipment. A leather interior with 4-way (driver) and 2-way (passenger) front seat adjustment, floor mats, Delco 2001 stereo, and remote keyless entry were standard

Unlike the 20th Anniversary Turbo Trans Am, the 25th and 30th Anniversary cars used regular Trans Am power teams. (Courtesy Bob & Edie Mohalley)

features, as well as a taller than standard Trans Am spoiler.

Fresh air fiends rejoiced in the return of the Firebird ragtop. The power top featured full headliner, heated glass rear window and a three-piece, hard plastic tonneau cover. Release two windshield frame header clamps, hit a button and your Firebird, Firebird Formula or Trans Am had suddenly lost its head! To combat the usual ragtop rigidity-loss structural adhesives in the cowl, plus body strengthening around the A pillars and rocker panels, sufficed. Convertibles can't be as rigid as their hardtop counterparts, but the new Firebird convertible was quite refined and relatively scuttle shake-free.

Cars are much like people in that with age, birthdays seem to come around that much sooner. Just when you thought it was safe to go back in the water, along came the 25th Anniversary Trans Am! Unlike the all-conquering 20th Anniversary Turbo Trans Am, the latest commemorative model was just cosmetic. Then again, given the regular LT1 Firebird's Mustang-stomping power, there was little need for the 25th Anniversary Trans Am to be anything else.

Reviving the livery of the first

Like the very first 1969½ Trans Am, the 25th Anniversary Trans Am had a crisp white exterior and blue trim decals. (Courtesy Andrew W Ten Eyck)

1969½ Trans Am, and echoing the 15th Anniversary Trans Am's color scheme, the latest Anniversary model had a white exterior, blue centerline stripe, and white 16x8in aluminum rims. The interior had white leather seating surfaces with blue embroidery 25th Anniversary insignia; there was also 25th Anniversary exterior decals and badging. A small blue Screamin' Chicken nose section decal recalled the similar decal on 1970½-1972 Trans Ams. The 25th Anniversary

package retailed for $995 and was available on Trans Am T-top or Trans Am ragtop models. The convertible version received the smaller rear spoiler seen on the Firebird and Firebird Formula.

It sounded good enough to pace the Daytona 500, which was just as well because the 25th Anniversary Trans Am was indeed the official pace car for the 1994 Daytona 500. As with the 20th Anniversary Turbo Trans Am Pace Car, no modifications were needed

for the 25th Anniversary edition to pace a race. However, whereas the 20th Anniversary car was a low volume, virtually custom job, the 25th Anniversary model was just a normal V8 Firebird adorned with fancy war paint. It just proved what potent firepower was available off the showroom floor. The 25th Anniversary Trans Am wasn't as quick as the 20th Anniversary version, but it was still more than adequate come race day. Testers were in agreement that the younger

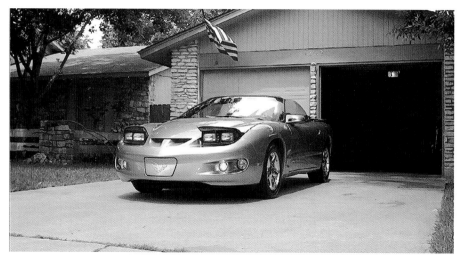

The Bird's Buick Series II 3800 featured a number of technical improvements. It was far removed from the version used in 1981 Firebirds. At 200bhp it was stronger than the Trans Am's 1983½ – 86 L69 5.0 HO V8. (Courtesy Ernesto Garcia)

car's normally-aspirated V8 provided more tractable performance than the 20th Anniversary Trans Am's fiery turbo V6.

A different V6 on Firebird duty

The mid 1990s witnessed a transition in V6 Firebird life, when the 60 degree Chevy V6 was replaced by the 90 degree Buick V6. Since 1982 the Chevy V6 had served lower level Firebirds in displacements from 2.8 to 3.4 liters. Now matters had come full circle and, for the first time since 1981, the Buick 3.8 V6 returned to the Firebird flock.

The changeover started with the 1995 Californian-spec V6 Firebirds. As of January 1995 the Chevy 3.4 V6 was no longer emissions legal in California, so the 1995 Firebird with the Buick V6 took over in that state. Of course, this wasn't the same

231-cube V6 known and loved from the days when it pushed around 1980 Yellowbirds, Bonnevilles and such. The 231 V6 now answered to the name of Series II 3800, sporting modified cylinder heads with symmetrical ports and better matched combustion chamber volumes. Improved production tolerances also permitted a 9.4:1 compression ratio. The revised 3.8 V6 made 200bhp and 225lb/ft of torque; unfortunately, those weren't the only things to rise: the V6 engine swap involved a $350 surcharge.

1995 gearbox choice was limited to the 4-speed auto, but in 1996 the twin balancer shaft

3.8 V6 became available with a 5-speed manual, as the Firebird 3.8 V6 became a 50 state model. 1996 saw the introduction of two packages that gave Formula flavor to the V6 Firebird. Something for Firebird fans that liked the V8 image, but didn't like the associated gas and insurance bills. The Y87 3800 Performance Package retailed at $535 and brought 4-wheel disks, 14.4 steering ratio, dual outlet exhaust, the base Formula P235/55R16 tires and a 3.42:1 final drive for automatic spec V6 Firebirds.

The W68 Sport Appearance Package, costing $1449, re-emerged at the same time and gave the Y87 V6 Firebird extra show to match the improved go. The reborn W68 was similar to the W68 package available during 1989-92, except that, back in the third generation days, it was only for V8 Firebirds.

As an aside; in 1996 the Firebird took center stage in the International Race of Champions (IROC). IROC organizers planned the construction of 24 new tube frame chassis race cars dressed in

V6 Firebirds changed over to the Buick 3.8 V6 during 1995/96 model years. The 3.8-liter V6 Firebird pictured is a 2000 model year car. (Courtesy Justin Kirkham)

The W68 Sport Appearance and Y87 3800 Performance packs gave the V6 Birds the look and feel of a Formula or Trans Am. The 2001 V6 model shown wasn't much slower than a regular 4.6 V8 Mustang. (Courtesy Stephanie M Sutphin & Knight Enterprises)

fourth generation Firebird attire for the 1996 season. The cars were powered by series-controlled, 500bhp Chevy sb V8s. Carrying on a theme that started in 1973, this series entertained many, as big name drivers battled it out in same-spec cars.

Don't imagine that the V8 Firebirds were missing out during all of these V6 Firebird self-improvements. Can you say Ram Air?

The IROC Firebirds looked like Firebirds, but behind that familiar face lay a custom tube frame racer. At least the Chevy sb V8 was a common link! (Courtesy James B McNatt)

The 1996 $2995 WS6 package comprised SLP's Ram Air cold air induction, and a serious handling kit. (Courtesy Chris Hall)

Try and breathe through your nose – WS6 and the return of Ram Air

A horsepower image storm was brewing for 1996. Ford was about to ditch its 302 V8, and a possible quad cam modular V8 Mustang Cobra loomed large. Regular Mustang V8s would now have the 2-valve, single overhead cam 4.6 V8, while the low volume Mustang Cobra would draw strength from the double overhead cam, 4-valve version of the 4.6 V8. Powerful as the LT1 Firebird already was, Pontiac wasn't going to let the blue oval steal all the thunder, and plans were made.

The F body LT1 received its first horsepower boost since 1993. A dual exhaust increased horsepower from 275 to 285bhp. Bigger news was confined to the Firebird and revival of two elements from the past: WS6 and Ram Air.

WS6 was a chassis/braking package introduced on late '70s Formulas and Trans Ams. In 1996 WS6 stood for suspension and power. Five spoke 17x8in rims shod with P275/40ZR17 Goodyear GS-C tires combined with stiffer springs, shocks and firmer bushes to reduce suspension yield and produce a more solid connection to the road. Front and rear sway bars now measured 32mm and 19mm respectively, and a firmer transmission mount completed the chassis changes.

While earlier fourth generation Firebirds were considered to have impressive grip courtesy of FE2 suspension, it was commonly felt that the latest cars had a softer feel when compared to the relatively raw bones, late third generation Formulas and Trans Ams. The new WS6 alterations gave greater control over what was a relatively large and heavy car.

$2995 WS6 also brought genuine Ram Air cold air induction.

The 1996 305bhp WS6 Formula and Trans Am took the fight right to the new 305bhp Ford SVT Mustang Cobra. The LT1's greater torque made cars like this 1997 WS6 Formula feel stronger than the Mustang Cobra. (Courtesy Chris Hall)

There's no doubt that the charge of cool, dense air delivered by the WS6 Ram Air kit would be useful when a car like this 1997 WS6 Trans Am visited the drag strip on a hot day. (Courtesy Cory Rose)

Firehawk #003 actually had the 'Firehawk' door decal. The legal wrangle between SLP and Firestone over the use of the name was ongoing, but some cars did receive the decal. Firehawk #003 had the hardcore $8995 Competition 'R' Option Package. Go Firehawk! (Courtesy Alex Claytor)

This Dark Jade gray metallic #026 Firehawk was one of the four non-red, non-B4U third generation Firehawks. #026 has the aluminum hood, Brembo brakes and aluminum Rodeck 366ci motor. (Courtesy Alex Claytor)

Dual hood apertures admitted cool, dense outside air into a sizeable air cleaner and the engine throttle body. It was alleged that, at speed, air entering the scoops became pressurized and contributed auxiliary horses to the LT1 paddock. The new hood looked impressive, but magazines were hard pressed to discern an improvement in acceleration compared to earlier, non-Ram Air LT1 Firebirds.

1996 also saw the Harley Davidson Edition Trans Am. Harley took 40 black WS6 Trans Ams and fitted black leather/cloth seats bearing the Harley Davidson logo. They had Harley Davidson front fender decals, and were mainly distributed in Southern California.

Once the dust of speculation had settled the WS6 Formula, Trans Am and quad cam Mustang Cobra all had the same 305bhp engine advertised power rating. Followers of the aftermarket would have noticed that Pontiac's new WS6 package had elements that looked surprisingly similar to the hardware present on recent SLP Firehawks. This was no coincidence.

Aftermarket afterburners – making the best even faster
The WS6 components offered by Pontiac on 1996 and later Formulas and Trans Ams were actually SLP sourced and fitted. Continuing the joint venture nature of SLP and Pontiac association, ticking the WS6 option box resulted in new cars built at the GM F body factory in Ste. Therese Canada being sent to SLP's Montreal facility for WS6 fitment. After the fire-breathing 1991/92 Firehawk, SLP's fourth generation Formula-based Firehawk had fewer modifications and a more affordable price tag. This move acknowledged the standard LT1 Formula's already good performance, and the opportunity to expand SLP Firehawk production.

1993 Firehawks featured a dual hood scoop sealed to a large, flat air cleaner connected to the LT1's intake plenum. The new Firehawk was available in hardtop and T-top forms with manual or auto transmission. An optional SLP cat back exhaust raised the Firehawk's output from 300bhp to 315bhp, at a time when V8 Firebirds had 275bhp. *Car and Driver* tested a 6-speed 315bhp Firehawk in April 1994 and this car produced 0 to 60mph and ¼ mile times of 4.9 and 13.6 seconds respectively.

The new fourth generation Firehawk wasn't much slower than its low volume 1991/92 predecessor. As with earlier Firehawks it was still emissions-legal fun all the way! In 1995 SLP enlisted the help of Herb Adams, creator of the Pontiac Fire Am whose suspension influence filtered through to Pontiac's late '70s WS6 package, to fortify the Firehawk's handling. So it was that the SLP fourth generation Firehawk hood scoop and suspension made their way onto WS6-equipped Pontiac Formulas and Trans Ams.

1995 also saw SLP diversify

It took the arrival of the LT1-powered fourth generation Firebird-based Firehawk to turn around SLP's fortunes. By this stage the legal dispute with Firestone had been resolved. (Courtesy Dan Taraban)

SLP Comp T/As were produced between 1995-97; this is a 1997 example. SLP didn't start building fourth generation Trans Am-based Firehawks until 1999. (Courtesy Ken Collings)

and become involved with the Trans Am. To commemorate the 25th Anniversary of the B F Goodrich Comp T/A radial tire, SLP produced a number of SLP Comp T/As with silver exterior and dark gray center stripe body decal. The cars had SLP rims, suspension and Ram Air system, but with a slightly differently-shaped hood compared to the Firehawk. Naturally, the SLP Comp T/A wore B F Goodrich Comp T/A radials. SLP Comp T/As were produced from 1995 to 1997. 1995 also marked the first year SLP started building Firehawks based on the Formula convertible.

Arrival of the WS6 V8 Firebirds obviously curtailed Firehawk production compared to 1994/95. SLP had to come up with

differentiated models offering even greater performance, and there were various diversions. A prototype 1998 Firehawk had a redesigned hood and non-flip-up headlamps.

The SLP Comp T/A celebrated the 25th Anniversary of the B F Goodrich Comp T/A radial tire. Apart from its unique decoration, the SLP Comp T/A also had a slightly different hood shape to that of the Firehawk. (Courtesy Ken Collings)

181

1996 was a low Firehawk production year. This is understandable given that Pontiac started to market its own WS6 Ram Air V8 Firebirds that year, albeit with SLP hardware and help. (Courtesy Jim Eberhart)

This Firehawk is one of only two 1996 bright metallic blue Firehawks built. The car's rarely ordered tan interior makes it one of a kind! (Courtesy Jim Eberhart)

For many, the stock level of performance offered by something like this 305bhp 1999 Firebird Formula is more than adequate. For others there will always be the tuners. (Courtesy Sabrina J Harootunian)

The charcoal interior is far more common on Firehawks. With the arrival of Pontiac's WS6 cars, SLP diversified and engaged in a number of projects. There was a 1998 Firehawk prototype with non-flip up headlamps, and 27 LT4-powered Firehawks were built. (Courtesy Jim Eberhart)

The design didn't reach production due to problems with the new style front lights. In addition, 27 LT4 Firehawks were constructed. The LT4 was a higher performance development of the LT1 V8 and appeared in 1996 Corvettes with 6-speed manual transmission. The LT4 engine had bigger valves, larger hydraulic roller cam, alloy roller rocker arms, forged crank, four bolt mains and a 10.75:1 compression ratio. It all added up to a 330bhp Firehawk.

Strictly speaking, no 1998 Firehawks were produced, but SLP did enhance six Formulas/Trans Ams with Firehawk equipment in Troy Michigan. Normal cars were purchased from GM dealers, converted in Troy and used for promotional work. These cars didn't have the GM RPO WU6 code and aren't official Firehawks. 1999 was the first year Trans Am-based Firehawks were constructed by SLP. The cars had a smoother Ram Air hood and 327bhp. SLP celebrated the Firehawk's 10th Anniversary with a special commemorative 335bhp model with black exterior, gold center stripe decals and gold alloys wearing 275/40ZR17 Firestone Firehawk radials.

On a lighter note, SLP made a

A 2002 NHRA SE Trans Am. The level of performance and convenience equipment supplied with late model Formulas and Trans Ams was very complete. (Courtesy Cary J Barrett)

one-off black and gold Trans Am-based Firehawk inspired by the 'X-Men' Hollywood motion picture. It had special X-Men related graphics, rims, exhaust and spoiler. The car didn't appear in the movie, but was built at the request of 20th Century Fox and Marvel Comics and used for publicity purposes. It traveled to comic book collector conventions around the country.

By the final year of SLP Firehawk involvement there was a 205bhp 2002 V6 Firebird GT, and the

The V8-powered Firebirds of the 1990s were a far cry, power-wise, from the LG4 and LU5-powered cars of the early '80s. The engineers achieved more power, economy and cleaner emissions using modern day alchemy. (Courtesy Cary J Barrett)

Firehawk's LS1 was up to 345bhp, thanks to a new, high flow induction system. To stress the legitimacy of SLP's automobiles, SLP packages carry RPO (Regular Production Option) GM codes, in addition to having a regular warranty and being street legal.

To maintain its reputation and quality, SLP sells replacement parts to registered SLP owners. Apart from actual car models SLP offers a range of build-up performance parts, such as the cold air induction system and engine hop-up parts, for cars already running around. SLP seemed to spark off interest in street legal mods with its initial work on the third generation Firebird. Government regulations were responsible for the demise of the hot rod car dealer shops by the early '70s, but the 1990s saw old and new parties enter the fray.

Former SLP regional manager, Matt Murphy, started GMMG Inc in Marietta, Georgia. GMMG worked in association with Carl Black Pontiac of Kennesaw to design, produce and distribute the Trans Am or WS6 Trans Am-based Black Bird. The Black Bird was another modified, street legal, fourth generation Trans Am. The 17 2002 Anniversary Black Birds had a freer flowing air box, special chambered cat back exhaust and improved engine

management software to increase horsepower.

Suspension changes involved shorter, 1.5in Eibach springs and polished, 17x9.5in American Racing Torq-Thrust II rims. There was a white instrument panel with a Firebird background for the tach, the oversize Hurst shift ball of the 6-speed manual was also white.

Anniversary insignia adorned the floor mats, front fenders and engine bay air box lid. Naturally, there were '380HP' hood scoop decals, not unlike the warning labels that urge 'Handle with care, appliance is hot!'

Dennis Mecham also became reinvolved with Firebirds in the late '90s. In 1997 Mecham Design & Performance of Glendale,

Mecham revived the Macho Trans Am in the late 1990s. Everyone was impressed with the four port heat extractor/Ram Air hood. (Courtesy Sheila Hartnagle)

Dennis Mecham signed the engine bay of this 2002 #2 Mecham T/A. Present Mecham Firebird work extends to more than just the Trans Am version. (Courtesy Sheila Hartnagle)

Arizona, started to produce higher performance, fourth generation Firebirds tailored to customer needs. The only Mecham caveat was that the chosen car had the QLC ZR tire option and be without WS6 or 1LE. Obviously, Mecham's work would clash with the suspension ingredients of WS6 and 1LE. Initially, the 'Macho T/A' tag was used with these fourth generation cars, but that quickly changed to 'Mecham T/A.' Indeed, subsequently a Mecham Formula and GTR Firebird were launched. The latter aimed at Pontiac's own

The sophisticated fuel injection and emissions control equipment found on cars like this 2000 WS6 Formula 6-speed, allow the aftermarket to create more powerful Birds whilst staying within the letter of the law. (Courtesy Glenn Brewer)

185

Like all those Chevy V8s before it, the LS1 V8 has been extended in size beyond its stock 346ci courtesy of stroker kits.
(Courtesy Glenn Brewer)

WS6 Trans Am and SLP's Firehawk. Who said fast domestic cars died out by the early '70s?

The Mecham options list is extensive, and a few items are worthy of special inspection. Mecham revived the Screamin' Chicken hood decal, which was made of 3M vinyl listed as 'Firebird Titan Hood Graphic' or 'Firebird Titan Hood Graphic in Paint w/ Clearcoat.' Other noteworthy items are the 5.7 HO and 6.3 HO engines. The numbers signify metric engine displacement. The 5.7 and 6.3-liter engines retail for $5161 and $15,618 respectively in 2003.

A 2003 6.5 HO (396ci) is also available for $16,813. Not exactly cheap compared to the $50 W72 400 1977 Trans Am option, but times have changed. Such engines

are developments of the all-alloy 346ci Chevy LS1 V8, with Mecham's tuning work resulting in displacements of 348, 383 and 396 cubes. Mecham also got noticed for its four port heat extractor/Ram Air hood. Want a Mecham car? As the sign in the shop window says, see Mecham Design & Performance's national sponsor dealer, Biddulph Pontiac-GMC, or make enquiries at your friendly local neighborhood Pontiac dealer.

Another company that offers special engine packages for fourth generation Firebirds is Lingenfelter Performance Engineering. In its performance listings are special 350 and 383 LT1 motors for 1993-97 Firebirds, not forgetting 346/383/427 LS1 engines for 1998-2002 models. Besides engine

packages Lingenfelter was involved with Hurst and Pontiac in the creation of a special 1997 'Hurst Firebird by Lingenfelter' that added $15,495 to a new 1997 WS6 Formula's price.

This LT1-powered car was the joint idea of Pontiac and Hurst, who called on tuner, John Lingenfelter, to make the first official Hurst car since the 1984 Hurst/Olds Cutlass 307 V8, more than just a paint and tape special. There was a special bodykit and gold paint for the hood, rear deck and aluminum rims. The leather seats had the insignia 'Hurst Firebird by Lingenfelter,' but the real story lay under the hood in the shape of a 350bhp Chevy LT1 V8.

Lingenfelter utilized 1996 Corvette Grand Sport LT4 intake manifold and cylinder heads, with

In Car and Driver's August 1999 'Keepers of the Flame' article, 1998 SCCA BF Goodrich Trans Am Series champ Paul Gentilozzi said Camaro Z/28 SS styling was like Penthouse compared to T/A's Hustler! (Courtesy Steve www.tripletransam.com)

The Ram Air 320 horse T/A's stats and value shone in the showroom, and were enough to leave the Corvette on the trailer at the track. No wonder GM wouldn't let F body have Vette power parity. (Courtesy Steve www.tripletransam.com)

custom porting of the latter. There were heftier valve springs, titanium retainers for the pushrods, longer roller rocker arms and a Lingenfelter Performance Engineering sports cam. New headers and Borla stainless steel exhaust system made the breathing easy. To better handle the increased power, a 3.5in aluminum driveshaft was pressed into service and Michelin Pilot SX tires replaced the usual WS6 Goodyear GS-Cs.

The 'Hurst Firebird by Lingenfelter' 6-speed did 0 to 60mph in 4.7 seconds and the ¼ mile in 13.1; terminal speed topped out at 182mph. This special Formula was tough enough to out-muscle the 345bhp LS1 Vette 6-speed. Lingenfelter produced 11 '97 MY LT1-based cars, with their conservatively rated 350 ponies. In '98 MY Lingenfelter built nine LS1 motivated Hurst Firebirds.

ASC & WS6

American Sunroof Corporation took over the WS6 program for fourth generation Firebirds from SLP for the 1998 MY. ASC's original build projection was for a figure of 6500 units, but, by the time production ceased on August 27 2002, ASC had processed 39,525 4th gen Firebird flyers! Amongst the cars completed were the 1999 30th Anniversary Trans Am and the 2002 Collector's Edition Trans Am.

The WS6 Firebird program worked up over three ASC factories. Bonding and priming took place at its Bowling Green facility in Kentucky, and the Livonia plant in Michigan handled paint for the special hoods. It was all put together at ASC's Lachine Montreal factory. The LS1 WS6 package looks different to the SLP version fitted to LT1 Birds, and ASC spent six months developing the kit. Indeed, there was a time lag intro between the final LT1 WS6 Firebirds, and the mid '98 MY arrival of the revised LS1 WS6 cars.

Still a live axle, like that original T/A, but C5 Corvette chassis engineer John Heinricy gave 4th gen LS1 Trans Am an okay ride comfort/track handling compromise. (Courtesy Steve www.tripletransam.com)

Sometimes ASC's work gets delivered far, far away. In this case, a brand new 2002 Collector's Edition Trans Am was Lilliputian compared to the minivans and SUVs also sold by this specialist car importer in Japan. The rear badge stated that the 2002 CE T/A was a proud product of ASC's WS6 program. (Courtesy Keishi Imai)

Firebird Convertibles ASC

1987	1988	1989	1991	1992	1995	1996	1997
173	104	330	1626	2092	3000	3000	3000

ASC WS6 Hood Program 1998-2002

1998	1999	2000	2001	2002
4653	6558	10,119	9195	9000

Special Collector Editions: 2390   Total: 39,525

(Courtesy ASC www.ascglobal.com/)

U-Haul with Hurst

Tradition is a big part of being a pony car, the Firebird is no exception. Following in the footsteps of the 2nd and 3rd gen Firebird sport wagons/show vehicles, came the 4th gen Hurst Hauler Firebird. This WS6 Trans Am-based speedy load lugger was revealed late in 2000, and may have been traveling in the guise of Hurst Hauler, but its genesis lay with a number of companies. Automotive Services, Inc. of Sterling Heights, Michigan, were on the starting grid with the body transformation that turned the Firebird coupe into a sport hatch, working with Custom Design Ltd of Trevor, Wisconsin along the way.

The Hurst Hauler connected with the road thanks to lowered sports suspension involving shocks and springs from Mr Gasket and Eibach, plus Lakewood rear control arms and Panhard rod. Large 18x10in American Racing Torque Thrust II rims with BF Goodrich g-Force P295/35ZR tires, created space for oversize Baer Racing brake hardware. Living up to its name, the 4-speed automatic Hauler utilised a Hurst shifter with integrated Line-Loc switch.

Unlike previous concept wagon experiments, this Bird packed greater-than-stock firepower with a worked LS1. Westech Automotive of Silver Lake, Wisconsin created a balanced and blueprinted LS1, with heavy duty valve springs, custom ground cam by Erson Cams, CNC'd heads and Accel fuel injectors/ sports air filter/spark plugs/ignition leads. TTS Power Systems burnt a special ECU chip for this 5.7-liter V8 and a Corsa Performance exhaust helped the Chevy sb reach 370bhp. The Hurst Hauler Firebird was a support vehicle for the 2001 *Hot Rod* Power Tour. With a custom Standox candy apple red exterior, with orange tinting, the HH Firebird was a standout!

Automotive Services, Inc and Custom Design Ltd turned the Firebird coupe into the Hurst Hauler Firebird sport wagon. The 18in rims were by American Racing, and the color was Standox candy apple red. (Courtesy John Zofko)

The car shown is a 1997 WS6 Trans Am. 1997 was the first year WS6 could be specified for a V8 Firebird convertible; it was also the first year for leather, 6-way power seats. (Courtesy James Fryhling)

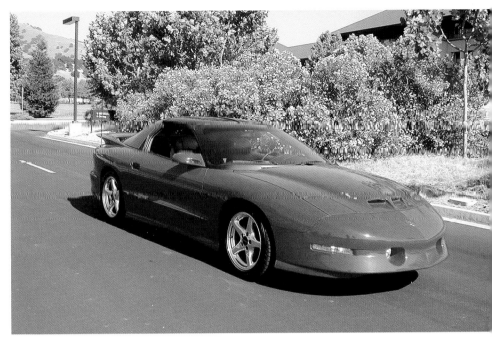

Firebird revisions for the late '90s

In 1997 the 1LE handling pack returned for the first time since the demise of the third generation Firebird. The difference this time was that it was just for the Formula. The 1LE Performance Package cost $1175 and contained 275 section tires, Koni shock absorbers and some special suspension tuning. There was some similarity to the WS6's suspension hardware, but front anti-sway bar diameter was boosted from 1.2 to 1.3in and even stiffer springs were used.

By 1999 1LE was available on the Trans Am, too. 1LE was discontinued by GM halfway through the 1999 model year, but SLP revived it for 2001.

1997 was also the first year that the fourth generation WS6 pack was available on a V8 Firebird convertible. Strangely enough, 1997 also marked the first year that leather power seats were available on the fourth generation cars. Previously, the choice was between 6-way power cloth seats and 4-way manually adjustable leather seats. Air conditioning became standard on all Firebirds, and so, too, did daytime running lights.

The bright purple metallic exterior of this 1998 Formula 6-speed was first introduced in the 1997 model year, along with bright green metallic paint. 1997 also saw 1LE become available on the Formula coupe. (Courtesy Phillip Lee)

1998 brought the first Firebird restyle since the fourth generation Bird originally flew in. There were new front and rear facias, and the Screamin' Chicken made a comeback as a molding at the center of the front facia. Dual front foglamps were now standard across the Firebird range. A pair of Ram Air-like apertures resided between the front flip-up lights. The flip-up pods were larger because they now accommodated a pair of headlamps, rather than the single lamps of pre-1998 Firebirds. This refinement greatly improved night driving vision.

One aspect of the restyle that

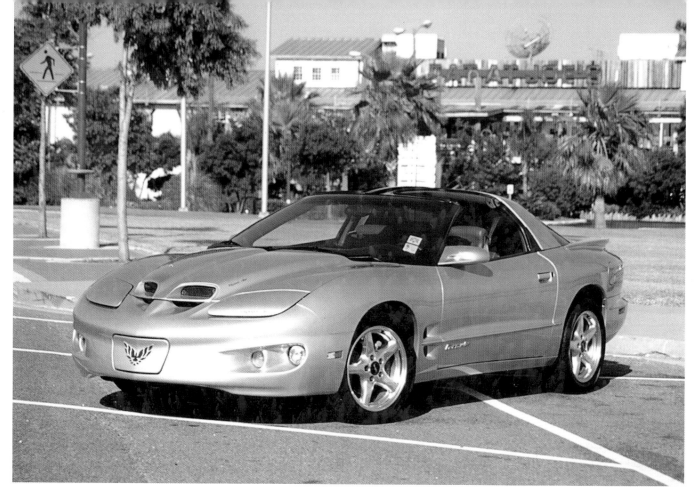

As shown by this 1998 Firebird Formula, nicknamed 'Silver Bullet,' the WS6 Ram Air option continued even after the Chevy V8 change from LT1 to LS1. (Courtesy Ginger Delvisco)

Formula and Trans Am were moving more upscale by the minute. So, a lavish interior and low volume ASC build number – only 223 1998 Formula WS6 cars – made this Formula pretty exclusive. (Courtesy Ginger Delvisco, www.thesilverbullet.f-bodygarage.com)

This 1998 Formula WS6 carries ASC conversion number # 1813. 'The Silver Bullet' was ASC converted in May, and delivered to Mossy Pontiac (New Orleans) on June 16th 1998. (Courtesy Ginger Delvisco, www.thesilverbullet.f-bodygarage.com)

This 2001 Formula auto uses CARTEK Stage 2 LSI heads, Comp Cam 224/224 580/580 113 LSA, Mac headers, Vigilante 4400 Torque Converter, and 4.10 final drive to achieve an 11.36 second ¼ mile time. (Courtesy Miriah Schramm, Steve Bell & Bob Brandoff)

made Firebird life a little easier was the four inches lost from the car's length. The substantial overhangs contributed to the sleek, zoomy image, but weren't much fun during slalom feats or tight parking travails. The latest Formula shared the revised Trans Am's pair of front fender air extractor slots, but had a different front facia with staggered fog and parking lights, reminiscent of the Jensen CV8.

The Trans Am was now set apart by dual intake moldings at the leading edge of the front facia. The upper aperture housed parking lights and the lower ones admitted cooling air to the front brakes. Need I mention that there was also an attention-grabbing raised rear spoiler?

LS1, anyone?

The most noteworthy Firebird news for 1998 was adoption of the Chevrolet LS1 V8. The LS1 – also sometimes known as the Gen III V8 – had arrived in the new 1997 C5 Corvette and was a major departure from the Chevy small block that started life in 1955. If one can imagine the first generation of Chevy small block V8s running in the 1950s-80s, and associate the second wave with the much revised Generation II LTI of 1992, then the late '90s witnessed generation number three.

So the still overhead valve LS1 made a fresh start with a reinforced aluminum block, aluminum heads, six bolt mains and tighter internal

tolerances. V8 Firebirds now had dual cats, even if the raised passenger footwell floorpan section, necessary to accommodate the previous single big cat, remained.

It wasn't even a Chevy 350 anymore; the LS1 had 346 cubes or 5665cc. It had a mainly plastic composite intake manifold and eight separate ignition coils mounted on the valve covers. The LS1 offered better breathing and higher rpm performance than the LT1. It's true that the LS1 doesn't have the low end torque many have come to expect from Chevy small blocks, but top end performance more than compensates.

The F body LS1 had a mechanically actuated throttle

The regular LS1 Formula and Trans Am had 305bhp, but a WS6 car had 320bhp. For 2001 those respective power figures rose to 310bhp and 325bhp respectively. (Courtesy Robert Pickens)

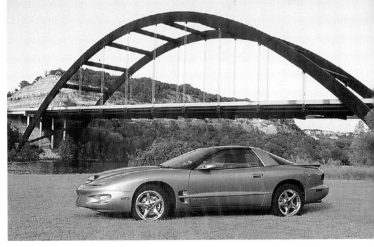

Since its 1987 rebirth the Firebird Formula has been regarded as a performance bargain. Careful optioning would yield a white hot, affordable V8 coupe like the 2000 WS6 Formula shown. (Courtesy Andrew)

This picture shows the styling differences between the 1998-2002 Formula and Trans Am. Both are WS6, T-top-equipped cars. Notice how the Formula on the left has a less elaborate rear spoiler, and the Trans Am on the right has its fog lamps more prominently positioned towards the front. (Courtesy Andrew)

body, milder cam and reduced valve overlap, plus EGR. All these changes meant that, on paper, the LS1 Firebird trailed the LS1 C5 Vette by 40bhp. Independent dyno tests and acceleration times recorded through formal magazine testing have revealed that the performance gulf between the LS1 Firebird and C5 Vette is smaller than that suggested by advertised horsepower ratings.

Car and Driver found the latest LS1 Trans Am to be almost 5 seconds quicker to 130mph than the earlier LT1 WS6 Formula it had tested. This was somewhat ironic because both cars were supposed to have 305 horses. Yes, that's right, an LT1 WS6 V8 Firebird and the new LS1 Firebird had engines with the same rated horsepower. Many pointed out that the new LS1 cars were a better deal because one was receiving 305bhp from a base rather than an optional V8.

Improvements to brakes and suspension welcomed the LS1 motor. There was a switch to Bosch 5.3 ABS and electronic front, rear brake proportioning utilizing the ABS's solenoid valves. Twin piston aluminum sliding calipers and 11.9in front disks replaced earlier single piston calipers and 10.7in rotors. Rear disk diameter jumped from 11.4 to 12in and separate auxiliary rear brake drums took over from the mechanical caliper clamping handbrake design.

Ride comfort was improved with no reduction in handling performance. John Heinricy was involved with chassis tuning of the 1997 C5 Vette. As Chief Engineer for the 1998 and later Firebirds, he oversaw the softening of springs and revalving of the DeCarbon shocks to produce better ride comfort with no loss in ultimate handling. Even the 1-4 skip shift device for the 6-speed manual was modified to reduce the likelihood of phantom shifting. In spite of a reduced chance of a skipped shift, the LS1 V8 Firebird EPA gas mileage rating improved by 1mpg.

I know what you're thinking; with the arrival of the LS1 there

Independent dyno tests have revealed that the on-paper power gap between the F body's LS1 and Vette's LS1 is exaggerated. This is a 320bhp 1999 WS6 Formula. (Courtesy Steve)

Some things just never go out of style! The flame paint job on this 2000 Formula blends old time hot rod tradition with today's modern American car. (Courtesy Michelle L Balmer)

would be no need for WS6/Ram Air, but that's wrong; an LS1-based WS6 option with four aperture Ram Air hood returned for a mid 1998 model year intro. It boasted 320bhp, compared to a normal F body LS1's 305 horses.

As displayed by this 2001 WS6 Trans Am, part of the Firebird's 1998 restyle involved incorporation of larger flip-up headlamp pods with a pair of lamps. The 1993-97 Birds had single lamps. (Courtesy Steve Hovis)

The last waltz

Sadly, declining sales resulted in the number of Firebird versions being reduced. From 1998 onwards, there were no more Formula convertibles and, from 1999, no more Trans Am hardtops. One thing 1999 did have was the 30th Anniversary Trans Am involving a $1575 package. Replicating the first Trans Am, the 30th Anniversary car had a white exterior with dual, body length blue stripe decals and 30th Anniversary badging. 17in aluminum rims had a sparkly blue clear coat tint with Trans Am centers.

As with the 25th Anniversary Trans Am, the 30th Anniversary edition had white leather seats with the 30th Anniversary insignia embroidered on the head restraints. 1600 30th Anniversary Trans Ams were produced, 535 in blue cloth convertible form. Naturally, the remaining cars were T-tops. All 30th Anniversary Trans Ams had WS6, which meant Ram Air hood scoops. There was little chance of one getting lost in the crowd!

2000 WS6 Firebirds featured new and elaborate 17in 'Torqued' style polished rims. The 2001 LS1 and Ram Air LS1 engines were up-gunned to 310bhp and 325bhp respectively. There was little doubt by this stage that the F body plant in Quebec Canada would cease production; it was more a question of when. The F body was able to ride out two world fuel crises and several recessions, but declining market share meant that GM would discontinue the Firebird and Camaro lines pretty soon. The pick-up truck and SUV segments had gathered momentum as the 1990s progressed, and had taken the place once occupied by V8 pony cars, at least in a marketing sense. Thus, it came as no surprise that, while trim and engine options for regular passenger cars were reduced, such options actually expanded for pick-up and SUV lines.

Another problem for the Firebird and F body in general was price. The Mustang hit pay dirt at the start of the '80s in terms of capturing

Declining sales brought range rationalization. From 1998 on there were no Formula convertibles, and from 1999 on there were no Trans Am hardtops. This is a 2002 Formula. (Courtesy Alan Day)

the affordable V8 coupe segment, and Ford exploited this in the years that followed. People like the idea of quality but, at the end of the day, buy on price. The fourth generation F body had a number of technical and performance strong points. GM had created a polished pony car, especially considering the company's less than rosy financial state at the start of the 1990s. However, there were indications that, good as it was, the F body had become too much car for mainstream buyers.

One indication of this was that just about every 1990s magazine comparison test featured the upscale

Once criticized for being too heavy and thirsty, it's ironic that this relatively light and frugal 2002 Formula V8 is being outsold by SUVs and pick-ups. (Courtesy Jim Scialabba)

Nothing like a special edition Trans Am to cheer you up! The bold WS6 30th Anniversary Trans Am combined the traditional white and blue color scheme with a long list of convenience features. (Courtesy Bill Jansen)

SVT Mustang Cobra against a normal, V8-powered Formula/Trans Am or Camaro Z/28. The regular 5.0 and 4.6 Mustangs were no performance match for the LT1 and LS1-motivated F body, so the low volume Cobra had to be included in reviews.

Detroit has generally moved on from the time when GM President, Ed Cole, walked into a comptroller meeting and stated that a carb upgrade would cost customers $50, and each additional cubic inch ran to a buck; early 1970s pricing meant it was possible to go from a 2bbl 350 V8 to a 4bbl 400 V8 for $100!

Car and Driver drew attention to the problem in its August 1999 'Keepers of the Flame' article, which described the awestruck, youthful McDonald's workers when magazine testers went for drive-thru service in the 30th Anniversary Trans Am convertible: "… the pimply slacker who waited on us could scarcely contain his bubbling hormones, immediately summoning a half-dozen fellow slackers to drool all over our Quarter Pounders." "Odd," wrote one tester, "this car is absolutely coveted by people who can't afford it."

Therein lay the problem; the Firebird Formula and Trans Am were performance bargains, depending where one was coming from. A buyer considering a new Vette or BMW M3 would note that the LS1 WS6 Formula 6-speed got very close to upper echelon competition in a number of performance areas for an incredible price. However, for those buyers counting the pennies, and concerned about insurance premiums, the regular 4.6 V8 Mustang was the pony car limit and LT1 or LS1 Firebirds were rarefied territory. Beauty is in the checkbook of the beholder.

That leaves us with time for one last, special edition Firebird, the

17in rims with a clear blue lacquer coat, plus a 500 watt Monsoon sound system, meant that the 30th Anniversary Trans Am was visually and audibly vocal. (Courtesy Bill Jansen)

The 2002 Collector Edition WS6 Trans Am marked the end of the Firebird line after 35 continuous production years. A 2002 Collector's Edition WS6 Trans Am driven by Jay Leno paced the 2002 Daytona 500. (Courtesy Kevin & Shannon Trahan)

Two of the last special edition Trans Ams. On the left the 2002 Collector's Edition WS6 Trans Am, and on the right the 30th Anniversary Trans Am. How long will we have to wait before the Firebird flies back? (Courtesy Kevin & Shannon Trahan)

2002 Collector's Edition Trans Am, resplendent in yellow exterior paint, custom stripes with black accents, black 17x9in rims with special centers and black brake calipers. There was exterior Collector's Edition badging and embroidery on the front seats. The interior featured ebony Prado leather with perforated inserts. It was all cosmetic, for sure, but the V8 fourth generation Firebird was no paper tiger, and the 2002 Collector Edition Trans Am was plenty spry enough to pace the 2002 Daytona 500.

Even as the 2002 Collector's Edition Trans Am dances the Firebird's last auto waltz, thoughts turn to the Firebird's return, with speculation about what form it will take and when, exactly, it will come back. In the meantime, the imported Pontiac GTO will have to satisfy those searching for high performance GM V8-powered rear drive 2+2 coupes.

As for the future, Firebird fans can only hope that market trends alter, and one day a new Firebird designed and built in North America will wing its way back.

Pontiac legends in Louisiana! From left to right: 2004 Pontiac GTO, 1998 Formula WS6 and 1981 Y85 Turbo Trans Am Daytona 500 Pace Car. (Courtesy Ginger Delvisco www.thesilverbullet.f-bodygarage.com)

Appendix

Model highlights from the Firebird's 40 years

Model	**1967½ Firebird 400 4-speed hardtop coupe**
Price	$3829 (price as tested)
Dimensions/curb weight	L: 188.8in W: 72.6in H: 51.5in/3580lb
Motor/gearbox	OHV, cast iron Pontiac 400 V8, (10.75:1 comp), 1xRochester Q-jet/4-speed Muncie, 3.36 final drive
Horsepower/torque	325bhp (gross) @ 4800rpm/410lb/ft @ 3400rpm
Chassis/suspension	Unibody & front subframe/#621 'Ride and Handling Package' (front), unequal length A arms, coil springs, tube shocks, (rear) live axle, single leaf springs, cushioned trailing arms
0-60mph	6.5 seconds
¼ mile	14.7 seconds
Overall gas mileage	11.9mpg
Source	*Car Life* August 1967

The 400 V8/4-speed power team could achieve its best when fitted to a lightly optioned hardtop coupe, rather than a heavier, loaded convertible.

Model	1969½ Firebird Trans Am Ram Air III 400 4-speed hardtop coupe
Price	Base Firebird 400 hardtop coupe $3087.83, WS4 Trans Am pack $724.60
Dimensions/curb weight	L: 191.1in W: 73.9in H: 49.6in/3375lb
Motor/gearbox	OHV, cast iron Pontiac 400 Ram Air III V8, (10.75:1 comp), 1xRochester Q-jet/4-speed Muncie, 3.55 final drive
Horsepower/torque	335bhp (gross) @ 5000rpm/430lb/ft @ 3400rpm
Chassis/suspension	Unibody & front subframe/Y96 heavy duty suspension (front), unequal length A arms, coil springs, tube shocks, sway bar (rear) live axle, multi leaf springs, tube shocks
0-60mph	6.5 seconds
¼ mile	14.3 seconds
Overall gas mileage	11.5mpg
Source	*Sports Car Graphic* April 1969

The Firebird Trans Am started as an optional package connected to the Firebird's SCCA Trans Am series activities. The car looked like the proposed T/G Racing 1969 season coupe, but used established Pontiac 400ci Ram Air motors. A 345bhp Ram Air IV 400 was an official option. A Ram Air IV Trans Am tested by *Road Test* magazine recorded 14.6 seconds for the ¼ mile. A solid lifter Ram Air V 400 was available on a crate motor basis.

Model	1970½ Firebird Trans Am Ram Air IV 400 4-speed
Price	$4663.63 (price as tested)
Dimensions/curb weight	L: 191.6in W: 73.4in H: 50.4in/3720lb
Motor/gearbox	OHV, cast iron Pontiac 400 Ram Air IV V8, (10.5:1 comp), 1xRochester Q-jet/4-speed Muncie, 3.73 final drive
Horsepower/torque	345bhp (gross) @ 5000rpm/430lb/ft @ 3400rpm
Chassis/suspension	Unibody & front subframe/[heavy duty] suspension (front), unequal length A arms, coil springs, tube shocks, sway bar (rear) live axle, multi leaf springs, tube shocks, sway bar
0-60mph	5.7 seconds
¼ mile	14.1 seconds
Overall gas mileage	11.5mpg (estimated)
Source	*Car and Driver* June 1970

The first of the second generation Firebird Trans Ams. Ram Air III & IV motors were available, but only with an automatic transmission specific camshaft. This was the last model year for a Trans Am designed to use 99 octane leaded premium gasoline.

Model	1972 Firebird Trans Am 455 HO 4-speed
Price	$4886.75 (price as tested)
Dimensions/curb weight	L: 191.6in W: 73.4in H: 50.4in/3701lb
Motor/gearbox	OHV, cast iron Pontiac 455 LS5 V8, (8.4:1 comp), 1xRochester Q-jet/ 4-speed Muncie, 3.42 final drive
Horsepower/torque	300bhp @ 4000rpm/415lb/ft @ 3200rpm (net power & torque figures)
Chassis/suspension	Unibody & front subframe/[heavy duty] suspension (front), unequal length A arms, coil springs, tube shocks, sway bar (rear) live axle, multi leaf springs, tube shocks, sway bar
0-60mph	7.0 seconds
¼ mile	14.04 seconds
Overall gas mileage	6.5mpg recorded during spirited usage; 11.5mpg (estimated for regular use)
Source	*High Performance Cars* September 1972

The first of the smog era Trans Ams. Engine size was upped to 455 cubes as compression dropped to accommodate low lead and no lead gasoline. The LS5 motor was available in the Firebird Formula and Trans Am, functional hood scoops continued to be available on both models. The LS5 dropped five net horsepower compared to the 1971 model year due to stricter pollution laws. Still a fast car, especially when compared to contemporary sport compacts and intermediates.

Model	1973 Firebird Trans Am SD 455 automatic
Price	$5295 (price as tested)
Dimensions/curb weight	L: 192.1in W: 73.4in H: 50.4in/3854lb
Motor/gearbox	OHV, cast iron Pontiac 455 Super Duty V8, (8.4:1 comp), 1xRochester Q-jet/THM 400 3-speed auto, 3.42 final drive
Horsepower/torque	310bhp @ 4000rpm/390lb/ft @ 3600rpm
Chassis/suspension	Unibody & front subframe/heavy duty suspension (front), unequal length A arms, coil springs, tube shocks, sway bar (rear) live axle, multi leaf springs, tube shocks, sway bar
0-60mph	5.4 seconds
¼ mile	13.8 seconds (required functional hood scoop)
Overall gas mileage	11.5mpg
Source	*Car and Driver* May 1973

The SD 455 package was Pontiac's high performance answer to the emissions conscious early 1970s. In spite of reduced compression and the use of 91 octane gas, SD 455-powered cars were quicker than earlier premium fuel Ram Air Firebirds/Trans Ams. It would take the arrival of the 1989 20th Anniversary Turbo Trans Am before such acceleration from an official, showroom, emissions legal Firebird would be seen again.

Model	1975½/76 Firebird Trans Am 455 HO 4-speed
Price	Trans Am base price $4740+$150=$4890 (1975½)
Dimensions/curb weight	L: 196.8in W: 73in H: 49.6in/3985lb (car tested fitted with a/c)
Motor/gearbox	OHV, cast iron Pontiac 455 L75 V8, (7.6:1 comp), 1xRochester Q-jet/BW Super T10, 3.23 final drive
Horsepower/torque	200bhp @ 3500rpm/330lb/ft @ 2000 rpm
Chassis/suspension	Unibody & front subframe/heavy duty suspension (front), unequal length A arms, coil springs, tube shocks, sway bar (rear) live axle, multi leaf springs, tube shocks, sway bar
0-60mph	8.8 seconds
¼ mile	16.35 seconds
Overall gas mileage	11.3mpg
Source	*Road Test* September 1975

The 1975½/76 Trans Am 455 HO used the L75 455 V8 as part of a $150 motor/gearbox/rear axle fun pack that tried to re-ignite Trans Am motoring after the demise of the SD 455 option at the end of 1974. The mid '70s 455 HO motor was only available with the BW Super T10 4-speed manual gearbox, and was only for the Trans Am. The ordinary nature of the L75 V8 precipitated media/public pressure to axe the 'HO' part of the model designation for 1976. However, the Trans Am driven and tested by *Road Test* magazine was a pre-release 1976 model that combined 1976 exterior styling with the '455 HO' hood scoop decal!

Model	1979 Firebird Trans Am W72 6.6-liter 4-speed
Price	$7285.45 (tested price includes WS6 $434 & W72 motor $90)
Dimensions/curb weight	L: 198.1in W: 73in H: 49.3in/3700lb (a/c not fitted on tested car)
Motor/gearbox	OHV, cast iron Pontiac 400 W72 V8, (8.1:1 comp), 1xRochester Q-jet/BW Super T10, 3.23 final drive
Horsepower/torque	220bhp @ 4000rpm/320lb/ft @ 2800rpm
Chassis/suspension	Unibody & front subframe/WS6 suspension (front), unequal length A arms, coil springs, tube shocks, sway bar (rear) live axle, multi leaf springs, tube shocks, sway bar
0-60mph	6.7 seconds
¼ mile	15.3 seconds
Overall gas mileage	12mpg EPA city
Source	*Car and Driver* January 1979

The final year for the W72 6.6-liter motor, as ever available on the Firebird Formula and Trans Am over 1977-79. Only 8690 W72 powerplants were set aside for 1979 and this model year saw 4-wheel disks officially become part of the WS6 package. 1979 was the last year for the big displacement, stick shift Firebird Formula and Trans Am.

W72 400 Production Totals	
1977	28,668
1978	34,886
1979	8690
Total	**72,244**

51% of W72 400-powered cars were automatic (36915)

49% of W72 400-powered cars were manual (35329)

N.B. During the 1979 model year the W72 400 motor option was officially listed as 'L78.'

Model	1980 Firebird Turbo Trans Am 4.9
Price	Trans Am base price $7178, 4.9 turbo motor ($350), WS6 ($481)
Dimensions/curb weight	L: 198.1in W: 73in H: 49.3in/3700lb
Motor/gearbox	OHV, cast iron Pontiac 4.9-liter V8, (7.5:1 comp), Garrett AiResearch TB0 305 turbocharger, Delco Electronic Spark Control, max boost pressure 9psi, 1xRochester Q-jet with boost enrichment provisions/GM THM 350 3-speed auto, 3.08:1 final drive
Horsepower/torque	210bhp @ 4000rpm/345lb/ft @ 2000rpm
Chassis/suspension	Unibody & front subframe/WS6 suspension (front), unequal length A arms, coil springs, tube shocks, sway bar (rear) live axle, multi leaf springs, tube shocks, sway bar
0-60mph	8.2 seconds
¼ mile	16.7 seconds
Overall gas mileage	14mpg EPA city (required high test)
Source	*Car and Driver* October 1979 performance figures

In 1980/81 the 4.9 turbo became Pontiac's top Firebird powerplant. A Turbo Trans Am 4.9 paced the 1980 Indy 500 with mods limited to dumping the a/c, rear gear swap to 2.56 and shaved tires. A wastegate limiting boost pressure to 9psi and electronic spark control first seen on the 1978 Buick Turbo Regal kept detonation at bay. The LU8 turbo motor implied automatic transmission and air conditioning as mandatory options. The LU8 was available on Firebird Formula and Trans Am. In 1981 LU8 output was re-rated at 200bhp, and the engine featured an electronic Q-jet.

Model	1982 Firebird Trans Am 'Crossfire' 5.0
Price	Trans Am base price $9658, LU5 motor ($899), WS6 ($387)
Dimensions/curb weight	L: 189.8in W: 72in H: 49.8in/3385lb
Motor/gearbox	OHV, cast iron Chevrolet 5.0-liter V8, (9.5:1 comp), Rochester dual throttle body electronic fuel injection/electronic ignition/GM THM 200C 3-speed auto, 3.23:1 final drive
Horsepower/torque	165bhp @ 4200rpm/240lb/ft @ 2400rpm
Chassis/suspension	Unibody/WS6 suspension (front) altered MacPherson struts, lower A arms, coil springs, tube shocks, sway bar (rear) live axle, torque tube and Panhard rod, coil springs, tube shocks, sway bar
0-60mph	9.2 seconds
¼ mile	17 seconds
Overall gas mileage	14.5mpg overall
Source	*Road & Track* September 1982

The first of the downsized Trans Ams, and the first year a Firebird was unavailable with a Pontiac designed V8. The Chevrolet 5.0 became an F body staple, with the 5.7 reserved for Mr Vette. The Crossfire injection system was shared by the top 1982 Trans Am, Camaro Z/28 and Corvette. Pontiac tried a softer WS6 suspension approach with the new Firebird S/E and Trans Am. The new Trans Am became famous on the small screen where it starred as the talking supercar K.I.T.T. (Knight Industries Two Thousand) in the television series *Knight Rider*.

Model	**1984 Firebird Trans Am 5.0 HO**
Price	Trans Am base price $10,699, L69 motor ($530)
Dimensions/curb weight	L: 189.9in W: 72.4in H: 49.7in/3250lb (car tested not fitted with a/c, but with W62 Aero Package)
Motor/gearbox	OHV, cast iron Chevrolet 5.0-liter L69 V8, (9.5:1 comp), 1xRochester Q-jet/5-speed BW T5, 3.73:1 final drive
Horsepower/torque	190bhp @ 4800rpm/240lb/ft @ 3200rpm
Chassis/suspension	Unibody/WS6 suspension (front) altered MacPherson struts, lower A arms, coil springs, tube shocks, sway bar (rear) live axle, torque tube and Panhard rod, coil springs, tube shocks, sway bar
0-60mph	7.9 seconds
1/4 mile	16.1 seconds
Overall gas mileage	16/27mpg EPA city/highway
Source	*Road & Track* November 1983 (performance figures)

The L69 5.0 HO & light shifting BW T5 spiced up Trans Am life from the middle of the 1983 model year. A number of technical changes to the Chevy 5.0 turned it into a high rpm motor. The new Borg Warner 5-speed overdrive transmission made it easy to exploit the new 5.0's improved breathing. From 1984 on the L69 could be teamed up with the GM 4A-700R4 4-speed automatic. The Trans Am-only L69 lived on into the 1986 model year when reliability problems and the existence of the TPI 5.0 caused its demise.

Model	**1987 Firebird Formula TPI 5.0 5-speed**
Price	Formula base price $11,844, LB9 TPI 5.0 $745 (WS6 standard)
Dimensions/curb weight	L: 188.8in W: 72.4in H: 49.7in/3350lb
Motor/gearbox	OHV, cast iron Chevrolet Tuned Port Injection 5.0-liter LB9 V8, (9.3:1 comp), Bosch Rochester multi point electronic fuel injection, electronic ignition/ 5-speed BW T5, 3.45:1 final drive
Horsepower/torque	205bhp @ 4400rpm/285lb/ft @ 3200rpm
Chassis/suspension	Unibody/WS6 suspension (front) altered MacPherson struts, lower A arms, coil springs, tube shocks, sway bar (rear) live axle, torque tube and Panhard rod, coil springs, tube shocks, sway bar
0-60mph	7.7 seconds
1/4 mile	16.09 seconds
Overall gas mileage	16mpg EPA city
Source	*Motor Trend* November 1986

The reintroduced Firebird Formula tried to put the fun back into Firebird at an affordable price, helping to deal with the successful 'bang for buck' Ford Mustang GT 5.0 format. The new Firebird Formula revived the Trans Am 'turbo hood' of the 1982-84 era, and 1976-81 W50-style Formula two-tone exterior graphics/appearance pack. A number of power teams were available on the Firebird Formula. The 5-liter TPI LB9/5-speed was considered the sportiest feeling combination.

Model	1987 Firebird Trans Am GTA
Price	Trans Am base price $13,259, Y84 GTA option $2700
Dimensions/curb weight	L: 191.6in W: 72in H: 49.7in/3530lb (usual loaded GTA with all the trimmings tested)
Motor/gearbox	OHV, cast iron Chevrolet Tuned Port Injection 5.7-liter L98 V8, (9.3:1 comp), Bosch Rochester multi point electronic fuel injection, electronic ignition/GM 4A-700R4 4-speed auto, 2.77:1 final drive
Horsepower/torque	210bhp @ 4000rpm/315lb/ft @ 3200rpm
Chassis/suspension	Unibody/WS6 suspension (front) altered MacPherson struts, lower A arms, coil springs, tube shocks, sway bar (rear) live axle, torque tube and Panhard rod, coil springs, tube shocks, sway bar
0-60mph	7.1 seconds
1/4 mile	15.5 seconds
Overall gas mileage	16mpg
Source	*Performance Cars* 1988

The upscale Trans Am GTA arrived in 1987, its package included items such as the L98 5.7 V8, 4-wheel disks, WS6 suspension, LSD, oil cooler and custom interior. The GTA took the Trans Am away from the Mustang GT 5.0/Camaro Z/28 'value for money' sales war. The GTA became available with the 5-liter TPI/5-speed power team in 1988. As ever, only the Vette could enjoy the L98 with a stick shift.

Model	1989 20th Anniversary Firebird Turbo Trans Am
Price	Base price $29,839
Dimensions/curb weight	L: 191.6in W: 72.4in H: 50in/3346lb
Motor/gearbox	OHV, cast iron Buick 3.8-liter V6 turbo (8.0:1 comp), Garrett T3 turbocharger, intercooler, max boost 16.5psi, multi point electronic sequential fuel injection, electronic ignition/GM THM 200R4 4-speed auto, 2.77:1 final drive, BW 'Australian' LSD
Horsepower/torque	250bhp @ 4400rpm/340lb/ft @ 2800rpm
Chassis/suspension	Unibody/WS6+1LE front brakes (front) altered MacPherson struts, lower A arms, coil springs, tube shocks, sway bar (rear) live axle, torque tube and Panhard rod, coil springs, tube shocks, sway bar
0-60mph	5.5 seconds
1/4 mile	13.5 seconds
Overall gas mileage	14mpg (estimated)
Source:	*Road & Track* January 1989

The 1989 20th Anniversary Turbo Trans Am was a low-volume, specialized model that revived the 3.8 turbo V6 of Buick Grand National fame for one more fast and furious rear drive fling. The turbocharged Trans Am paced the 1989 Indy 500 without modification and had performance that overshadowed the regular 1989 Vette. 1550 production examples of this automatic-only Trans Am were created to commemorate the Trans Am's 20th Anniversary.

A 1988 GTA with a Blue Angels F/A 18 Hornet. (Courtesy Benjamin English)

Model	1993 Firebird Trans Am LT1
Price	Trans Am base price $21,395
Dimensions/curb weight	L: 197in W: 74.5in H: 51.7in/3455lb
Motor/gearbox	OHV, cast iron block/aluminum heads Chevrolet 5.7-liter LT1 V8, (10.3:1 comp), Rochester multi point electronic fuel injection, electronic ignition/BW T56 6-speed manual, 3.23:1 final drive
Horsepower/torque	275bhp @ 5000rpm/325lb/ft @ 2400rpm
Chassis/suspension	Unibody/FE2 suspension (front) upper & lower control arms, coil springs, tube shocks, sway bar (rear) live axle, dual lower trailing links, Panhard rod, torque arm, coil springs, tube shocks, sway bar
0-60mph	6.3 seconds
$\frac{1}{4}$ mile	14.8 seconds
Overall gas mileage	20.5mpg
Source	*Road & Track Specials* 1993

The virtually all-new fourth generation Trans Am brought new front suspension and rack & pinion steering, plus the Vette sourced Chevy LT1 5.7-liter V8. This time around the top 5.7 V8 could be teamed with a manual box, the BW T56. The fourth generation body used SMC and RIM plastic exterior panels in a manner reminiscent of the 1984-88 Pontiac Fiero.

Model	1996 Firebird Formula WS6
Price	Formula base price $19,464 + (WS6) Ram Air Performance & Handling Package $2995
Dimensions/curb weight	L: 197in W: 74.5in H: 52in/3435lb
Motor/gearbox	OHV, cast iron block/aluminum heads Chevrolet 5.7-liter LT1 V8, (10.5:1 comp), Rochester multi point sequential electronic fuel injection/electronic ignition/BW T56 6-speed manual, 3.42:1 final drive
Horsepower/torque	305bhp @ 5400rpm/335lb/ft @ 3200rpm
Chassis/suspension	Unibody/WS6 suspension (front) upper & lower control arms, coil springs, tube shocks, sway bar (rear) live axle, dual lower trailing links, Panhard rod, torque arm, coil springs, tube shocks, sway bar
0-60mph	5.5 seconds
$\frac{1}{4}$ mile	14.1 seconds
Overall gas mileage	17mpg city/25mpg highway (EPA ratings)
Source	*Car and Driver* August 1995

The WS6 package available on the Firebird Formula and Trans Am from 1996 reflected SLP's work with the Firehawk; in fact, SLP installed WS6 components on the Firebird for Pontiac. The Firebird hadn't seen the Ram Air nomenclature since the 1970$\frac{1}{2}$ models. The WS6 code had been absent since the final 1992 third generation F body days. It could truly be said that the WS6-equipped, fourth generation Firebird Formulas and Trans Ams were a blast from the past!

Model	1999 30th Anniversary Firebird Trans Am WS6 Convertible
Price	Trans Am base price $34,255, 30th Anniversary pack: $1575
Dimensions/curb weight	L: 193.8in W: 74.5in H: 52.4in/3617lb
Motor/gearbox	OHV, all alloy Chevrolet 5.7-liter LS1 V8, (10.1:1comp), Rochester multi point sequential electronic fuel injection/electronic ignition/BW T56 6-speed manual, 3.42:1 final drive
Horsepower/torque	320bhp @ 5200rpm/335lb/ft @ 4000rpm
Chassis/suspension	Unibody/WS6 suspension (front) upper & lower control arms, coil springs, tube shocks, sway bar (rear) live axle, dual lower trailing links, Panhard rod, torque arm, coil springs, tube shocks, sway bar
0-60mph	5.3 seconds
1⁄4 mile	13.9 seconds
Overall gas mileage	19mpg city/28mpg highway (EPA ratings)
Source	*Car and Driver* August 1999

Pontiac celebrated the Trans Am's 30th Anniversary with this commemorative model featuring a white and blue color scheme reminiscent of the first 1969½ Trans Am. 1600 30th Anniversary Trans Ams were built; 535 as convertibles. All cars featured the revised suspension tuning and LS1 V8 introduced for the 1998 model year. As ever, if you wanted to get noticed a special edition Trans Am was still a standout.

| \multicolumn{6}{c}{SLP production totals} |

Year	Firehawk	Firehawk Convert	Comp T/A	Formula	T/A
1992	25				
1993	201				
1994	500				
1995	569	102	72		
1996	32	9	45		
1997	100	16	47		
1998	Not applicable, Firehawks based on Formula & T/A from 1999 model year onwards				
1999	719			106	613
2000	741			62	679
2001	540			70	470
2002	1501			167	1334

NB. 1999 onwards Formula-based Firehawks used T-top/coupe.
1999 onwards T/A-based Firehawks used T-top/conv.

Clubs and organizations

www.poci.org
Pontiac-Oakland Club International(POCI), established in 1972 and covers all Pontiac and Oakland vehicles. A club with national headquarters, local chapters and an international membership.

www.firebirdtaclub.com
The National Firebird & T/A Club was founded in Chicago in 1984 for all Firebird, Formula and Trans Am owners.
National Firebird & T/A Club, P.O. Box 11238, Chicago, IL 60611, USA

www.historictransam.com
The Historic Trans Am group showcases the cars fielded during the SCCA's Trans Am series, focusing on 1966-72. Find out about the cars that participated in this golden era and where they are today.

www.firebirdtransamparts.com/redsky/ladybirds.htm
Hoghead's Skybird, Redbird and Yellowbird Page.

www.wwfirebirds.com
The Western Washington Firebirds club.

www.sdpoci.com
The San Diego Chapter of the Pontiac Oakland Club International.
San Diego Chapter of POCI, 2926 Oak Hill Drive, Escondido, Ca 92027, USA

www.poc-uk.org
The Pontiac Owners Club (UK), 'Chamberlains', Chalk Lane, Matching Tye, Essex CM17 0PQ. England

www.tacs.nu
Trans Am Club of Sweden, Economics & Memberships registry, Gårdsvägen 24A, SE-141 70 Huddinge, Sweden

www.camaro-firebird.org
Camaro-Firebird.org Inc (Australia). An Australian internet-based club for all US GM vehicles. Camaro-Firebird.org Inc (NSW), PO Box 1025, Albion Park Rail, NSW 2527, Australia

www.transamcountry.com
Trans Am Country, if you like second generation T/As then come and visit!

www.delorean.com
DeLorean Motor Company takes care of all enthusiast needs concerning the DMC-12

www.transamdepot.com
Trans Am Depot is an auto conversion company that does new Camaro-based Trans Ams, plus resto-mods and restorations.

www.thesilverbullet.f-bodygarage.com
Johnny and Ginger Delvisco's Silver Bullet 4th gen garage.

Yanque Tanque Racing, 129 Ridgeway Pointe, Ellenwood, Georgia, 30294, USA
Phone no. 770-389-9680
Vintage Racing Team (Est. 1990), involved in historic racing.

www.ultimategto.com
The ultimate Pontiac GTO picture site, run by Sean Mattingly.

clubs.hemmings.com/frameset.cfm?club=chrommettes
The Chrommettes of America, a car club for women that covers all types of cars and trucks.

www.aarcuda.com
The AARchives – home page of the 1970 Plymouth AAR 'Cuda.

www.challengertaregistry.com
The Challenger T/A Registry.

Specific model areas

www.theformulasource.com
The place to be if you like
Firebird Formulas, dedicated to
all Formula models from 1970½
onwards.

www.firehawk.com
The official Firehawk website. For
those custom SLP 3rd and 4th
gen Formulas with the extra pep!

www.301garage.com/Rehorn/
index.html
The Rehorn Brothers' Page Of The
Second Generation Trans Am.

John M Witzke
POCI Tech Advisor
1977-79 W72 Performance
Package Historian
email jmwitzke@prodigy.net
A contact for W72 research.

www.gtasourcepage.com
Devoted to the Gran Turismo
Americano (GTA) sports luxury
third gen Firebird of 1987-92.

www.thirdgen.org
Home of the third generation
F body.

www.superduty455.com
Douglas Sciberras 1974 SD 455
T/A.

bencar.freeyellow.com/76TAPage.
html
Ben Deutschman 1976 L-78 T/A.

www.eonet.ne.jp/~ben/transam/
index.htm
Keishi and Maki Imai 1985 T/A.

www.78ta.com
Hitman's Pontiac Trans Am
Information Site

www.lchr.org/a/24/or/
Michael Russell's 1980 Turbo
Trans Am SE Site

www.cardomain.com/
member/1fastformula/
Todd Canter 1989 Formula 5.7 TPI

www.smpcorp.com
Standard Motor Products Inc.
carries a range of replacement
parts to keep your Firebird flying.
Standard Motor Products Inc.
37-18 Northern Boulevard,
Long Island City, New York
11101, USA Tel: 718-392-020

www.thefierofactory.com
Providing Fiero owners with
car servicing/spare parts on a
worldwide basis, plus Chevrolet
3.4 V6 & Cadillac 4.9 V8 engine
conversions. Founded by
Ed Parks.

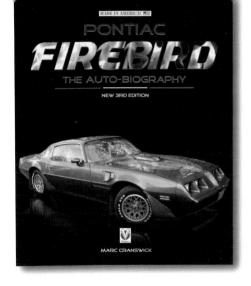

Index